Turned Funny

Turned Funny

A Memoir by

Celestine Sibley

1817

HARPER & ROW, PUBLISHERS, New York
Cambridge, Philadelphia, San Francisco
London, Mexico City, São Paulo, Singapore, Sydney

Photographs follow pages 86 and 214.

FIRST EDITION

Copyeditor: Margaret Cheney

Designer: Erich Hobbing

Library of Congress Cataloging-in-Publication Data

Sibley, Celestine.
　Turned funny.

　1. Sibley, Celestine—Biography. 2. Authors, American—20th century—Biography. 3. Georgia— Social life and customs. 3. Humorists, American— 20th century—Biography. I. Title.
PS3569.I256Z477　1988　　　813'.54　[B]　　　85-42591
ISBN 0-06-015990-1

---

88 89 90 91 92 CC/HC 10 9 8 7 6 5 4 3 2 1

For my family, of course, and for all those unsung heroes, the city editors, living and dead, who sent me forth in quest of who-what-when-where-how and, if possible, why.

Prologue

Some time ago a reviewer, who gave a book of mine perhaps more attention than it merited, described a couple of my relatives as "eccentric." I was stunned. I wanted to look her up and shout childishly, "No such thing! My kinfolks aren't what-you-said, 'eccentric.'"

There's a gentler, kinder, maybe more southern term I think more applicable. I first encountered it when I was about four or five years old. We lived for a time on old Seville Square in Pensacola, Florida, and had as a neighbor a lady named Miss Derby.

Every seaport city probably has what is called a "waving girl," some odd old lady, who according to local legend, lost her lover at sea and goes every day to the waterfront to wave a welcome or a goodbye to passing ships. Miss Derby was Pensacola's and I was her assistant, perhaps the youngest "waving girl" on record.

We became friends when we happened to run away from home together one afternoon, following an organ grinder man and his monkey. I was hopelessly lost. Miss Derby had sufficient grasp of our whereabouts to get us home. After that I saw a lot of the old lady, who lived in what they call a light housekeeping room upstairs in an old house with galleries all around it. She had many cats and was probably thin because she spent whatever little money she had to feed them. She was nourished mainly by water sweetened with cane syrup and we drank a lot of it sitting on the upstairs gallery, looking out through the branches of a great live oak tree at the sailors and their girls walking in the square or sitting on its iron benches.

Miss Derby may have been unusual looking but a four-year-old's experience with the usual is small. I thought her richly hennaed hair was beautiful. Her long dresses of georgette and chiffon, I suppose now, were tattered and not very clean and there was a musty smell about her person that didn't offend me. I hated to bathe myself. But, best of all, she wore bedroom slippers everywhere, little kid slippers with the heels bent in so she walked on them and toes ornamented with yarn pompoms, which she made herself and changed often to get a variety of color. She taught me how to make them, a skill that I still proudly possess.

Between making pompoms out of yarn, drinking syrup-flavored water and playing with her cats, Miss Derby and I made frequent trips through the park to a long rock jetty that thrust out into Pensacola Bay. Sometimes we had to wait a long time for a big ship to go by but we waved impartially at anything passing—sailboats, fishing smacks, little oyster boats. I didn't know why we were doing it but I enjoyed it. Miss Derby always had a white handkerchief to wave and finally she gave me one, on the theory, I suppose, that bare-handed waving wasn't as visible to the seafarers as a big white handkerchief.

The best part of our waving vigil was that the ships' masters whose home port was Pensacola and some of the foreign captains saluted us by blowing a whistle when they passed. We left the jetty in a fine glow of pleasure at the recognition.

One afternoon we were walking homeward through the park and a group of older children started following us shouting derisively. I remember to this day that they yelled at me:

> *"Cel-us-stine, Cel-us-stine,*
> *Ballheaded Yankee bean!*
> *High ball, low ball,*
> *Ball-headed Cel-us-stine!"*

Miss Derby took my hand and started walking fast, her little heelless slippers going slip-slap on the pavement.

"Crazy, crazee!" shouted one of the meaner children. "Old lady Derby is *crazy!*"

It wasn't an indictment I understood but it made Miss Derby cry, something so surprising and distressing that I told my mother about it when I got home. I don't know where she thought I was all those afternoons I was out waving but she didn't seem surprised at my friendship with Miss Derby.

"Is Miss Derby crazy?" I asked.

"No, honey," said my mother. "She's not crazy, she's just turned funny."

There it is, the term that I have heard applied over and over again through the years to the odd, the unusual, the nonconforming. Not crazy, not insane, not eccentric, for goodness' sake, but turned funny. There's a patience with the turned funny, even an enjoyment of the foibles, which people have in practically every family I know in the South and, I suspect, in families all over the world. Some of them have a piquant singularity, some of them—the ones at the other extreme— are behind bars. But from Miss Derby, I suppose, I learned to value them. I once thought it was because they were more *interesting* than regular, run-of-the-mill mortals. Now I wonder if it is because they and I have a certain bond born of compatibility.

Of this I am certain, life has interested me a great deal because of my acquaintance with turned funny citizens—murderers, politicians, street preachers, beggars, actors, cops and robbers, and even a few rich and stylish people like the old lady in Mobile who used to say she loved to sit on her front porch on Government Street and watch "the cars go pro and con." I have loved the never-the-sameness of people and time and places and events. Only an idiot would suggest that it has all been easy—not for me or any single soul I have known. But when E. B. White assembled some of his old, largely autobiographical pieces for the delightful collection, *The Second Tree from the Corner,* he spoke of putting his affairs in order "such as they are," harvesting "what fruit he has not already picked up and stored away against the winter" and tying his "love for the world into a convenient bundle accessible to all."

So in spite of the inevitable pains and griefs, the occasional hardship and tragedy, this purports to be my bundle of love for the world, convenient, I hope, and accessible to all.

Part One

Chapter One

Before my mother died in early summer of 1976 she wanted to talk about it. The subject of her own death fascinated her, and the long-unremembered details of her childhood and the lives of the relatives who reared her came back to her mind with undimmed freshness.

"Come, sit down and let's talk," she would say as the twilight deepened around her little house in the northwest Florida town of Alford, where she had lived in her girlhood and to which she had returned in the early 1940s.

I couldn't bear to. I didn't want to believe she would not recover from the pains that had begun to rack her eighty-three-year-old body. I didn't want to know where she had put the deed to her house, the only thing she owned, or the name of the man to whom she had been paying her burial insurance for nearly forty years. The stories of the hard times through which her family had lived were painful to me.

"I'll be there in a minute," I'd lie and tackle with renewed frenzy cleaning out the utility room, where she had been saving brown paper bags since World War II. I scrubbed her oven and cleared out kitchen cupboards and replaced shelf papers. In the daytime I dragged the ladder around the house and washed windows with a mindless, obsessive fury.

She sighed and turned her attention to any neighbor who might be passing the gate.

"Come in," she would say hospitably, "and tell me the news."

While two old ladies talked, I cleaned madly, relieved that I didn't have to sit still and listen. Now I grieve that I didn't listen. Now I know there's nobody left to tell me things about my family in general

3

but especially the things about my mother, who was the most important person in all our lives for as long as she lived. When she died, I believe in her sleep, one hot afternoon in June, I was overwhelmed with guilt that I hadn't been with her.

She had called Atlanta to tell me, I think. At least she said "that pain" was back in her chest.

"Get Bessie to take you to the hospital," I said, referring to her next-door neighbor and unfailingly kind friend, Bessie Powell. "I'll be there as fast as I can."

"No, I'll wait for you," she said.

"Muv, I'm six hours away," I said, exasperated. "I'll get there as fast as I can but go on to the hospital."

"I may and I may not," she said obstinately and hung up.

Four of my grandchildren were spending time with me in the country and I had obligations at the Atlanta *Constitution,* where I worked, but I made arrangements as fast as I could, and my son, Jimmy, and I took off for Muv's house. We stopped for gas in Columbus and I called her. No answer. I called her neighbor, Bessie.

"She's asleep," said Bessie. "I was just over there and she seems to be resting."

Three hours later we drove up to her gate to find a police car parked under one of the big oak trees and neighbors standing about on the porch and in the yard. Stupidly, I didn't realize what had happened.

"What's going on?" I asked Buck Barnes, who lived across the street from her.

"Your mother has died," he said. "About an hour ago, they think."

It took me a long time, months, maybe years, to realize she had done what she wanted to do. She had no stomach for going back to the hospital and putting up with tubes and needles and the hideous exposure of tests and examinations. She had loved life but she knew she had death coming to her, and she was ready to claim it. I think she walked into her room and got in her bed and willed herself to die.

She may even have been sure the day before that death was imminent because when I went into the kitchen I found that she had done what she always liked to do when she knew that we were coming—"prepare" with turnip greens and a jelly cake, fresh cooked and waiting for us.

Through the years I listened to stories of my forebears, alternately

4

embarrassed and uncomfortable. They sounded so poor, so dirt poor, so heartbreakingly hangdog and hopeless. Even Muv's grandmother, who was said to be a "real lady," looks stringy and hard-bitten in the murky tintype that was left to us. Muv liked to talk about her beloved Grandma, who grew up in south Georgia and "had advantages," which included a melodeon in the parlor and some education at a nearby female academy.

Her undoing, as Muv used to tell it, was that she fell in love with "a sorry renter." Anybody who didn't have the git-up-and-git to own a piece of land was patently poor husband material. And Susan Nix's parents didn't want her to marry King Hinson. He must have had charms that were never perceived by his children and grandchildren because Susan was determined to marry him, and she started assembling pots and pans and dishes and quilts with marriage in mind. For years we had a little glass cream pitcher, all that was left of Susan's house fixings, which Muv said she bought at Henry Paulk's store in Willacoochee back in 1845.

Her mother, who was obviously no more gentle or diplomatic than women in our family have ever been, is said to have remarked: "You might as well buy dishes. *He'll* never get you any."

He must have bought dishes because they had twelve children who had to eat out of something. But apparently he was not given to indulging his Susan or their children in many of life's amenities. He stopped being a "sorry renter" and acquired land, a lot of land, which he tilled with the passionate devotion of the formerly landless. I know so little about him except that his children and grandchildren hated him as a harsh taskmaster, who made them work in the fields from can-till-can't. The older boys went off to fight with the Confederate Army and the girls took over the farm work. All I know about them is fragments, passed on by Muv from time to time through the years.

They weren't sent to school, she said, because "old King," as they called their father, did not consider education important, especially to females. Aunt Rose Ann, according to the stories, married a well-to-do widower, who lived in a painted house with glass windows, and since she couldn't read or write, she had to dictate the exuberant accounts of her new affluence to the folks at home.

"Just put down there," she directed to a niece or nephew, "that I'm a-settin' up here a-lookin' out my glass winders."

Aunt Dilly, the eldest of the girls, had been "promised" to a boy named John, who went off to fight in the Civil War and never returned, leaving her, at the age of fifteen years, a confirmed spinster, who would live the rest of her life in the role of servant and poor kin to the rest of the family.

Elizabeth, called Babe, was a sharp-tongued old lady when I knew her and I suppose she had good reason to be.

As a young girl she was working in the cotton field one day when some young people from a neighboring plantation passed by on their horses. She knew the young man in the crowd and, I suppose, thought that he had noticed her and been attracted to her. To have him catch her in the cotton field in a dirty, draggle-tailed skirt and sunbonnet, laboring like the slaves on his father's land, was more than she could bear.

She hid, face down, on the ground between the rows and refused to budge until the laughing and carefree young riders had gone their way. On her knees on her cotton sack, according to the story, she took a solemn vow that she would never, never work in the fields again. She would do anything that needed doing around the house but she would not pick cotton or hoe corn or harvest tobacco or ever again be caught in the role of field hand.

"Pa can beat me," she said, "but he can't make a field hand out of me."

I don't know if her pa did beat her. He may have had hands enough among his other children. But he didn't help them to the schooling they longed for or see that they learned to read and write. I know now that he wasn't alone in this. There were no public schools and only those who could afford private schooling were taught. But Aunt Babe was never reconciled. She taught herself, as well as she could, and when she was an old lady I remember her letters to my mother sometimes broke off and became drawings. We laughed when she wrote about getting some rabbits to raise and, unable to spell "rabbit," drew pictures of one. Now I know that it wasn't funny. Nor was it funny that Aunt Dilly, in her eighties, insisted on going to a circus with me and some of my teenage friends.

Why would an old lady like that want to horn in on the outing of a group of young folks? I asked my mother.

"Because," Muv said, "she wanted to go to the circus all her life. Once when she was a girl a circus came to Berrien County, Georgia, and she wanted to go bad. She found somebody who would pay a few cents apiece for guana sacks if she washed them. It wasn't easy work. Guana is smelly fertilizer. But she made enough money to buy tickets for herself and Aunt Babe and Aunt Molly. The day of the circus was Saturday, and they knocked off work and filled washtubs and bathed themselves and got dressed and ready to walk the five miles to Nashville to see it. Their father drove up in the yard as they were getting ready to leave and made them get back to the field."

What was the matter with that "real lady," Grandma, that she didn't intercede for her children? I don't know. But my impression is that she was relieved when the old tyrant died and she was free to travel around and visit with her married children.

Aunt Molly married a fun-loving Irishman named John Welch, who drank a little whiskey and played the fiddle and left her with three children when he died young and penniless. Aunt Babe married a railroadman named David Alonzo Kennedy, who was solid citizen enough to establish a home for his family, which became a refuge for all his wife's poor kin. Aunt Dilly and Aunt Molly and my mother were among this number, as was Aunt Babe and Uncle Lon's daughter, Theda, called Sister, when she divorced Uncle George Chapman and came home with their son, Roy. My mother's mother, my grand-mother, named Susan for her mother, was the most puzzling of the lot to me.

Sue, as her sisters called her, was said to be the prettiest of the girls, fair-skinned and red-headed, and full of mischief and fire. At the age of sixteen she married an older man of forty named John Barber and went to live in the little south Georgia town of Pearson. I know nothing of John except that my mother always regarded him as a gentleman from a good family, who was able to provide his wife with a nice two-story white house on the town's main street. He might not have been a good husband, but, on the other hand, Sue was not the most biddable wife. When her first and only child, my mother, was born in that tall white house, she took her and went home to the farm, where she dumped her baby and took off.

Muv, named Evelyn but called Dixie, found out later that John came looking for them, but her grandparents hid her and told him they didn't know where Sue had gone. He never found either of them and, according to family lore, was so grief-stricken his reason slipped and he was eventually committed to Milledgeville State Hospital for the Insane, where he died. My mother told me she wasn't sure of that

7

and always meant to visit the hospital and ask them to check their records for her father's name. Years later, when I was a reporter covering stories at the hospital, I saw a cemetery with many unmarked graves and I wondered but did not ask if my grandfather John Barber lay there.

Meanwhile, Sue became what my mother called "a traveling woman." Restless, never content to stay in one place more than a few days, she prowled the countryside, stopping to visit relatives, occasionally taking a job of some kind, usually as a housekeeper. When her daughter was old enough to go with her she took her along.

"Going, going, walking, walking, always traveling," Muv said.

Once they had a berth with a widower, who fell in love with Sue and asked her to marry him. She agreed and little Dixie was ecstatic.

"A good home and plenty at it," she told me.

The wedding was set and the bridegroom's married daughters came home to take a hand with the arrangements, helping to outfit Sue and Dixie with new finery and launching a cooking marathon to have a suitable feast for the wedding guests.

"I was so happy," Muv told me. "I loved that house and that old man, and I thought I was going to get to stay put and maybe go to school and church like other children."

The night before the wedding Sue slipped out of the house, taking Dixie with her. They walked to the nearest railroad line and flagged the first passing train.

"I never got over it," Muv said. "My, that would have been a nice home!"

I don't know how many years Sue's traveling went on before Dixie parted company with her. One night when they were visiting some aunt or cousin little Dixie saw the signs she had come to recognize in her mother—a restless tramping around and singing, too-ready laughter.

"I knew she was fixing to go again," she told me. "I knew I couldn't do it anymore. I was done with it. I went to the woods and hid out, and when she looked for me in my bed and I wasn't there, she left without me."

Somehow, Dixie made her way back to her grandmother's house, and there she stayed, except for periodic excursions to homes of relatives to "help out" where there was illness or a new baby.

"I knew I was always welcome where they had a lot of shitty

diapers to be washed," she said, using the word which was acceptable in that day but became scatological later.

Like the others, she wound up at Aunt Babe's, first in south Georgia and then in the little northwest Florida town that Alford Brothers, a sawmilling family, had laid out as a trading center. The Atlanta & St. Andrews Bay Railroad went through there and Uncle Lon was a foreman on the maintenance crew, traveling by handcar and spending weeks in camp cars on railroad sidings.

They bought a big weathered gray house with a barn and ample room for a mule and cows and pigs and a garden spot, and they acquired acreage out from town, where they grew velvet beans and corn and peanuts to feed animals and perhaps bring in a little cash from time to time. It was tended, not by Aunt Babe, happily, but by a hired man. When Uncle John Welch died Aunt Molly arrived, and when Grandma died Aunt Dilly arrived.

I was always moved by the story of how Aunt Dilly set off to make her home with her sister, carrying as her only worldly goods a basket of baby chickens on her arm. She was settled in the day coach and the train had traveled quite a distance before the conductor came for her fare and found she didn't have money enough to get her to Cottondale, where she would transfer to the A. & St. A. B. for Alford.

He could have put Aunt Dilly and her biddies off. She was timid, frightened, and helpless. Naïvely, she asked for credit. She told him her brother-in-law was a railroadman and he would send the money for her fare when she got to Alford.

Magnanimously, the conductor not only let her ride but accorded her the treatment members of the railroad fraternity reserved for relatives of the brotherhood in those days. She and her biddies arrived in triumph, and she stayed to help in time of sickness and sorrow, on washdays and with quiltings and yard sweepings, until she died at the age of ninety-six years.

My mother may not have been so useful, although I can't imagine any set of circumstances in which she didn't pitch in and do her share. At the age of sixteen she had worked as a printer's devil and later a reporter for the *Fitzgerald Enterprise* in south Georgia. She learned to set type by hand and she did enough writing of community personals and death notices to initiate a lifelong interest in the written word. One summer she took a flier into acting. She and a friend named Bessie Blum got jobs with a traveling stock company, which was touring south Georgia. Bessie, who was blonde and blue-eyed and a real beauty, according to Muv, signed on as a ticket seller, making such an enchanting picture at the box office that she later married the star-actor-director-producer of the company, an Englishman named Browning.

Surprisingly, it was Dixie, no beauty to hear her tell it, but feisty and uninhibited, who got a job acting. She played a cowgirl named Nugget Nell, and as long as she lived she could strike a pose and triumphantly deliver the punchlines of the play.

"Three aces and a king!" she would proclaim, holding aloft an imaginary poker hand, which, I think, saved the old homestead.

Muv wanted a picture as a keepsake of that halcyon experience, but the stock company had traveled on, taking with it not only her chum Bessie Blum but Nugget Nell's divided riding skirt and broad-brimmed cowgirl hat. Ever one to improvise, Dixie pinned back the broad brim of a straw hat and converted a regular skirt into a riding costume for the camera.

All her life she was to remember that summer's work as a tour de force, and when she yearned over movie stars and the stock-company performers who came to Mobile's Lyric Theatre in my childhood, I used to say, "Muv, why didn't you keep on being an actress?"

"My narrow-minded kinfolks," she would say. "They thought actresses were bad women."

Southern families who fled their homes at the approach of Union troops during the Civil War spoke of "refugeeing" as a desperate journey made with the devil at their heels. Forty years later Muv knew exactly how they felt. She refugeed to Aunt Babe's and Uncle Lon's in Alford "because I had no place else to go." The work she did there didn't provoke any criticism from her relatives because it certainly wasn't of the dubious moral caliber of newspapering or acting.

She trimmed hats and tried to get a husband—worthy occupations for any girl of that day.

She and a friend, Ezella Gilbert, opened a millinery shop in a vacant store building on Alford's main street, a dirt thoroughfare that ran parallel to the railroad tracks.

"We didn't sell many hats but we made some mighty pretty ones for ourselves," she told me later.

A becoming hat was a help to a girl trying to find a husband, and Dixie's confidence was high when a well-to-do young railroadman came a-courting.

"I should have married Tom, I reckon," she used to muse. "I'd have had a good home and plenty at it. But it was so funny about those pills."

A group of young people, including Dixie and Tom as her date, had gone in buggies to an all-day church meeting and sing at Chipley fifteen miles away. The heat and the music and maybe the unaccustomed travel gave Dixie a headache. Tom, the considerate suitor, sought out a drugstore and bought her some pills.

Reared by man-fearing aunts, Dixie wasn't about to take any potion administered by a young man. There was always the danger that he would, as they said, drug her to get her in his power. Dixie declined the pills and Tom doggedly took every one of them.

"Did he have a headache, too?" I used to ask.

"No!" Muv snorted. "He had a bad case of stingy. He said, 'I paid good money for these pills, I might as well get the use out of them.'"

That effectively scotched his case as prospective husband for Dixie. She didn't want a tightwad.

Her aunts thought they saw a likely candidate in the town's leading dry-goods merchant, a widower named Thompson. He was old for Dixie but he had that requisite, a good home and plenty at it, and he seemed to like her. He picked a propitious time for his first call on her—Christmas Day—arriving with a paper bag that obviously contained a present. Dixie met him at the front door and, since it was a warm day, invited him to take a seat beside her in the porch swing.

Sister, who saw the arrival of the suitor, noting the package in his hand, hurried to set up a listening post behind the concealing vines, which screened the porch.

After some throat clearing and preliminary comments on the weather Mr. Thompson got to the point. "Miss Dixie," he said abruptly, "I'm obleeged to tell you, you've somewhat won my affictions. I brung you a gift."

And he unwrapped an orange.

Back of the vines Sister broke into uncontrollable giggles.

"Huh!" snorted the startled merchant, peering near-sightedly over his shoulder. "I gotta go!"

And he stampeded, said Muv, like a spooked horse. He ran down the steps and cleared the gate without opening it. She would have been impressed by that physical feat in a man his age but he suddenly turned, fumbled for the latch, and galloped back up the walk, red-faced and apoplectic.

"Huh!" he snorted again. "I fergot my hat!"

Then Dixie broke up. When they were old ladies she and Sister could still giggle over the ignominious departure of Mr. Thompson.

That brought her down to Henry Colley, a blue-eyed, dark-haired giant of a fellow, who came through Jackson County on a cattle drive. He was six feet six inches tall, in his early twenties, and shyly interested in her. In all probability he talked about his father's house and store on East Bay in Santa Rosa County a hundred miles to the east. His mother was dead, his older brother had married and moved a mile or so down the beach, and he and his father ran the store and post office and kept house for themselves. It most certainly wasn't love at first sight for Dixie, if love at all, but she must have kept Henry in mind, because when he got back home and started writing to her she answered.

She never told me that he proposed marriage but she knew the option existed. One morning while most of the household slept she heard Aunt Babe and Uncle Lon stirring. He was ready to leave for his job on the railroad and Aunt Babe was assembling the things he would need for a week's stay in the camp car.

"I'm sorry you have to start so early," Muv heard her say, looking out at the predawn sky. "If you didn't have so many of my poor kinfolks a-laying up here on you, you wouldn't have to work so hard."

Stung to the quick, Dixie wrote to Henry Colley that day, and shortly afterward she made herself a tweed suit and a blouse with a white lace fichu to dress it up and caught the train to Pensacola, where he met her and they were married. He later told East Bay friends that they agreed to meet on "neutral ground," each of them going by train to Cottondale, where they lunched together and he bought her a watch and a pistol. My mother never mentioned the Cottondale meeting, but she talked often of the home she found on East Bay.

"I didn't know I was driving my ducks to a bad market," she would confess with a rueful smile. "How could I? He told me his papa was a big landowner and had a store and a post office and a nice house overlooking the water. It was true then. But it changed. At first it was as good a stay-place as anybody would want. Grandpa Colley was a

12

fine gentleman—always wore a suit and a tie and a black felt hat. He treated me like his own daughter. In fact, he called me 'Daughter,' instead of by my name."

It was a journey from the security of the known world of her mother's safe, if grudging family, to the unknown world of her bridegroom's family, but Dixie took to it with enthusiasm and high hopes.

Although little more than a hundred miles from Aunt Babe's house and the defunct millinery shop, it was a new and strange land to her, beautiful and isolated but in some ways more cosmopolitan than any place she had lived. To get to Holley (named for a preacher, not a tree) and her father-in-law's homestead and post office a mile to the east down the beach, she had to take a boat from Pensacola. When the wind blew and storms brewed, travel to the outside world was hazardous, if not impossible. And yet the citizens of East Bay didn't feel deprived. They felt that they had nearly everything they needed within reach—two or three stores, two churches, employment in logging, crosstie cutting, turpentining, and boatbuilding.

The land, rich, untamed "new ground" mostly, produced abundantly—sugar-cane crops for the coveted winter supply of "long sweetening," corn, and, most sustaining of all, the great carmine-fleshed sweet potatoes, which would be banked in straw-laced mounds and last all winter. Peach trees did well and the woods abounded in huckleberries and blackberries. There was succulent grass aplenty for the small range cattle, and acorns and palmetto berries and roots for roaming razorback hogs. The sheltered bay, which curved in front of them, and the big Yellow River, which sprang up in Alabama and flowed behind them, yielded a seemingly endless supply of fish and oysters. The forests were nearly impenetrable, with a virgin growth of pine, oak, cypress, and juniper, and full of deer, wild turkey, and fur-bearing animals, which they trapped for their hides.

On the map East Bay looked—and still does—like the tail on the big blue rooster of Pensacola Bay, a south-curving prong of indigo water. Century-old live oaks, twisted and lichened by the turbulent winds, shaded the white-sand shoreline.

The main street was a dirt road running along the bayside, but it was a lively thoroughfare, lined with the bright-painted houses of Swedish settlers named Anderson, Nelson, and Bengston. From them came the laughter and play sounds of many children because families in that community frequently numbered ten or twelve children each. (One of my father's uncles had a record eighteen by two wives and a neighbor known only as Florence. He claimed them all.) There was also the smell of good cooking, exotic foreign-named cakes and strudels, brought from Scandinavia, and rich fish chowders, which my mother could never quite emulate and never quite forgot.

The Broxsons, my father's maternal ancestors, may have come from Sweden originally but they had been in the United States for generations. Robert Broxson, the first one to settle in the Florida panhandle, was born in South Carolina in 1812 and was apparently a planter there, because he had thirteen slaves.

He moved to Florida several years before it attained statehood in 1845 and, according to William J. Wells, who wrote a delightful book about the area (*Pioneering in the Panhandle*), farmed until the Emancipation Proclamation freed his slaves in 1863. Then he switched to lumbering. According to a family story, some of the slaves followed the Broxsons to Miller Point on East Bay, where they moved into a mill house next door and continued to work for and were fed by the Broxsons.

Robert and his wife, the former Mary Ellen Lovett, of Holmes County, Florida, had ten children, the second of whom was my grandmother, Susan, born in 1850. According to the stories told to my mother, who, of course, didn't arrive until a few years after Susan's death in 1911, she was a beautiful woman and well loved by countless East Bay children, who called her Aunt Sook.

William Henry Colley was in the logging business on Yellow River with her younger brother, Joseph, and must have begun to pay court to Susan when he came home from the Civil War. For, although he was a native of Barbour County, Alabama, he fought with a Florida company, Company F, First Florida Regiment, which went on to Shiloh. He may have been married twice, although I never heard that, but there is a headstone in the Holley Cemetery that reads "W. H. Colley, Jr. Born April 22, 1862. Died October 31, 1889." There is no marked grave of a first wife. Anyhow, Henry and Susan were married July 20, 1871, and were elderly for that time, forty-eight and forty respectively, when my father, called Little Henry, was born in 1890. (I don't know when his older brother, Clark, was born.)

According to legend still current on East Bay, there were "salt-water Broxsons and fresh-water Broxsons." Many of them were both, moving from river to bay and bay to river and back again. Henry Colley, Sr., made a salt-water Broxson of his bride, Susan, taking her from Yellow River to a beautiful wooded spot on the bay. There they built a neat white house back of the Harper post office and store and the substantial wharf, from which barrels of turpentine, from L. D. Bryan's still a couple of miles inland, were shipped out to Pensacola three days a week.

The bridegroom had bought from the government a full lot of land, less four and a half acres designated for a Baptist church and grave-yard. There they reared their two sons, Clark and Henry, establishing them on neighboring homesteads—the great land bonanza responsi-ble for settling much of the area. In order to persuade settlers to go west, the Homestead Act of 1862 had offered 160 acres to anybody who would settle on the land and care for it for five years. The offer also applied to Florida, a newcomer among states and still largely unsettled. Clark and Henry claimed 160 acres each, which gave that branch of the Colley family a fair chunk of the beautiful Santa Rosa peninsula.

Years later, when my mother grew restless and dissatisfied with life as she was living it, she would say, "I'm going to get me a homestead." I don't think she knew that the offer was withdrawn in 1934 when President Franklin D. Roosevelt abolished the homestead system.

But her arrival at East Bay in 1915 was an occasion for celebration among Little Henry's friends and relatives. His brother, Clark, had married Ellen Anderson, daughter of Swedish neighbors, and moved down near the mouth of the bay on a tract from the Andersons' homestead. Little Henry and Henry, Sr., batched together and defi-nitely felt the need of a woman's hand in the house. When Henry had reached the age of twenty-three with no indication that he was inter-ested in the local girls, his friends and neighbors were concerned. According to William James Wells, a friend told Little Henry about the Lonely Hearts Club, which published a matrimonial bulletin. It was the place to write to get himself a bride, they said. Little Henry gave it a try and had response enough, according to Bill Wells, who thought my mother had been one of the applicants. (She emphatically denied it.)

Anyhow, he met and married Dixie, and when he brought her home to the bay, the population, numbering chiefly his kinfolks, turned out to welcome them. Their first night, to my mother's chagrin, they were "shivareed" by the exuberant young blades of the bay. French settlers of Florida had called it a *charivari,* a noisy serenade to newlyweds. The American pioneers pronounced it "shivaree" and it meant the same—a tumultuous night-long commotion around the honeymoon house, engendered by moonshine and good feelings and punctuated by pistol shots. My mother hated it and the series of "frolics" that followed.

She never forgot one such party in the little white clapboard Methodist-Congregational church at Holley, where there were bountiful food and drink and fiddle music and singing, interrupted by the arrival of a bunch of roistering young fellows, who rode their horses around the church, cracking the long whips used on oxen logging teams, and shooting off their pistols. She had already backed timidly into a corner when the young bucks dismounted and came rolling merrily into the church with the avowed intention of kissing the bride.

Little Henry, to her surprise, did not attempt to rescue her.

"I had to look after myself and I was ready for them," she recalled. "I had a hatpin and I used it!"

That night may have been the tip-off that Little Henry wasn't going to look after her. She didn't notice it as long as his father lived, for they truly had a good home and plenty at it. And, when she became pregnant with me, Henry, Sr., was delighted and spoiled her, ordering off to Pensacola for special foods not available in the store, and yard goods from which to make baby clothes. He encouraged her efforts to fix up the house and was apparently far more interested than his son when she bought cheesecloth to paste over the plank walls and flower-sprigged wallpaper to paste on the cheesecloth. She made scrim curtains and cut fancy paper valances for the mantels and planted flowers everywhere, drawing freely on seeds and cuttings from her neighbors, as well as ordering from the catalogues.

Henry, Sr., bought her a saddle horse, and she rode around the bay visiting families she was to remember with affection all her life. Aunt Sister and her little boy Roy arrived to spend the winter with Dixie, and the two cousins put in many happy hours making baby clothes for the expected one. Grandpa ordered a pair of Keen Kutter scissors for the enterprise and Dixie cherished them as long as she lived, keeping them sharp and frequently angrily rescuing them from various playhouses when I reached doll-clothes and paperdoll age. The day after her funeral when my children and I were preparing to go back to Atlanta, my daughter Susan said, "Maybe you should take some of Muv's things that you want to keep. Her silver?"

Muv had bought a service for eight with money she saved from teaching school during World War II years and I knew she valued it. But I had no inclination to pick through her things and take them out of her house. Not so soon. Then I remembered her scissors, the ones the grandfather I never knew bought, the ones she used to cut out my baby dresses and those of my children and grandchildren. I opened her work basket and picked them up and took them home with me.

Grandpa died in 1917 shortly after I was born and by that time my little brother was on the way. Things at the Colley homestead seem to have changed drastically. The store closed. My father lost the post office. Storms buffeted the little house, and Little Henry's legs broke out with sores, which were to bedevil him all his life.

"He wouldn't get out of bed to put the mail bag on the boat," Muv told me later. "I did it until I was so pregnant I was ashamed to be seen. I'd call and call him, trying to get him out of bed, and one morning I saw him flying down the wharf with the mail bag, wearing nothing but his shirt, the tail flapping in the breeze!"

Dixie was delighted with my little brother, naming him Vernon Castle for the famous dancer. But there was no indulgent grandfather to buy him Horlick's Malted Milk and a silver cup, as he had bought me, and life was getting increasingly precarious for the whole family. Dixie, proud and energetic and determined never to be anybody's "poor kin" again, did not want help from even the kindest of Little Henry's relatives, although most of them were considered well-off by local standards, and all of them treated her husband with the affection and indulgence they had accorded the gangling, good-humored giant all his life.

"Old High Pockets," they would say fondly. "Nary a bit of harm in him."

Dixie agreed. He was amiable and gentle and kind to her and his children, but he wouldn't or couldn't earn a living. When the house and store and post office were gone, they moved to Bagdad, a little mill town to the north, and Little Henry went out looking for work.

I don't know how long he was gone, but we ran out of food and

17

my little brother, never robust, seemed to sicken on biscuits and flour gravy, which was all that was left in the larder. Taking him in her arms and me by the hand, my mother walked across the railroad trestle to a store where she had bought food in the past.

She asked to get a few things on credit. Her husband was away looking for work and would pay when he returned.

"I'm sorry, Miss Dixie," the grocer said. "I can't give you any more credit. Little Henry ain't good for it."

Dixie lifted her chin proudly and turned away quickly. The baby in her arms saw a pile of bright red apples on the counter and reached out his hand.

"Ap, Ma," he implored. "Ap?"

Humiliated and angry at him for reaching for what she was powerless to give him, Dixie slapped her baby's hand—a blow that left a bruised place in her own heart as long as she lived.

"He got sicker during the night," she told me. "I knew he needed nourishment and my colored neighbors—Lord, they was good!—they must have known it too. They came and brought a frying-size chicken cooked tender and juicy with gruel. We tried to feed him, a spoonful at the time, but it was too late. He died that day."

They took his body back to East Bay on the *Monroe W.,* the passenger launch that ran between the bay and Pensacola. It was a windy, rainy day, but Dixie sat in the stern of the boat and held on to the little coffin, which swayed and rocked with the boat's rough passage.

Vernon Castle was buried in an unmarked grave in the Harper cemetery beside his Colley grandparents. Muv never meant to leave his grave without a headstone, and months later in Pensacola she bought a small angel of some insubstantial material. She had it on a table by her bed, ready to take back to East Bay, when she could go, but I was bouncing on the bed one day, pretending to drive a horse, and I knocked the angel to the floor. It shattered.

When anyone speaks of ineradicable childhood guilts I remember that. Muv slapped me and I cried and then she held me in her arms and we cried together.

Although the marriage was not legally severed (it never was, as a matter of fact), it was over. Whatever affection she had once had for the awkward, boyish fellow she married turned to hatred. She despised the slow, plodding way he moved. The country occupation of whittling, universally pursued by a man with a sharp knife, a good piece of wood, and time on his hands, filled her with rage. She hated the way he smelled, the sores he wouldn't get treated, and the way he dressed. And, when he took up Bible reading and quoting scriptures to answer any question she had about some workaday matter, she took a perverse pleasure in attacking God, the church, and all religions—this despite her own previously strong religious convictions.

There must have been some effort at reconciliation on Little Henry's part, and I think his relatives probably considered Dixie unreasonable and peremptory to leave him. I have a foggy recollection of being on the bay with him when she wasn't there and being taken to a little house beside a bridge where it crossed a beautiful stream that flowed like amber over white sand. He must have told me that mama was coming and that we might live there, because I found a left-behind broom and swept the vacant rooms. There was a crape-myrtle bush by the back door and I broke off a flowering branch and set it in a jar of creek water. Like my mother, I wanted a home and I clung to the fantasy, fostered by my father, that we would all be together again.

When Dixie came she looked at the little house sadly and hugged me and shook her head. We must have been staying with some of the Broxson relatives because I remember that she gave them most of her household goods. I don't know what she saved or how she took care of it in the wanderings that followed, but years later, when she was back in Alford and I was grown up, she gave me a little pink-flowered cup, which, she said, had belonged to my Grandmother Colley.

Ah, I thought, she's just telling me that because she knows that an old cup is thrice valuable to me if it has a family connection. Later we drove down to East Bay and in the Harper cemetery I found the mate to Grandma Colley's cup on her grave. It had held flowers at some time or other but winter rains had frozen and broken it and summer suns had faded its pretty pattern, but it was from the same set of dishes. I picked up the pieces and wiped the sand from them and took them home with me. I keep the whole cup on the guest-room mantel to hold matches and the broken one carefully wrapped in a cupboard.

Once one of my daughters asked me why I kept a broken cup and

19

I couldn't think why. It's a legacy, I suppose, from the grandmother I never knew, a tenuous connection with the whole big East Bay family, known to me mostly because my mother remembered them with affection and a sense of regret that she couldn't be closer to them.

A few years before her death a friend from her East Bay days, Frances Hurst, came to see us in Atlanta and later took my mother and me, my daughter Mary, and granddaughter Sibley around East Bay to visit the cemeteries and a couple of friends of long ago. An old lady who had been a beautiful young girl when Muv first knew her lived in a trailer in a grove of trees a few yards from where the Colley homestead, my birthplace, had been. While she and Muv reunioned, Mary and Sibley and I wandered down to the water to see if there was any trace of the old house. There was none.

Later we stopped by a weathered gray house by the East River. It was home and business enterprise, a fishing camp, to a handsome, lively, barefoot old lady named Ola Broxson. Sibley, who up until then had been the only female among my four grandchildren, met the eighty-odd-year-old Ola (called Oler) with delight.

"At last!" she cried. "A girl cousin!"

I was equally moved at meeting a cousin—any cousin—having practically no relatives at all. We hugged Cousin Ola and begged her to visit us in Atlanta and she promised she would but she never did. Frances wrote us that she died a few months later.

We went back to the old cemeteries and Muv read the headstones of people who had been young and full of ebullient life when she knew them. The wind soughed through the moss-strung oaks and whipped a ruffle of foam on the waves rolling in to the beach. The small church, where she had fended off her well-wishers with a hatpin, was there and little changed, its white clapboard only stained by time and weather, its dusty interior inhabited by dirt daubers and spiders. Down the road at Harper the original church had been replaced with an expanded concrete-block structure to accommodate new worshipers, who had followed the paved road from the Santa Rosa Sound inland or come down from the new superhighway a few miles to the north to build ranch houses along the bay shore and up to the edge of lands once homesteaded by my kinfolks, now Eglin Air Force reservation.

Muv sat long moments on a tombstone feeling the wind from the bay and thinking about Grandpa, whom she had loved and the little baby she had lost.

"I think I'd like to be buried here," she said, even then thinking of her own death. "It's beautiful and peaceful. You'll see to it, won't you?" she asked me.

Later she told me not to bother. She had changed her mind.

"They're not my people anymore. I gave them up and went away. I have no right to be there now. I'll stick with my own kinfolks in Alford."

Chapter Two

A few years ago I wrote a novel called *Jincey,* which I hoped was a "road" book, the story of the journey of a courageous, spirited woman with little education and no resources to find a home for herself and her child. It was, of course, fiction, but no less a writer than E. B. White has pointed out that everything a writer writes is to some extent autobiographical. *Jincey* is, perhaps, more than I intended it to be.

My mother, like Della in the book, lost a baby and fled from a husband she despised. She did it clumsily, not always playing by the rules, but she did it. Once when the scorned husband attempted to deter her with a ploy reminiscent of a country-song title—"If I can't have you, we'll die together"—my mother bluffed him by pulling the pistol first. At times she was frightened and hungry. At times she was desperately worried about me, fearful of fire if she left me alone, frightened of a child molester if she took me to the park to play where she could keep an eye on me while she worked in a Pensacola store. She was terrified that I would be hungry in Mobile, where she couldn't seem to find a job, and applied to the Salvation Army for milk. When it came she couldn't bring herself to accept it, and haughtily told the delivery man that there must be some mistake, we had plenty of milk.

Two or three times when things got bad or when my father was on trail of us (once he wrote the police and asked help in finding a "kidnaped" child), she would let me go back to East Bay as per the agreement to "go halvers" on me. The next to the last time she did, indeed, kidnap me, snatching me from under the noses of the couple my father was supposedly boarding me with. That time, determined to put as much distance as possible between him and us, we went to Mobile. We lived in the tiny hall bedroom of a St. Joseph Street rooming house, and she spent every day job-hunting.

It must have seemed like the ultimate defeat when she had to wire Sister in Alford and ask for railroad fare to send me back to that set of relatives. They were, after all, the ones she meant to "show" when she married Henry Colley. But Dixie was young and tough and determined, and she prevailed. She got a job in an overall factory—hard work and low, low pay—and found a room with a couple of friends from her youth in Georgia. They were Aunt Ida and Uncle J. C. Pumphrey. (I called them "aunt" and "uncle," as I called all older relatives, near-relatives, and friends of my parents. I think it might have been a southern custom, but then what do I know about the form of address in Dubuque or Ithaca?) They lived at 219 South Jackson Street, an address I remember with a sense of guilt because, after my mother drilled it into my memory in case I should get lost, I went back to East Bay for a short time and I inadvertently told it to my father. I don't know how old I was. School on East Bay was very sketchy for me. I went for maybe a month once, enough to learn my ABCs and after that I think the term ended. But I remember being terribly agitated when my father took out a pencil and wrote the address down on an envelope. I begged him not to and tried to wrest it from his hand and cried until he promised me that he would never use it and never, never come there. For a long time I feared that he would appear at 219 South Jackson and my mother would regard that as a disaster—a disaster, worse yet, of my making. But he kept his promise and never appeared.

The house we lived in at 219 South Jackson was, I know now, an exceptionally nice one. A music teacher (I think her name was Miss Nellie Sumerall) owned it and must have loved it. I haven't seen it since I was about seven years old, but I think of it as white clapboard, vaguely Victorian, with decorative bannisters along a small front porch, a cupola room at one corner, a bay window in the dining room, screened in spring by a magnificently fragrant purple wisteria, and spacious double parlors with sliding doors between them. I think Miss Sumerall rented it out and moved to the eastern shore of Mobile bay and I hope that she never saw the pass it came to when we lived there.

23

Aunt Ida and Uncle J. C. and their son Joel lived in the front parlor, with two beds and an armoire to hold their clothes, a rocking chair for Aunt Ida, who did a lot of sitting and rocking, and a leather davenport in the front hall. Muv and I lived in the back parlor—bed, dresser, and a two-burner oil stove in the corner for our kitchen. Floor-to-ceiling windows flanked a marble fireplace, where we rarely had a fire, lacking twenty-five cents for a bucket of coal. We usually hovered around the front-room fire with Aunt Ida and Uncle J. C. The windows opened out on a two-story porch, where the delicate coral vine, with deep pink flowers strung along its length like rosy beads, made a screen. Aunt Ida let her son Joel and me strip the vine of its flowers to make play jewelry and laughed when we broke the central stalk out of a handsome palm tree and Joel held it aloft striking a pose and yelling, "Statue of Liberty!"

My mother loved flowers and planted them when she could, and she would have been horrified at the carnage in Miss Sumerall's yard—the trampled lilies, the opulent elephant ears we broke for shields for fencing à la Douglas Fairbanks, the banana fronds we pulled to fashion into sunhats. But Muv was too busy to notice Miss Sumerall's yard or our destructive play.

She was back at her old quest—trying to get a husband.

There was a serious obstacle to getting a good home and plenty at it: me. There had been a young lawyer who took an interest in her when she worked as cashier in a drugstore in Pensacola during one of my sojourns on East Bay. He had proposed marriage and taken her to a house his family owned in the then-fashionable North Hill district. (I read recently that they now call it the North Hill Restoration District.) When she picked a room and murmured that it would be mine he was plainly upset. He had thought that I would be living with my father. Dixie walked out on the young lawyer, the North Hill house, and all.

We were back where we started. This time she meant to be careful. But working in a factory wasn't the best place to meet men. All the workers at the big power-driven sewing machines were women, and the foreman, who drove them to work ever harder and harder, was middle-aged and married, with two or three hungry female hirelings eager to grab him if he should become available. Occasionally there was a chance to go out with a seaman from one of the ships that came into port, and after a date or two with one of these awkward lads, Muv was strengthened in her conviction that a child was a drawback to getting a husband.

So when she met Bob Sibley it was time for strategy.

As in *Jincey,* Dixie got a night job working on the gown of the Mardi Gras queen, Mobile society's most magnificent production. Somebody told her extra seamstresses were needed in a last-minute push toward carnival. She applied and was hired. Every day, after a full shift at the overall factory, she would catch the streetcar out Government Street and sew beads on the sumptuous stately white satin gown that season's luckiest debutante would wear to her coronation at the peak of the Fat Tuesday revelry.

It happened that one night she worked so late the streetcars had stopped running and the queen's cousin, a young fellow with a high country haircut and well-shined but old-man-style hightop shoes, took her home. He had a Model-T Ford with a canary-bird whistle rigged under the hood and a string attached to the steering column for trilling it as he sped around corners. She laughed delightedly at his musical whistle and frankly exulted in the heady excitement of car riding, a rare experience in those days.

The cousin was Wesley Reeder Sibley and he liked her.

Although he lived way out in the country—eighteen miles—he found it possible to swing by his cousin's house and take the seamstress home on several nights. Sometimes they stopped at the Metropolitan Restaurant on Royal Street for a crab omelet, and they must have taken an occasional drive out Cedar Point Road, where you could buy Hires root beer in a frosted mug and watch the miracle of moonlight on Mobile Bay.

They both loved to sing, and I heard them laughing together and trying to harmonize the barbershop favorite "On Mobile Bay" one night when they sat parked late in front of the house.

After a while it became standard procedure for us to listen for the canary-bird whistle on Saturday nights, and when we heard it I would disappear and my mother would head for the front door. If Mr. Sibley came in and caught me—and he never got beyond the front hall—I was to call her not Mama but "Miss Evelyn."

Aunt Ida and I both asked "Why?" at the same time.

"Because it's my name," Muv told Aunt Ida. "My father named me that and my mama's poor country kin stuck me with Dixie. I'm sick and tired of having the kind of name every whore in the world has. From now on I'm Evelyn."

But why "Miss Evelyn" to me?

Muv elucidated. We were embarking on the biggest scam ever pulled at 219 South Jackson Street or its vicinity. From that moment on she was my guardian, not my mother. If we succeeded, we were headed for a good home and plenty at it, never to be separated again.

I was game, thrice game after Mr. Sibley took Joel and me out for root beers and car riding a couple of times and let us blow the canary whistle. And then there was the circus.

I was seven years old and not having a very good time in the second grade at Tucker School. Looking back, I am bewildered by my misery there. When children in our family have been miserable in school I have tried repeatedly but usually unsuccessfully to fathom it. Because she could sew, my mother kept me dressed presentably, usually in dresses made from some grown person's hand-me-downs. Except for Joel, who was older and in the fifth or sixth grade, I knew nobody at the school, and circles of friendship were already formed when I got there and were seemingly closed against me. It shouldn't have mattered. I had a good teacher, a kind gray-haired woman named Miss Parker, who was patient and encouraging. But nothing I tried seemed to work.

If we were told to memorize a poem I could do it, only to have it go right out of my head when I got to school. Once we had to write a paragraph about a bird. When I think of all the paragraphs I have written since about birds and otherwise, I am dumfounded that I could not think of a single sentence that day. I was frozen in blankness, my mind locked tight.

The circus came to town and all the children who could go brought notes from their parents and were dismissed from school early. It never occurred to me that I could go. I don't think I even knew what a circus was.

But about noon a strange and fearful thing happened. I was called to the principal's office. There stood my mother and Mr. Sibley, come to take me to the circus!

Many wonderful and astounding things have happened to me since that fall day in 1924 but nothing to compare with that circus. Mr. Sibley made sure that I didn't miss a clown or an elephant or a spangled lady aerialist. He bought me cotton candy in a paper cone and a cardboard clown so cunningly put together that when you pull a string he dances (I still have him). Professor Eddy was there with his trained seals and a man with a pistol and a chair fearlessly made ferocious lions and tigers do his bidding. A fat lady in boots with a beribboned whip put ponies and poodle dogs through a marvelous act.

I went home full of peanuts and popcorn and a grand weariness. Oddly enough, after that school seemed better—and we married Mr. Sibley!

One Sunday afternoon Miss Evelyn and Mr. Sibley drove to Pascagoula, Mississippi, the Gretna Green for that part of the country, and were married by a justice of the peace. There was some talk back at 219 South Jackson about a tiresome thing called bigamy. I didn't know what it was but Uncle J. C. was a policeman and he seemed to take it seriously. I remember that my mother dismissed it lightly.

"Go catch a murderer," she told him.

The newlyweds went to Mr. Sibley's family seat—Hatter's Mill at Creola—to pick one of the quarters houses and move into it. And I, left behind temporarily, broke out with chicken pox.

They came to get me at the end of the week. In *Jincey* I quoted Uncle J. C. as saying (and I believe it to be true) that the poor bridegroom didn't deserve what he was getting—a bigamist wife and a poxy youngun.

For me it was a memorable time for two reasons. On that Sunday morning, while the rest of the household slept, I got up with my itching, running welts and went out on the side porch. Mr. Sibley was in the yard in khaki coveralls doing something to his car, and he saw me and came and looked at my rash and sympathized with me. Then he told me about where we were going to live—a place where he had spent most of his childhood and which he loved more than any place in the world. It was to be my home, too, he said, and he solemnly took my hand and said a sentence that was, of course, a cliché and he knew it. But to this day it is a line that holds for me imperishable beauty.

"You're as welcome," he said, "as the flowers in May."

The other thing happened as we neared the mill. We stopped by the side of the road before a dark rectangle of sawmill house with lamplight showing at the door. It was where Mr. Jimmy Myers, of a long-time Hatter's Mill family, and his wife, Miss Lillie, and their five children lived. Mr. Sibley trilled the canary-bird whistle and three of

27

the children came out to the car bringing me a puppy.

Living in furnished rooms and other people's houses, I had never had a pet of any kind. I held that warm, loving little animal in my arms and I think I knew instinctively that he, better than all else, represented my at-homeness.

For years my mother was to laugh at how awed I was the first night by the beauty and splendor that were ours. It was a plain little sawmill house made of rough unpainted pine, and it consisted of five rooms, lined up two by two with a shed room tacked on the back for a kitchen, one porch across the front two rooms and another porch opening into the kitchen at the back. Muv had picked it from all the vacant houses at the mill because it was bigger than most, on a little hill and had a fine stand of water oaks and one big chinquapin tree shading it. There was also the advantage of a nearby water supply, a pitcher pump on a little platform a few yards up the road. Everybody had to "tote water" in the country in those days and we not as far as most.

In the week between their marriage and my arrival Miss Evelyn had scrubbed the house, walls and floors, removing layers of newspaper that some previous tenant had flour-pasted to the walls. Then she and Mr. Sibley had taken a man with a truck from the mill and gone into Mobile to borrow furniture from the big Victorian house on LaFayette Street that belonged to his mother, then a patient and for many years before at the state hospital for the insane at Tuscaloosa. A servant's house in the backyard held an overflow of out-of-service furniture, and Miss Evelyn picked a horsehair loveseat and two platform rockers to match and a dark oak library table for what was to be our parlor, a brass bed and mattress and springs and a marble-topped dresser for their bedroom, a big oak dining table with chairs and a sideboard, and best of all, for me, a neat little daybed with a Roman-striped fringed cover.

Incongruous for a rough sawmill shanty? We didn't know it. We thought it was beautiful. And there was one other touch of elegance that night—a folding deck chair of bright-colored duck with a handy footrest set up in one corner of the dining room. Muv directed me to sit in it and put my feet up, and then she brought me Lucullan fare—a piece of raisin bread and a glass of buttermilk.

It was an auspicious beginning for an exceptionally happy life, for I was very happy at Hatter's Mill in Creola, Alabama, for all my growing-up years.

28

The night before I was married a banker friend of my husband-to-be mentioned that he had served on a jury in a lawsuit against the Southern Railway for a small piece of Hatter land taken by the line.

"Old Hatter," he said of my stepfather's uncle, had gone crazy over losing a little strip of worthless land—part of a big tract of sorry cut-over pine woods—that his family had owned.

I was aghast at that description and I suppose I still am. It was the most beautiful spot on earth to me, and I well understood that they couldn't bear to lose any small part of it.

Thomas Aaron Hatter, as I've always heard—and I haven't really checked it—came to Mobile County from Virginia and acquired hundreds of acres of pine forest north of Mobile. He built a sawmill and a turpentine still, which would later supply lumber and naval stores to Admiral Raphael Semmes's pitiful little Confederate Navy. He dammed up a creek and made a beautiful big pond, designed, I suppose, to float the logs to the steam-powered sawmill, but he must have recognized that it was a jewel-like ornament to the landscape, for he built his bride, Miss Virginia Reeder, also from Virginia, a handsome three-story house facing the water and planted an avenue of water oaks leading to it. The house had burned before I came along but the pond endured, a deep amber reservoir of bright water, where I learned to swim and fish and paddle a pirogue. I rode my horse to the head of the pond and picnicked on its banks, sometimes alone, later with friends from town. I met my first alligators in that body of water, peaceful loglike fellows that drifted by with only their big eye knobs breaking the surface, harming no one. Once I, too, drifted, lying in the bottom of my boat for an afternoon of reading. I heard a splash and saw a deer, big and heavily-antlered, come to the pond to drink.

The place was full of magic.

Marrying Wesley Reeder Sibley was some kind of magic in itself. I felt that I helped bring that miracle to pass because I was such an *unnoticeable* child. I knew how to "go play" at crucial moments. I learned quickly the lines Muv drilled me in: "Thank you, Mr. Sibley, I had a nice time. . . . Thank you, sir, for my new shoes."

My mother dictated and I laboriously wrote down thank-you jingles to him. One memorable one began: "Dear Mister Sibley, I'm writing this note To thank you for my new brown coat."

He loved them—and he loved us.

My mother wasn't a pretty woman. At least, she always said she

29

wasn't. The looks in her family had gone to her Cousin Kate Welch, a candy-box blue-eyed blonde. Dixie had luxuriant dark brown hair with mahogany lights in it, bright, coffee-bean brown eyes with thick silky black eyebrows arching over. Her nose and her teeth may have been too prominent, her mouth was thin, her chin strong, and her figure was slim and erect. Most of her life she lamented having a small bosom and slender legs. She remedied the flat-chestedness by making herself some pink pin-cushion-looking contrivances, which she wore in her bra long before falsies were manufactured commercially. But she couldn't do anything about the legs except admire anybody who was endowed with plump piano-leg-shaped ones. She kept her waist nipped in, her back rigid, and her hips small but shapely by wearing a steel-ribbed corset, available in the Sears Roebuck catalogue for $1.98 most of her life. When the price went up to $10 and $12 she was outraged and wrote a letter to the president, but she continued to stock that corset until the day of her death and was, I hope, buried in it.

She knew her husband, who was related to rich people on Government Street, with debutante daughters, could have done better, and she determined that he wouldn't notice that fact by keeping herself clean and freshly dressed when he was due home, by having hot meals ready to put on the table, and by keeping from him as many unpleasant truths as possible. If she was ill she didn't tell him unless it became obvious and urgent. Men, she instructed me, can't bear sick women, and just before he came home she would pull herself out of bed, put on a clean starched and ironed "bungalow apron" (what the *Delineator* magazine was calling a housedress in those days), brush her hair, put on lipstick, and greet him with a smile. She might fall back in bed the minute he was out the gate but at least he never knew she was in anything but radiant health. He certainly didn't know that she had a live husband walking the earth and that we both worried that someday Henry Colley would find us and get the word to him. If he suspected that I was his wife's child and not just her ward, he never said so. He called me *his* child, "My ugly little freckle-faced gal," and it was pure music to my ears.

Although he was given two family names, Wesley, his mother's middle name, and Reeder, his grandmother's maiden name, Mr. Sibley was never called anything but Bob except by his mother and sister. They called him Wes. When he was born in his grandparents' home at the mill, his Uncle Lyles took one look at him, professed to see a marked resemblance to his father, Robert Sibley, and said, "Old ugly Bob!"

He was Bob to his friends and his brother, to my mother and her family, and Mister Bob to the workers at the mill. He always referred to himself by his initials, W. R. Sibley.

He was Mr. Sibley to me for the longest time, although he urged me to call him Uncle Bob. I don't know why I couldn't do it, the same reason perhaps that made me shy about touching him. I couldn't sit in his lap or kiss him, as so many other children were glad to do. I was always eager to be with him, and when he whistled for me on his way home from the office I ran to meet him and put my feet on his big work shoes, my hands in his, and thus be "walked" to the house. He liked to sing or whistle Sousa marches as we progressed and that always brought my mother out of the kitchen to laugh and join in. When radio came along I found a name for him. There was a song he liked so much I started teasingly calling him by its title, "Old Pappy." Almost immediately we shortened it to "Pap" and I called him that the rest of his life.

Grandpa Thomas Aaron Hatter was said to have studied medicine for a time in Virginia but it didn't take, except that he was moved to brew up a remedy for malaria—a bitter quinine-heavy concoction called Hatter's Chill & Fever Tonic, which all the people on the place took by the bottleful during mosquito season. Everybody loyally professed to find it efficacious, but somehow it never caught on and made him a fortune, as other patent medicines were doing for their concocters in that day. Grandpa died without amassing a fortune beyond pinelands, which extended for miles in every direction, and some rental property in Mobile. He left his property in a peculiarly chauvinistic way—everything to his two sons, Roy and Lyles, except for $100 each to his daughters, Kate, Julia, Talley, and Ophelia, on the theory that they had husbands who would care for them.

Ophelia did not.

The story that was handed down in the quarters was that Ophelia did not want to marry Robert Sibley but was pressured into the match by her parents. Many of the blacks I knew were the children and grandchildren of slaves who had served the family since before the Civil War. Their romantic version of the alliance was that Ophelia's wedding cake was made for her by her older sister Kate (later the

31

wife of a Mobile banker), and the servant who was helping her brought salt out of the pantry instead of sugar. When the bride tasted the cake after the ceremony she is quoted as having said, "All the sweetness has gone out of my life."

None of us had the nerve to check that story with the principals when they lived, and now I don't know if it's true or false. But, after she and Robert had built the big gingerbread-trimmed house on La-Fayette Street in Mobile and brought three children into the world, Ophelia divorced him. When the eldest son, Clarence, reached college age she packed them all up and moved to Auburn, where she rented a house big enough to take in student boarders, financing her own children's education.

Her former husband moved across Mobile Bay and remarried, but Pap's mother, who always called herself by her full name—Ophelia Wesley Hatter—never, so far as I ever heard, acknowledged his existence again.

She and her children spent their summers at her old home at Hatter's Mill. Pap returned there again and again after his brother and sister were grown and his mother no longer came, and would stay with his grandfather and his uncles. When he left home to join the Army in World War I his Uncle Lyles saw him off and promised him then that if he came home and ran the place after the war it would one day be his.

Pap never collected this inheritance in the sense of legal ownership, but if it is true, as I firmly believe, that you own what you see and love and work at, he and I were both inheritors. He went off to work whistling every morning, glad to have books to keep, a commissary to run, men to oversee in mill and turpentine still, in the woods and on the farm. Many of the hands had been his childhood playmates, and he laughed and joked with them, treated their injuries and ailments from his own stock of medicines and bandages on a commissary shelf and worried when they overcharged rations and had no money on payday.

They were my friends, too, and I wandered freely, assured that wherever I was, in woods or on the pond, there was a cheerful Hatter's hand, black or white, to look after me and help me if I needed it. They taught me to saddle a horse and picked me up when she threw me. They took me fishing and shared their lunches of fried fatback and cold biscuits when I showed up at dinnertime where they were loading logs or dipping gum or hoeing in a field. The Myers children got me a job hoeing around satsuma trees with them, and when Saturday payday came Pap gravely made out a time sheet and put my name on a pay envelope containing ten cents an hour for the labor I put in. They showed me where to look for arrowheads in the washed places at the edge of fields, and Lizabeth, a Cajun woman, spent hours roaming through the woods with me, teaching me the names of plants and trees and sometimes their uses in home remedies.

Our house seemed to grow more splendid every day, as Miss Evelyn stained the rough weathered walls dark green and wheedled Pap into sending her a carpenter from the mill to tack on porches and move walls around. When we got used to one big screened porch she would want it enclosed. She put in glass windows and tacked on a new kitchen, which was sunny and bright and, as she later decided, looking at it from the road, somewhat resembled "a wart on somebody's nose." She knocked down a wall to make a big living room and added a generously wide-hearthed fireplace. I thought it was grander than any mansion on Mobile's fabled Government Street.

Recently, going through some of my mother's old snapshots, I found a picture of it and I was amazed at what a plain, poor little house it was. It's really a deficiency in the camera that it didn't see and record the quality of life in that little house—the warmth, the good smells, the music, the laughter. The picture failed entirely to show that we always had plenty to eat. Not everybody did.

Mr. Eastman's little gadget had no way of picturing the summer evenings when, damp and cool from swimming in the millpond, we ate watermelon on the back porch and played card games on the dining table there. It couldn't recapture the winter Sunday nights by the fire when we ate a cold supper off the wicker teacart and listened to Jack Benny and Fred Allen on our wonderful battery radio. (The electricity that was generated in the mill was not compatible with radios.) A funny open porch my mother had built doesn't show in that snapshot, but I can see it in my mind's eye and the moonlight nights we sat there, listening to her playing the piano in the darkness of the living room. She wasn't a good pianist but she loved it so, and playing in the darkness seemed to give her confidence and improve her performance. We never reminded her that we were listening by calling out to her, but Pap, who loved to sing, would sometimes hum

33

along softly such songs as "Marcheta" and, if her playing turned frisky, "The Darktown Strutters' Ball" or "Yes, We Have No Bananas."

The roses my mother planted don't show in that picture. The dogs and the cats, the baby goats and chickens are not present. There's no Christmas scene to show that we always had a beautiful tree and presents and good food, no interiors to show the books we had to read or the awkward, wide-carriaged old L. C. Smith typewriter, which my mother plunked along on, writing limericks and Burma Shave rhymes and slogans for contests. She and Pap were indefatigable contestants, laboring many a night to try to win $1,000 for naming a new bar of soap or cure-all tonic. I still think that somewhere in their hundreds of entries there must have been one superior to the slogan Malbis' bakery selected for its new loaf of bread—"Pride of Alabama's Seaport."

Creola grammar school, three miles away across the Southern Railway tracks and beside the gravel road, which was the main highway from Mobile north, was our two-room social and intellectual center. I was enrolled in the third grade when the fall term started, and, far from being lonely and at odds with the place, as I had been at Tucker School in town, I was popular, happy, and even an academic achiever. (At least I could do third-grade work.) I walked from the mill every day with the Myers children, who were kin to nearly everybody in the settlement and therefore the best of sponsors. We took our lunches and I always had somebody to sit beside when we ate them in the shade of the big oak tree back of the school. They soon learned not to choose me when we played scrub baseball at recess. (I don't know if this is a real game or one Creola children invented when they didn't have enough people to make up two teams. I just know that the second the teacher jangled the recess bell the bigger boys would set up a litany: "Scrub *one!*" which meant first up at bat; "Scrub *two!*" second at bat, and on down the line.) I never seemed able to hit the ball, but I was a good runner, and one of the older seventh-grade girls, who was a regular Babe Ruth at bat, elected me to run for her on certain days of the month when she was something called "that way" and feeling languid.

My deficiencies on the playing field were more than compensated for on Friday afternoons when the whole school chose up sides for a spelling match. Boy, could I spell! Although only a third grader, I could spell toughies straight out of the back of the seventh-grade English book—for the good reason that my mother borrowed the book from Mamie Myers, who was *in* the seventh grade, so she could learn grammar herself.

She was determined that Pap's "proper-talking," college-educated relatives wouldn't catch her "talking ignorant and country." When she mastered seventh-grade grammar and spelling, which she taught me as she went along, we went to the library in Mobile and took out more advanced books. At least, Muv did. I took out fiction, which she frowned on.

"You're just reading for entertainment," she accused. "Get something that will do you some good."

She didn't know how much good those lovely fairy stories and Roman and Greek myths did me. She guessed that James Fenimore Cooper had turned me into an Indian scout with the Leatherstocking series, and she broke down and steered me to *Little Women* when I was twelve years old and Creola got a glorious box of new books from the school board. (Up until that time we had four or five skimpy shelves salvaged from the Grand Bay School fire years before. They ran to dark tomes like *The Mill on the Floss* and Augusta Evans Wilson's *Beulah,* which I doggedly read anyhow.)

In her pursuit of learning Muv made some mistakes. She knew that the verb "was" couldn't cut it in every case. It was the standby of Alford and East Bay syntax: "They *was* going. . . . Them *was* good people. . . . You *was* wrong." Proper-talking people used "were," she learned, and studied it carefully in Mamie's book. But she had a hard time with the pronunciation. "Were" . . . "wear"? She tried it. Pap, too much of a gentleman to point out her mistakes, pointedly pronounced the tiresome verb "wur" every chance he got. She wasn't such a lady that she didn't correct *him.* "Wear!" she would proclaim. "You *wear.* . . . They *wear!*"

He let it go because sooner or later she would listen and learn from somebody else. She did. And she couldn't understand why everybody couldn't do the same. Once we got a letter from Henry Colley, sent in care of Uncle J. C. at the Mobile police station. The implied threat that he might track us down and show up was horrifying and traumatic, but as the fright eased down her scorn at his writing, spelling, and grammar rose.

"Nobody has to be illiterate," she said. "Only a sorry, good-for-nothing won't *learn.*"

Oddly enough, when she was an old lady and had had a term at Florida State University and taught at Alford school, she was secure enough to revert to the speech of her childhood and of her neighbors. She let "were-wear-wur" return to the grammar books.

She had told the Alford principal that she was "privately educated" and she was. The suggestion was that she had a pride of governesses and tutors. She had the Mobile Public Library and Uncle Lyles Hatter's personal collection of books. A bachelor, he lived upstairs over the commissary and office, which sat beside the millpond. Before Pap was married and we moved to the house on the hill, he, too, had a room up there. Some time later they tore down the old weathered commissary building and replaced it with a substantial new structure, which had a basement for storing apples Pap's cousin Clayton Haines sent from Virginia every fall, and the tawny scuppernong wine that Uncle Lyles made from the grapes his father had planted, prohibition notwithstanding. It also had several bedrooms, an indoor bath—the first on the place—and a big room facing the pond, which we called "the library" because it had floor-to-ceiling shelves of books. I don't know what Uncle Lyles called it. We never went there when he was at home but sneaked in when he was away and slipped out one book at the time. Like the city library, you had to put before you could take.

Because of her theatrical experience Muv felt qualified to coach me for school plays and even arranged for me to take both "expression" and piano from a Yankee lady up at Axis, who taught in her home. I flunked piano but I excelled at showy dramatic gestures and facial grimaces, putting such feeling into my rendition of "Who Killed Cock Robin?" that it had me and the entire third grade in tears before the dénouement.

The schoolhouse was also our church and Sunday school. I don't know who started it, but I think our Yankee neighbors at Creola, the Mayes, who ran the store and post office, and the Howlands, a Pennsylvania family who lived nearby, felt the community would benefit by a little spiritual nourishment. There were twenty-four registered voters in that precinct, which meant, in those days, landowners. That could have produced a hundred church and Sunday-school members, but I'm sure we never had that many except possibly for the annual Christmas tree and carol service or the wonderful midsummer picnic on Gunnison Creek, to which the area's prime sight and wonder—Mr. Winter, a Yankee, a Republican, *and* a Catholic!—also came. Everybody brought their most prized dishes, but Mr. Winter, true to his reputation for singularity, brought something nobody had ever heard of—rich, pork-flavored, tomato-sauced Yankee beans, which had been simmered in an iron pot buried in the ground under a slow fire overnight! I don't remember that we found Mr. Winter's offering memorably delicious. After all, most of us had lived on beans most of the time. But the cooking process was so fantastic we lined up and ate helping after helping just because they were different, perhaps feeling intuitively that our lives were broadened and expanded by viands so exotically wrought.

I don't remember if the Mayes and the Howlands made any kind of canvass to determine what denomination church we should have. I think it may have been a sort of accidental taking what we could get. There was a Methodist mission to the Cajuns up the river, and the minister, a weekday railroadman, a Sunday preacher, passed through Creola in his goings and comings. What more natural than to have him stop off and give us a Sunday, say, the first Sunday in the month?

The deal was made. Baptists, Holy Rollers, and even my father, who had been reared in Mobile's stately Government Street Presbyterian church, historically the denomination of the Sibleys, joined up. We were in for a year-round siege of sociability—Sunday school every Sunday, preaching night and morning every first Sunday, with the minister and his family taking turns visiting around the community and having dinner with any family confident enough to invite them. (The Howlands and the Mayes were the most regular and reliable. Muv could be counted on intermittently.) Our Sunday table was prized by the minister for two reasons: Muv prepared early and had dinner ready to put on the table when they arrived from church. Many families didn't even catch the chicken and scald and clean him until the preacher was in the door. She also initiated the custom of excusing the preacher shortly after dinner so he could go take a nap. Other families kept him up earning his dinner by talking to them.

So Muv's invitations were gladly accepted, although the preacher felt duty-bound to go anywhere he was asked. But after several seasons of cooking for such company Muv wearied of it and took to urging us out of the schoolhouse at the last "Amen" and on the road to Mobile. There were two great attractions—the new Morrison's cafeteria and about four movie houses. That Morrison's, the flagship of the now nationwide chain, was the first cafeteria any of us had encountered, and we were spellbound by the opulence of the steam table, the variety of pies and salads and marvelous new vegetables. Potatoes baked in their skins? Heavens! And what was this new slippery kind of greens called spinach? Muv, ever venturesome, tried it out and vowed that it was as good as turnip greens. After dinner we separated, Pap to go to the ballpark to see the Mobile Bears play, Muv to the Saenger or Bijou or the Lyric for a wonderful session with John Gilbert and Corinne Griffith, the Bennett sisters, Ruth Chatterton, Bebe Daniels, and Vilma Banky. I was off to the Crescent or the Queen to the cowboy movies, the incomparable Tom Mix, Hoot Gibson, Tim Holt, and Ruth Roland. Often I was allowed to invite a friend or two from Creola, nearly always Elsie and Mildred Ellison or the youngest Myers girl, Kathleen. Lacking a new friend, I could always count on a friend of our days at 219 South Jackson—Timmy Beale. Timmy, being a Catholic, went to parochial school instead of to Tucker so she was only a Saturday or Sunday friend but a good one. She could see any Ruth Roland picture three times without budging, unless she was forced to bring along her little brother, Vander. Vander had the most unobliging kidneys either of us ever saw. When the movie unfolding before us reached its most exciting point, when the music of the player piano wheezed and clacked to a heart-stopping crescendo, Vander had to go to the bathroom. Apparently there were no facilities at the Crescent or the Queen because we always had to grab Vander by the hand he was not using to clutch his aching privates, and rush him down Dauphin Street to the lavatory under the bandstand at Bienville Square.

Sunday movies and Elsie Dinsmore brought me to what was the first and maybe most severe ethical and spiritual crisis in my life. On our periodic forays into the servants' house-storage rooms back of Pap's mother's house on LaFayette, we found boxes of books. Some of them were books that Pap had as a little boy and which I still cherish, among them *Treasure Island,* which certainly never upset anybody's Sunday plans. I can't say the same for the musty, yellowed old Elsie Dinsmore books, which must have belonged to his mother when she was a little girl.

Elsie was the most insufferable little prig anybody ever encountered but I didn't know it then. She was my ideal. Elsie wouldn't do anything to violate the Sabbath, including playing the piano. When her dear papa asked her to play something for a gentleman friend of his, she piously pointed out that to do so was a desecration of the Sabbath.

Papa, the infidel, insisted. Elsie tearfully refused. Lacerated by the twin dilemma—to disobey her papa in violation of the fifth commandment, or to break the Sabbath-keeping fourth commandment?—she opted for the fourth.

Papa ordered, Elsie refused, and finally the hedonistic scoundrel commanded her to sit on the piano stool until she was willing to obey him and play. Wouldn't you know Elsie sat there until she fainted?

Now I suspect she faked it, but then I was all choked up over her martyrdom. It was clear to me that going to the movies on Sunday was bad, bad and I was ready to renounce Hoot Gibson and Ruth Roland forever.

My mother was thoroughly disgusted. If I wouldn't darken a moviehouse door what would I do while she darkened one? Clearly I couldn't go watch the Mobile Bears play either. In fact, there didn't seem to be much that I could do. Muv would have throttled my new piety at the source, burning the Elsie books and dragging me along to the Bijou whether or no.

But Pap had a great respect for conscience. He didn't want me to go against mine, even if it was inconvenient for them. He suggested that I have a talk with Brother Webber, the minister.

Brother Webber was a gentle, kind man and clearly embarrassed by my ethical problem. He liked movies. He specially liked in summer the big blower systems that cooled the theatres in that era just before air-conditioning. He was willing to wrestle the devil for my soul but he couldn't believe that Hoot Gibson was the devil. I don't remember the ethical and philosophical tenets he advanced, but I emerged from that first counseling session with what may be a rather limber theological rule of thumb but one which, I have to confess, I've used a lot in my life. If you don't *think* it's a sin, it isn't.

Convenient? It certainly was. I resumed Sunday movies immediately—just in time for the talkies.

There was a lot more to church and Sunday school than conscience, of course. We had box socials and song fests. There was Epworth League every Sunday night, a young people's service, which was not as spiritually instructive as it was socially broadening. Older girls came with dates, at least with young males who sat with them in the too-small school desks and walked them home afterward. By the time I got to be an older girl myself I was running the Epworth League meetings, instead of lingering in the dark cloakroom with boys. I had learned to enjoy the sound of my own voice, and I was either directing the weekly program or I *was* the weekly program. If it hadn't been for the infinitely more-interesting gropings in the cloakroom, attendance at Epworth League would probably have fallen off beyond recovery.

Meanwhile, I found that I liked school. Walking to school with the Myers children was an educational experience. They knew all the side trips to find the prettiest white violets and cowslips in the spring. They taught me how to harvest the wild sweet persimmons when the frost ripened them, and that mayhaws that grew on thorny bushes at the edge of ponds offered minute apple-tasting little berries, which didn't amount to much if you ate them raw, out of hand, but were wonderful if you picked enough and took them home for mayhaw jelly. They knew a ditch where calla lilies grew, the only ones I've ever seen wild, and a fine fern that foamed and sudsed like soap when you crushed it in your hands to wash them on the creek bank.

The oldest son in the family also told me my first dirty joke. Like the hopeless little tattletale that I was, I hurried home and related it at the supper table: Why is the doctor different from a billy goat? The doctor rolls his pills with his hands, silly!

My mother lifted her eyebrows at Pap. Neither laughed. I think Pap may have thought that one unspeakable riddle like that could open the door to all kinds of disrespectful behavior from our boy neighbor. After supper he went across the creek and had a talk with the joke teller's father, and after that we weren't allowed to walk to school together anymore. He either preceded or followed his sisters and me by a country mile. I was embarrassed and apologetic, particularly because he had been fun on the trips home, knowing more wood lore than his sisters and being a big help when we stopped and bent down pine saplings and rode them like horses.

Prudery has its price.

Later, when I was in high school, driving our Model-A Ford to and from town with my friend Dot (I'll call her that) accompanying me, the compulsion to hurry home and tell everything hit me again. (I suppose this practice was to expiate my guilt. I later learned that as far as my mother was concerned, a little decent reticence or sneakiness would have been more acceptable.) Anyway my friend and I played hooky.

We decided a day on the town looked a lot better than a day in class at Murphy High School, and I drove our car as close to the main business district as I dared. Having had no experience with downtown traffic, I was afraid to brave the principal thoroughfares of Dauphin, Royal, and lower Government. We stopped out by big old St. Joseph's Catholic Church near Father Ryan Park, parked the car and set out on foot from there. After we had looked in the church and eaten our lunches in the park there didn't seem to be anything else to do and it was still only about 10 A.M.

"We could go see Aunt Myrtis," my friend said. "She lives right down yonder."

She pointed to a store building with an upstairs apartment opening out on an iron-lace-trimmed gallery over the sidewalk, the graceful fashion of so many old Mobile and New Orleans structures then.

I was afraid that Aunt Myrtis, being grownup, would make us go to school. Dot knew that was unlikely. She always let people do what they wanted to do, Dottie said, and I knew her status in the family. She had married a Mobile fireman and was the source of every new thing Dottie and her sisters got or hoped to get. When Muv made new curtains for my room Dottie would admire them and say, "I'm gon get Aunt Myrtis to get me some." When I got a new dress she would say, "Maybe Aunt Myrtis will buy me one like it."

This fairy-godmother-type aunt had bought their mother a rayon taffeta bedspread and their little sister, who was born with a misshapen head, trips to the doctor. She sent birthday and Christmas money—the fount of all good things, Aunt Myrtis. I couldn't wait to meet her.

She was a rather striking-looking lady, I had to admit, weighing about three hundred pounds with richly hennaed hair in what was the rage that year, a Mae Murray friz similar to today's Afro. She wore a purple rayon robe with gold dragons on it, and she greeted us cordially, ushering us into a bedroom where two young women I took to be relatives sprawled on the bed looking at movie magazines.

They were warm and welcoming, were Maxine and Mabel, making room on the bed for us and sharing their movie magazines. When we wearied of that, they showed us how to pluck our eyebrows and put on makeup, and as the morning progressed they talked about order-

41

ing up sandwiches from the barbecue stand on the corner.

Our lunch long gone, even our candy money spent, Dottie and I were hungry, too. We listened hopefully as the young ladies spoke of ordering the sliced beef and maybe some pork ribs and pickle to go with it. But they didn't act and we finally found out why. They had no money.

"If I had two dollars I would go down to Weatherby's and pay it on Mama's furnitoor," Mabel said. "I bought her a bedroom soot a year ago and I just can't seem to get it paid for. The collector's been twice this week."

Hooky playing was beginning to pall on Dottie and me.

We were hungry and bored and beginning to feel twinges of guilt when Aunt Myrtis came in and told us to "skedaddle" to the back porch and play with Prince, her German shepherd. Mabel and Maxine had some gentlemen callers.

The porch was hot and Prince had fleas and smelled bad. But we stayed and pretended to be enjoying it, having to keep up a front for one another, until Aunt Myrtis came and invited us back into the apartment. Maxine was on the phone to the Palace of Pork, ordering barbecue.

We ate and decided it was time to start walking back to St. Joseph's Catholic Church and the car. That night at the supper table again I *talked.*

There was an initial chill when I said I had played hooky. But when I got into the details they bit their lips and looked at one another and burst out laughing. They were still laughing when Muv sent me out to feed Bertha, my dog, and I heard her say to Pap: "She's spent the day in a *whore*house!"

Later I got the serious lecture from my mother about my obligation to go to school and make Pap proud of me, all the money he was spending. She pointed out something I had already found out, that neglecting your duty never turned out to be as much fun as you thought it was going to be.

She also had something to say about visiting other people's relatives uninvited and unannounced. Dottie's Aunt Myrtis was probably a fine woman and certainly good to her Creola relatives, but her house was not a suitable place for young girls to visit.

Actually I was past needing that lecture. I had already decided that Aunt Myrtis's dog had mange and the Palace of Pork ribs had given me heartburn. It wasn't exactly a Noel Coward–type penthouse like the movies were showing that year. Besides, I had found another locale for hooky—the airport.

Dottie had to drop out of school and get a job, and I started riding to town with a boy named Buford Martin, who lived up at Buck's Crossing, five or six miles north, and drove his father's big touring car to school. For a weekly fee of $2 each, he took four other students and could work me in if I sat on a Brown Mule tobacco box on the floor of the back seat. My mother called it "riding the mule," a joke that was intended to make my position in the car less ignominious. I was tongue-tied with shyness anyhow. The other students were older and three of them, were, of course, Yankees—a breed of people who didn't think it farfetched and unreasonable to send their children all the way into Mobile to high school. Most of our country neighbors didn't think high school important or even feasible.

One of my fellow passengers was a glamorous older man, all of sixteen years old, from Minnesota. I had spotted him arriving at his sister's house to live when I was eleven years old and had fallen so desperately in love with him I stopped skinning the cat on the neighbor's pasture fence and started wearing shoes. Somehow he never noticed this newly acquired maturity. Now that I spent more than an hour each day literally at his feet on the Brown Mule tobacco box, he still didn't notice.

But one day my hero was absent and the other passengers in the car voted to skip school and go to the airport to watch the barnstorming pilots, who came in and set their planes down on the muddy field, offering rides over Mobile Bay for $5 a head.

We didn't have that kind of money, of course, but just being there in the presence of those exciting flying fellows in their puttees and riding pants, their open-at-the-throat and flapping leather helmets, was better than anything formal education had to offer. They were used to the adulation—and the poverty—of the young and they treated us kindly. We were to go back again and again, and on one memorable day they were idle and at loose ends, with no paid passengers to fly over the bay, and they took us up!

My idol, who was an earnest and hard-working honor student, later to win the state declamation contest and a scholarship to the University of Alabama, gave me a little lecture about such escapades. He wasn't particularly concerned about me personally, I realize now, but

43

I was the youngest in the carload and his sister and my mother were best friends and, I suppose, he felt an obligation to set my feet on the straight and narrow.

I'm afraid I took it as proof of a great burning passion. Would he have gone to the trouble if he didn't adore me? It was the only straw I had to grab at, the only evidence that he ever saw me, but it was enough. I renounced hooky forever.

Murphy High School was almost exciting enough anyhow. On our Sunday trips to Mobile, when I was still in grammar school and they were building what they called "the new million-dollar high school," we often went to see it. It was unlike any high school anybody had ever seen, certainly unlike the old and classic white-walled Barton Academy back of its iron fence on Government Street. Generations of Mobile children, including Pap and his mother, had gone to Barton. But, instead of being a single building, the new million-dollar school was a university-like spread of buildings—a central structure for offices and classrooms; an auditorium, rich and splendid and velvet-curtained; a cafeteria bigger than any restaurant in Mobile; arts, biology, math, and language buildings; greenhouses and athletic fields and a vast parking area. All buildings were connected by colonnades strung with flowering vines, which softened the saffron-colored stucco walls of the main buildings, too. Some lobbies, that of the biology building especially, were paved with colored tile, making it suitable for small dances. Everybody who saw the high school was dazzled by it, and the three of us examined each week's building progress and exulted that it would be finished and going by the time I was free of Creola Grammar School and could go there.

The problem of getting me there was tricky at first. I spent a month or two boarding with our old pastor, Brother Webber, and his wife, who had me calling them Uncle Ernest and Aunt Rachel, and his aged mother, in a new little house in walking distance of the school. I should have been perfectly happy there, but they were old people and uncompromisingly pious, despite Brother Webber's liberal attitude toward Sunday movies. I got a new hat and preened in it before the mirror. They scolded me for my worldliness. I brought home a movie magazine and they put it in the trash. I had the words of a new song copied down in a notebook, courtesy of a girl who sat next to me in General Science class, and my effort to share it with them—"Pale

44

Hands I Love, Beside the Shalimar"—earned me frosty disapproval from Aunt Rachel.

Uncle Ernest, who worked in a machine shop at one of the railroads, rightly thought his greasy clothes unfit to be worn in the house, and he always went to a washroom on the back porch and changed before he entered the kitchen. His greetings were timid: "Good evening, Rachel; good evening, Mother; good evening, Celestine." I was wild with homesickness for our house, where Pap, dirty clothes or not, came striding up the front walk whistling and singing and calling out to us: "Where is that vimmens?" (Katzenjammer funny-paper German.) "Where is my ugly little freckle-faced gal?"

Distressed at the blue fog that hit me every Sunday night when they returned me to the Webbers' after a weekend at home, Pap suggested as an alternative that I move in with his mother in the old Victorian house on LaFayette Street. A singer and a reciter of poetry and scripture, Ophelia was a jolly greeter and welcomer. She hadn't been home from the state mental hospital long and had just taken possession of her house, which had been rented out. By the time I got there she was established in five or six dim and densely fumed-oak thicketed rooms on the second floor. For some reason she had not had the lights or gas turned on, using kerosene lamps and a new thing—canned Sterno heat—to cook on. She was not much of a cook anyhow, so a small fifteen-cent can of the blue gummy stuff with the pungent smell served very well to heat up a can of something. Pap promptly got the electric lights on and had a telephone installed, but as long as I lived there—a matter of months—we cooked on the Sterno.

A big room at the top of the stairs served us as living room, dining room, and kitchen. There was a small room off the back porch that would have made a handy kitchen, since the big one downstairs was not in use for some reason, but by combining everything in the big central former bedroom we could make maximum use of the grate fire. It saved coal.

Ophelia slept in a spacious front bedroom with a towering Victorian bed, a dresser, and an armoire. I was assigned the little connecting dressing room, which now had a small bed and a dresser and windows that offered easy access to the big crape-myrtle trees in the front yard. When grandmother settled down for her afternoon naps, sending me to my room for the same, I slipped out the window and

45

shinnied down a crape-myrtle tree and either sneaked to the corner grocer across the street for a Popsicle, a new five-cent treat that year, or sat on the front porch and read *The Clansman,* the newest book in Ophelia's library.

It wasn't home and I had bouts of longing for the open sunny house at the mill and Miss Evelyn and Pap and my dog, Bertha. But it wasn't as bad as living with pious, low-voiced strangers. Ophelia was a plump cushiony old lady but beautiful, with the skin of a baby, a headful of white curls, blue eyes, and a happy, noisy way of singing, reciting, and talking in a loud voice to her nervous little fox terrier, Cuty Sweetie. She loved to dress up and go to town on the streetcar to prowl the stores, and it wasn't unusual for some friend of the past, who hadn't seen her since before she went off to the mental hospital, to recognize her and cry, "Isn't this Ophelia Hatter?"

She was pleased to reunion and seemed to me to take on a girlishness odd in an old fat woman. Sometimes she rummaged through her jewelry box and gave me things. I remember going to school wearing three enameled bluebirds in full flight across my flat thirteen-year-old chest.

Then her daughter and son-in-law, Lillian and Charles Moore, came to live in the dark and closed downstairs rooms, refugees from the Depression. Charles, a silent, elegantly tailored man, who looked almost exactly like the movie star Herbert Marshall, had kept them fashionably situated in the St. Charles Apartments on Government Street (the first apartment building I ever saw). Then he lost his job in imports of some kind. They moved their Windsor chairs with the pretty blue cushions and the grand piano to what had been the back parlor and set up housekeeping. Oddly enough, they never straightened out the furniture or seemed to settle in. While Charles job-hunted Lillian reupholstered her mother's horsehair loveseats and platform rockers in blue velvet and brought order and beauty to the hall and front parlor, although they slept on a mattress on the floor in the back parlor, surrounded by boxes and bags and cast-off furniture. When their grand piano disappeared, probably sold for carfare and grocery money, they had more room but still no order. The big kitchen with its great wood stove was never used, and I don't remember ever eating a full meal in that house. We had potted-meat sandwiches and canned soup a lot and apples and pecans because they came from home and were free. It must have been nourishing enough.

I liked Lillian, who was pretty and funny and always stylishly dressed when she went out. She was full of suggestions for my making friends at Murphy High. She professed to know all the so-called "cute" girls that I talked about, even Dot Pettus, the cheerleader, who was my heroine. I didn't find out until years later that it was sheer pretense. There was no doubt that she had many affluent and socially well-placed friends but that didn't guarantee that she was acquainted with those of cute-girl status. She had suggestions about my clothes and hair and made me leave off the enameled bluebirds. But I had no friends to walk home from school with or check out homework assignments with over the telephone. Nobody came to visit. Lillian opened the long windows and aired the front parlor—rare in that house, where fresh air wasn't considered healthful. Sometimes she lit a fire in the corner grate and I would tiptoe in and sit beside her mother's square rosewood piano and admire the room. But it was not really used any time I lived there.

The next year I was deemed old enough to drive the car to school. There was no age limit then, so far as I know, and I suppose my parents thought fourteen was plenty old enough since I had had a lot of practice, driving the back roads between the mill and Creola. So I drove with Dottie to keep me company until she had to quit school, and I switched to "riding the mule." It was an altogether happier arrangement because I loved being at home, truly a good home and plenty at it.

There was always something cooking for supper and, if the day was cool, a fire crackling on the hearth in the living room. My mother was always busy with some project—scraping and refinishing a ladder-back chair she found in the barn, raising chickens, writing Burma Shave jingles and once a confession story. She sewed a lot and loved handwork, in which she attempted to interest me. And she found much of my schoolwork totally fascinating.

If I had to write a theme she studied the assignment and, her eyes alight with ideas, followed me about reeling off her suggestions. My first emergence from anonymity at the big school was when Miss Ruth Moore in freshman English read aloud a theme I had written.

"Describe a room," the assignment had said.

I had in mind something I had never seen, of course, an Arabian-nights-type ballroom.

My mother shook her head. "Write about what you know," she

directed from what was innate rather than acquired knowledge. "Do a kitchen."

A kitchen wasn't glamorous but she made it so. Put down how it feels, she said, how it smells, the color, the taste. There had to be flowers (she *always* had flowers) and something fragrant simmering on the stove. The floor could be damp from a fresh scrubbing, the windows should gleam. If the room was big enough, why not a rocking chair by the window and a shelf with a few books? (She kept a mammoth mildewed volume of Tennyson and the White House cookbook in hers.)

Although I don't remember a line I wrote, I remember the feel of that theme, and it brought me momentary celebrity in Miss Moore's class. She had thought I was just another C student "from the rural." My grades weren't impressive after that but she did recommend me for journalism in my junior year, and you had to have a B average to skip the regular English course and take that.

Journalism wasn't my first choice. I planned to be a movie star (didn't everyone?) or a lawyer. I hadn't decided. English students who averaged a B could also take drama, and I went so far as to try out for the high school Players, missing by a mile. The piece I wrote about the trauma of looking on the bulletin board in the Four Arts Building after tryouts and not finding my name listed among the chosen made the school paper, a success my dramatic performance never achieved. But it was all right. I had a friend who showed me that journalism can be a door to high drama. She was on the way, unsummoned, uninvited, to the office of Principal K. J. Clark to *interview* him, instead of the other way around. Furthermore, she had collaborated on an editorial calling on the streetcar company to run its line from Dauphin two blocks down Carlin Street to the school so students would not have to walk that distance in bad weather. (I wonder if it ever did?) A mere student acting so boldly?

Not just a student, said my friend, the *press,* inquiring into matters of the common weal. Not effrontery, duty.

I applied for journalism and was accepted. It was love, pure love, from there on out.

A young woman named Anita Wagner is largely responsible. A Georgian, she had served as the Atlanta *Constitution*'s campus correspondent when she was a student at Wesleyan College, and she had great respect for newspapering. Until she took over as journalism teacher and faculty adviser to the Murphy *Hi Times,* it had been largely the stepchild of Miss Aline Bright, head of the English Department, a pseudo-literary paper with many silly gossipy columns devoted to who was seen with whom at the biology dance. Miss Wagner wanted to make it a real newspaper filled with hard news, and she persuaded the editors of the downtown dailies to inspire and instruct us. They came out and talked to our class, and the editor of the *Press* went beyond that. They would publish, if we could write, edit, and make up, a page of school news in the Sunday edition.

Miss Wagner was jubilant. As her acolyte, I was jubilant, too. It meant late hours in the little *Hi Times* office on the second floor, but Miss Wagner saw in me a deathless devotion very like her own. I gladly stayed until they turned out the lights and locked the building. (My car pool would leave me but Muv was willing to drive to town to get me, realizing the importance of the mission.) I would go home and sit up until daylight struggling with stories and headlines for this stellar publication. We won medalist honors from the Columbia University Scholastic Press Association that year, and Miss Wagner persuaded the editors of the Mobile *Press* to take me on to work on Saturdays for experience.

My mother, as excited as I was, made me a new dress and drove me to town and waited outside while I went in to be interviewed. When I came out, not hired—there was no money involved—but taken on to work for experience, she was as excited as I was.

"Oh, honey," she exulted, her dark eyes shining. "Do good."

Miss Wagner was equally pleased. When she died at her home near Swainsboro, Georgia, the winter of 1985 I remembered the gray, rainy afternoon in 1932 when I lingered before her desk to discuss my future. To work for a newspaper, she told me, was a very great privilege—a genuine public service, and the best thing she could wish for me was that someday I would write things that people would read "and remember for a little while."

To this day it seems a worthy ambition.

Chapter Three

The *Press* was the new paper in town, launched by Ralph B. Chandler of the Los Angeles *Times* family, to challenge the hold of the century-old morning *Register* and its afternoon compatriot, the *Item*. The editors of the *Press* were young and bright and venturesome. Somewhere Henry P. Ewald had picked up one of those Kentucky colonelships, and he shamelessly listed himself on the masthead as Colonel H. P. Ewald, editor-in-chief, a mischievous ploy to cover his youth with an aura of age and dignity. We called him "Colonel" without knowing any better for years. He had assembled a lively and literate staff and set up shop in an abandoned church building on downtown St. Michael Street, near neighbor to courts and jails and governmental buildings and the waterfront.

The mechanical and business departments were on the street floor, the editorial offices and newsroom in what had been the pulpit and choir loft. We had a balcony-like view of the composing room, and I learned to stand at the water fountain and follow any piece of copy I had written all the way from the city desk to the copy desk to the typesetter, in his little sawed-off chair in the composing room, to the stereotype department, which had a wondrous hot-lead-scorched matrix smell, to the pressroom. It was a dim and dusty aerie we worked in and totally glamorous to me. The Taj Mahal couldn't have impressed me more, even after something fell into my hair from the ceiling one day and, when I plucked it out, it was easily identified as a head louse.

They let me come on Saturdays until school was out. Then they gave me a summer job for pay—$5 a week. Looking back, I marvel at the things they let me do. There was plenty of routine but it was never dull to me. I loved weather stories, which older, better reporters scorned. I was ecstatic when they let me fill in as movie critic. Already a fan—*everybody* was a fan in those years—I went on my own time five nights a week to review the new offerings. Unfortunately, I wasn't an astute critic. Intellectuals had gone wild over the outrageous comedy of Mae West. I thought she was a vulgar, overweight old lady. Bing Crosby struck me as a conceited fellow who couldn't last, and Shirley Temple was a precocious but tiresome sugar-mouthed tyke. To do them justice, my bosses laughed at my priggishness and let me write it as I saw it. I suppose they knew that I would come to rue these childish judgments.

Obituaries, the plague of most beginning reporters, fascinated me. I was so young I had never known personally anybody who died except Waverly Taylor, a black fieldhand-preacher at the mill, and I had never been to a funeral.

My superiors at the *Press* corrected that. A policeman shot his girlfriend and turned the gun on himself one night on a bayside lovers' lane off Cedar Point Road.

"Celestine, run out to the house and interview the girl's family and get pictures," ordered Jim Taylor, the city editor.

That was long before television, of course, and the blessed public hadn't taken up the practice of going on the air with their most intimate griefs and tragedies. A little reticence, a desire for privacy, was still left to people, and the relatives of the principals in that shooting hung on to theirs. They didn't want any truck with me. But they were courteous about it. The mother of the slain girl came out on the front porch and talked to me, while the girl's little boy trundled his tricycle up and down the sidewalk. She didn't agree with me that a photograph of her daughter would "dress up" the story and show that she was a nice person despite the fact that she was getting around lovers' lanes with a married man. But finally, to get rid of me, she let me borrow a photograph she had on the piano in the living room, and I trudged back to the office, feeling terribly sorry for everybody, particularly the little boy on the tricycle.

My story was about him and, for some strange reason, better than the city editor had hoped for. He played it on page one and sent me to the funerals the next day.

The girl's funeral was so civilized it was pallid. The minister contented himself with a sort of impartial recital of Tennyson's "Crossing the Bar," tactfully avoiding any mention of the deceased and certainly not speculating on her chances of heaven.

But ah, the policeman's funeral! It was held in the bedroom of an old downtown house where the young man and his family had lived in comparative squalor. The day was hot and the room was crowded with neighbors and his brother officers. I found a spot in a corner against an old wardrobe and was trapped there when they wheeled in the coffin and set up the standards of flowers. Foremost among these was a big wreath emblazoned with the words "My Beloved Husband."

Then they escorted in the widow, a little crippled woman who had recently had all her teeth pulled. They put a chair for her at the head of the coffin, pinioning me securely to the wardrobe, and she began to cry.

The minister didn't shilly-shally around about what had happened to the young man in that coffin.

"Here, my friends," he cried, waving at the body, "you see before you the results of S-I-N SIN!"

The little widow covered her face and wept loudly. I shuffled and sweated and, for the first time, questioned my right to be there.

Fortunately, something of more urgent interest had happened in the news and the two funerals were shunted to an inside page and allowed only a few routine paragraphs. I hadn't known about pallbearers and had to scuffle at the last minute to get their names.

Because the paper was short-handed during summer vacations I got a chance at every beat in town, covering for two weeks at a time the big gray granite customs house, the weather bureau, the city hall, courthouse, county jail, and police station. Prohibition was still alive and the revenuers, undoubtedly bored with it, sometimes took me along for the shock value in showing me dead or drunk hogs in mash barrels in the swamp. I got to ride with them around the bay in pursuit of rumrunners we never caught. The Coast Guard was hospitable about letting me join the regular rescue missions that went on almost any moonlight night in the summertime, when young couples got becalmed on sailboats in Mobile Bay.

By the time my newspaper job got me to a murder trial I was already a bedazzled convert to courtroom drama.

My first murderers had been neighbors, two young men in a big clan who worked at the mill. We wouldn't have dreamed that they would do murder, although it was generally agreed that they were po' white trash. That's a tired and out-of-fashion term used to clothe the unlettered and the unwashed, sometimes unjustly. To be poor and white was pretty usual, but if you scrubbed your floors and sent your children to school clean, if you went to church and were careful not to drink moonshine or to cuss in front of women, you missed being trash. The Hickses didn't bother.

They were a noisy, roistering set of people noted for roaming, which is to say they never spent more than a season or two anywhere. Somebody in the family died while they were at Hatter's Mill, and the matriarch of the clan, an enormously fat woman called "old Lissy," collected $200 in insurance. They hitched a ride into Mobile with my father to spend it.

"I expect we got as much cash money now as Mr. Hatter has," old Lissy told my father.

She was probably right. Nobody had $200 loose in those years of the Great Depression. And the Hickses didn't have it long, not more than half a day. They went on a riotous spending spree, buying honey jumble teacakes and Oh Henry! candy bars for all the children, a month's supply of snuff for old Lissy, patent-leather shoes for all the women, play-pretties for the babies, and a red rayon dress for Georgia, who, by virtue of having crossed eyes, was the only female in the family who didn't have a husband or at least one illegitimate child. And then they bought a car—a Model-T Ford with considerable age on it.

Pap passed them on the way back to the mill that night. They were walking single file down the shoulder of the gravel road, carrying their shoes. The car had run out of gas and they had abandoned it seven miles away by Bayou Sara bridge. They never retrieved it.

Shortly after that, Waverly Taylor disappeared. Waverly was the farmer on the place, the one who brought us vegetables from the fields every morning during growing season, and a peerless singer and pray-er in the quarters church across the road from our house. I often went to that church with whatever black woman was washing or cleaning or cooking for us at the time, and I loved Waverly's prayers, which always had a fresh and original twist to them. No standard "Our Father, which art in heaven" for Waverly. He cried,

"Oh, Lord, come out on the front porch of heaven!"

And he was missing. He didn't show up for work and he didn't show up for church. He wasn't seen at the pump that stood by the road in the middle of the quarters, source of water for all the black families and a nightly gathering place for most of the black men.

Nobody knew what had happened to Waverly until a woods rider, a horseman assigned to keep a lookout for fire in the pine woods, followed the skywriting of a flock of buzzards and found his body in the swamp. He had been shot to death.

I was as eager as anybody to get to the scene. Everybody at the mill, including women and children, went and looked. Pap and Muv went but made me stay at home. The position and condition of the body were talked about for weeks. Sheriff's officers came out from Mobile and took the body away.

And then two of the Hicks men were arrested.

Weeks later Pap received a summons to appear in court as a witness against the Hickses. Muv and I went with him, making a day of it—my first murder trial and, after all these years, it remains one of the memorable ones.

The atmosphere of the courtroom awed me. The pattern of selecting a jury and questioning the witnesses was fascinating—to me and to Pap. His testimony was brief. Hatter's Mill paid off its workers not in U.S. currency but a kind of play money called "chex" and good only at the company store. My father was able to recognize and identify the "chex" he had paid Waverly Taylor on Saturday afternoon as the same money the Hicks men had brought into the commissary to buy rations a day or two later. With his testimony in the record we were free to leave the courthouse, but we couldn't tear ourselves away. We had to know the end of the drama that played itself out in that courtroom. We had to know if the Hickses had killed Waverly and robbed him in an argument over moonshine, as the state contended.

Solicitor Bart Chamberlain, the prosecutor, was the greatest showman I had ever beheld. He addressed old Lissy Hicks with a wonderful, courtly old-school deference that had my mother and me in stitches.

"Miss Melissa," he said unctuously, giving her a name we had never heard before. "Tell the gentlemen of the jury . . ."

And Lissy, easing her fat feet out of the too-tight patent-leather shoes, bridled and bobbed her head and settled down to the momentous business of testifying. Skillfully, Mr. Chamberlain led her through a recital of events leading up to her son's and son-in-law's departure for their liquor still in the swamp and their return hours later with grocery money.

He drew from her the information that they lived in a three-room house and all the family were at home except the two young men.

"And how many was that, ma'am?" asked the solicitor.

Lissy couldn't count but she knew their names, and she recited them while the prosecutor ticked them off on his fingers.

"And your daughter Georgia and your son Luke and his wife Parizettie and their baby . . . let's see, that makes twelve in your three-room home!" he said in warmly congratulatory tones. "Now was there anybody else?"

"Yes, sir," said old Lissy, pleased that he had asked. "There was our boarder."

Mr. Chamberlain rolled his eyes at the jury. "Miss Melissa, you amaze me," he said. "You were able to accommodate a boarder amongst your big family!"

"Oh, no, sir," said Lissy hastily. "We didn't accommodate him. He jes' stayed with us."

Even the jury laughed, and Lissy, pleased to have been a hit, wriggled her bare feet and got ready for another triumph in the interrogation.

"Tell us, Miss Melissa," wheedled the prosecutor, "where did the boarder sleep?"

The boarder's sleeping arrangements were irrelevant and immaterial but obviously the judge and the defense attorneys were curious, too.

"Why, with first one and then another," answered Lissy.

When laughter in the courtroom had subsided, Mr. Chamberlain led old Lissy back to her recital of how her son and son-in-law came home with blood on their clothes. What was she doing when she saw this? asked the prosecutor.

"Well, I was out there in the yard a-baking a hoecake on a spider," said the witness.

"You were a *what* on a *what?*" gasped the solicitor.

Lissy smiled benignly on his ignorance. "Don't you know what a arn three-legged spider is?" she asked, chuckling indulgently.

The city lawyer was certainly unacquainted with arn spiders. Later, when the jury was out, he came and sat with my parents and they were able to explain this utensil, all-important in the lives of nomadic sawmill workers. A spider is a three-legged iron skillet, which cooks splendidly when set over coals on the hearth or out-of-doors and handily takes the place of a stove, which the Hickses didn't have anyhow.

The jury returned a verdict of guilty.

Old Lissy had helped to send her son and son-in-law up for life. I think she was philosophical about it. It may have been that their going made room in the house or that it gave the family someplace to go on Sunday afternoon when prison camps had visiting hours.

The tragedy of the Hickses' poverty and ignorance didn't strike me then. I was well used to both poverty and ignorance. What impressed me was that the state of Alabama and the county of Mobile *cared* what the Hickses did, that it mattered to officialdom that a lone black man, who had no family and was not even a particularly valued worker, had died while engaged in an illegal act, stealing moonshine whiskey.

The whole machinery of justice back of the tall white columns in that awesome county courthouse had operated for two days, seeking the truth about the Hickses and Waverly Taylor. Smart lawyers, a judge, twelve jurymen had assembled in the stately marble chamber, which was the courtroom, and had questioned and listened. They had laughed but they had listened and had truly striven to avenge the wronged and punish the guilty.

I was impressed then and I still am. For a year or two I told everybody at Murphy High School that I was going to be a lawyer when I grew up.

But then I was hooked on newspapers.

It was a school-board assignment that got me involved in my second murder trial. Dr. John O. Rush, a urologist, was chairman of the school board, and the city editor sent me to his office on some simple story of little impact. I had to wait and I was getting bored with the doctor's magazines when I saw a man and a woman come into the hall outside the doctor's reception room. They stood and talked a moment and then he kissed her and left. The woman came in and sat next to me.

The afternoon wore on and the woman became increasingly restless. Finally she started talking to me, reasoning that a sixteen-year-old girl was better than no audience at all, and she had a lot she wanted to say. She was from some little country place up the river and had the misfortune at the age of fourteen to meet this handsome, debonaire married man from Mobile. They fell madly in love and he took her away from the farm and set her up in an apartment in Mobile. She was happy for years and then she contracted tuberculosis and had to go away to a sanitarium. When she came out she found that the man she loved had grown cold and no longer wanted her. Now she suspected that she had an even worse disease.

She nodded meaningfully, not wishing to spell it out to a teenager. But I thought I knew what she meant. My mother had told me about "social diseases" and warned me against sitting down on the public toilet under Bienville Square bandstand, no matter how urgent the need. My waiting-room friend probably hadn't minded her mother, I decided.

The doctor saw me and gave me the story I sought on educational matters, but he wasn't, I know now, as educational as his patient had been. The next morning I picked up the *Register* and there was the woman's picture on page one. Her name was Willie Mae Clausen, and she was in jail charged with murder!

Immediately after leaving the doctor's office she had, it was alleged, gone straight to the office of her erstwhile lover, a prominent Mobile attorney, and shot him dead.

I had told friends at the office about the strange, talkative woman in the doctor's office and now I babbled, "She's the one. . . . I know her!"

Sam Johnston, the town's most glamorous defense lawyer and father of my schoolmate, Annie Ruth, heard about it and subpoenaed me as a witness. My mother tried to persuade him that I was too young and tender to be mixed up in anything so sordid, but Mr. Johnston rightly contended that a woman's life was at stake and if I was going to be a newspaper reporter I would be encountering sordid things the rest of my life.

The day the trial opened I was sworn in as a witness and assigned to sit out the morning in a room with a lot of other witnesses. But we caught the drift of the trial, of course. Willie Mae pleaded not guilty by reason of insanity brought on by that "social disease," coupled with the rejection by the man who had brought her from the country as an innocent little girl of fourteen and made her "a slave to love." To me she looked like an awfully old woman to be a slave to love but I doubt if she was more than forty.

My testimony was brief. Mr. Johnston wanted to show that by engaging me in all that personal conversation Willie Mae was not just turned funny but stone-cold crazy. The prosecution naturally objected to any conclusions from this immature witness, and a legal squabble ensued. When they finally got back to me Mr. Johnston asked one question, "Was she garrulous?"

Glad that I knew what the word meant, I said carefully, "Yes, sir. She was very talkative."

"Come down, honey," said my old friend Solicitor Chamberlain.

It wasn't exactly courtroom stardom, but when I climbed the stairs to the newsroom back at the *Press* the city editor and all the reporters waited for me at the top.

Our veteran trial reporter, Rhodes McPhail, had phoned in the burning details of my testimony and they cried in unison, "Was she *garrulous?*"

Then they sent me back to help Mr. McPhail cover the trial.

Willie Mae served a year in prison and married her jailer.

Every newspaper reporter who has seen people in trouble or in need and been able to help them by writing about them or seen social and political evils corrected or improved because the public was informed has a mighty respect for the so-called power of the press. My experience with the magic in "letting the people know" came in a small way but it was an awesome thing to me—and it still is.

That first summer on the Mobile *Press,* when news seemed dull or nonexistent and little seemed to be stirring in the sleepy old seaport town except an occasional breeze, which died when it hit the sun-baked pavements, our city editor got a call about a minor crisis at the Family Welfare Bureau. You have to understand that welfare was a small business then. Miss Florence Van Sickler, the director, a secretary, and one caseworker constituted the staff, and they operated from two rooms over a downtown store. Their budget had to have been infinitesimal or they wouldn't have called for help for three newborn babies.

But they did call and the city editor sent me down to talk to Miss Van Sickler. There were three infants just born who had not a diaper to their names and were literally crying for milk, which their scrawny, undernourished mothers could not provide. If by some miracle we could get milk contributed to them, there was then the problem of ice to keep it. Perhaps a small notice in the paper, Miss Van suggested.

Distressed and alarmed that the babies might die (infant mortality rate was still high then), I wrote a little story, which the paper carried on page one.

The response was overwhelming. Layettes enough to outfit hundreds of babies to come poured in. Milk enough for the newborns and all the children in many families was provided. Ice companies rallied, not only with every-other-day delivery of the standard fifty pounds of ice but with old wooden iceboxes in which to keep it. I was both astonished and perhaps a little impressed that words of mine had wrought such a miracle.

Miss Van saved me from smugness. She praised me for caring and for the words that evoked the response, but she showed me that the problem of hunger and need was still big and heartbreaking and certainly beyond the skill, if not the comprehension, of a kid who could use a typewriter. For the Depression was on the land and just beginning to reach out octopus tentacles to our town.

I spent a lot of time around the Family Welfare Bureau that summer. Miss Dorothy Bennett, the sole caseworker, was finding that her load was growing, and she took on her first assistant, a college girl named Mary McMullen, who came to intern with them.

Between them they introduced me to many things I had not dreamed of. Hookworm was rampant. (I had thought it was inevitable.) Pellagra, which many old people I knew took for granted, was a deficiency disease that could be cured. We distributed many cans of salmon to old people in cottonmill villages, convincing them—and me—that nutrition could save them. I, who only dimly suspected where babies came from, heard about birth control, a procedure my social-worker friends favored for cutting down on the number of feeble-minded and demented couples. They told me about incest, which was a way of life in some of the itinerant families who lived under bridges and culverts not too far from where I lived. I had thought, when I found out about it, that the little girls who had sex with their fathers and uncles were maybe a shade more respectable than those who did the abhorrent act with strangers. Keeping it in the family made it less . . . well, "nasty." Miss Van and her staff laughed but then they sat me down for a serious talk.

As the Depression deepened, my visits to the Family Welfare

Bureau and my stories about need increased. People called me about cases that were unknown even to the caseworkers. There was a family living in an empty store building out on the edge of town—a mother and half a dozen little children. I don't remember where the father was but he had probably joined that vast army of men who tramped over the country looking for work. The family was cold and hungry, and, to make things more acute, the mother had given birth in the night to a baby. She had stretched out on one of the store's old counters, after she had bedded down the children, and managed to bring a new baby into the world alone and unattended.

I caught the streetcar and went out to see them.

My story that afternoon evoked a response that impresses me to this day. I don't recall that there was any effort to put the mother and baby in the hospital, but they seemed well enough, considering that they had no beds or stove or food in that old store.

The man who owned the store had not even known that they were there, but he made no objection when he found out, and I began to haul in furniture and mattresses, boxes of groceries, blankets, clothes. One man gave them a heater and installed it himself. There was a ton of coal waiting for somebody to pick it up. The paper gave me a truck from the circulation department and I went and hauled the coal. I went into basements and attics to get the gifts proffered by sympathetic Mobilians. Darkness had settled and I was making my last haul. Excitement over the response and the satisfaction of seeing the family taken care of had begun to pall. I was wet—my own shoes had cardboard over the holes in the soles—cold, and utterly exhausted.

One more stop, I said to myself, and pulled up in front of the home of a prominent lawyer. His wife met me at the door. She alone among all the people who gave me things had thought to prepare something the family could eat immediately. She had a big pot of hot soup on the stove.

Taking a look at me, she said softly, "My dear, *you* need to eat. Take off your coat and those wet shoes. Sit down. Warm a little and eat some of this soup."

The warmth of the kitchen, the first food of the day, and the kindness of the old couple were a moving end to what had been one of the momentous days of my life—an exhausting day in which pain and need had been met by an outpouring of concern and generosity.

60

I sat there in my stocking feet and cried a little.

But those tears were nothing to the ones I would shed in rage and frustration a few years later when I heard that the kind couple whose soup I had eaten had become victims of the first instance of anti-Semitism I had ever known about.

For years they had spent their summers at an ancient, sand and windswept hotel on the eastern shore of Mobile Bay, and they assumed that they would continue to do so after the hotel was bought and replaced with a far grander structure. They wrote to make their annual reservation and were turned down. Clientele, they were told, was "restricted," which meant no Jews.

As far as I know they made no protest, and if the gentle, grandmotherly woman who had warmed and fed me cried a little, nobody knew about it. But it was the first time I had encountered senseless prejudice against *white* people. We took segregation of our black friends for granted, not even suspecting that they minded it. After all, we had never heard of black people who considered applying for a reservation at any hotel, much less a fancy resort hotel. I think it was the first glimmering I had of an idea that there were many wrongs in the world that a few published words of mine could not change.

Franklin D. Roosevelt had been elected President and welfare was suddenly one of Mobile's most flourishing industries. Miss Van enlarged her staff and set up offices in one of the big, beautiful, empty old mansions on St. Louis Street. She had been named to head one of the new alphabet agencies charged with distributing relief. The jobless and the hungry poured in. A waterfront warehouse was converted into a dormitory for rootless, roaming men and called the Transient Bureau.

The city editor sent me down on Christmas Eve to talk to some of the men who had found refuge there, to learn who they were and where they came from.

I didn't know they had any right to privacy. Miss Van hadn't taught me then that to publicize the name of a person who was homeless and hungry was to "pauperize" him. I sailed in, confident that ex-bankers, stockbrokers, merchants, and teachers would sit up on their dinky little cots and pour out the stories of their lives to me. I didn't understand the helpless desolation they endured, the shame.

I did understand when one unshaven, bleary-eyed fellow lifted his head from his pillow and yelled, "God damn, kid, get out of here! If

61

you don't somebody's gon knock hell out of you!"

How could the man know I was more afraid of the city editor than I was of him? I moved away from him but I hung around outside long enough to find one not-too-proud transient who talked to me about better days, a family, a home somewhere, and rebirth of hope at the Christmas season.

It served. The story I wrote passed muster, but even then I knew it was inadequate. It didn't reveal and I was far from understanding the bitterness and defeat I had seen in that waterfront warehouse, much less those that were spreading across the country.

Some sense of the scope of the problem of breadlines and soup kitchens and flophouses came to me one rainy, cold day when I went to see Miss Van in her new office. I was suffering from a cold and a sore throat, and the sight of lines of men waiting patiently to make application for WPA jobs depressed me. The old house, which had been kept comfortable in its better days by coveys of servants running with scuttles of coal to its many grates, was dank and chilly. A small grate fire flickered feebly in one of the old parlors, now converted to an office, and I went in to find a couple of volunteers unpacking some boxes of clothing sent by two rich and stylish Mobile women. Their names were well-known to me because of their prominence on our society pages, and their homes were showplaces I had often passed on Government Street.

Their contribution to the lines of jobless men outside was dozens of pairs of shoes—women's beach sandals, satin slippers, silver and gold gilded dancing shoes, all in sizes 3 and 4. The volunteers and I stood and looked at them aghast.

Miss Van came in and saw the shoes and our faces.

"They're rich women!" I cried indignantly. "Look what they sent!"

Miss Van picked up a little gold slipper and turned it in her hand. "And the feet of the poor are always so big," she said ruefully.

"It's not right," I persisted. "They're *rich* and they're *horrible!* You should throw these silly shoes back at them and spit in their faces!"

Miss Van took me by the arm and led me into her office, which was only slightly warmer. She pushed a chair closer to the hearth and bade me dry my shoes.

"Celestine, it's a bad time our country is having," she said slowly. "But good will come out of it. I don't know what or how but I don't believe we'll ever have another depression when we're through with

62

this one. We're going to do better than this. People are learning."

"But those rich women!" I said.

"They'll learn if we're patient," she said. "They don't know any-thing about poverty and need. It's not their fault. They have to be taught. We mustn't be contemptuous of their pretty little party shoes. I hope you will be careful, if you write anything, not to make them feel ridiculous, because I'm going to call them and thank them and ask them to come down and spend an hour or two every day helping us."

I didn't write anything, but years later when I met one of the women at a party I said, "You sent those silver slippers and pastel satin pumps . . ."

"Oh, Lord," she moaned. "Wasn't that awful? Florrie Van Sickler made me pay for my stupidity. My husband had to find jobs in his business for a whole bunch of men and I can't tell you the work shirts and warm jackets she made me buy!"

People decried the "give-away" programs and politicians fought over dispensing the government's largesse. There were jokes about shovel leaners, but the lines of the needy and job hunters scarcely diminished, and Miss Van handled it all with great warmth and human-ity and boundless patience. Countless families lived on the city dump in ramshackle shacks thrown together from scraps of tin, old signs, and whatever else the occupant could put hand to.

One bleak day when the lines seemed longer than usual and our paper had carried a story about funds being depleted, I found Miss Van sitting alone in her office. She was watching the rain coursing down the dusty window panes.

"Do you ever get discouraged?" I asked out of boundless naïveté.

She laughed her pleasant throaty laugh. "Oh, my dear, we all do. On a day like today I indulge myself by remembering Florence and the sunshine and flowers. I was in Italy with the Red Cross during the Great War and I have always dreamed of going back. Especially to Florence. Ah, the beautiful buildings and the warmth and flowers everywhere! I won't go back but you must go for me someday."

My shoe sole had just come loose and it flapped distractingly when I walked. I had lost my handkerchief and my nose was raw and red from constant swiping at it with toilet paper. But I left Miss Van and walked down St. Louis Street in a kind of rosy haze.

Florence, Italy. Abroad. Miss Van thought I might go there one day. I had never been more than twenty-five miles from the Gulf of

Mexico. This was the only world I knew. It had never occurred to me that I would travel to another beyond the curve of Mobile Bay, beyond the smell of the marshes and the banana dock or the turpentine and sawdust fragrance of home. But Miss Van was wise and she knew. The dreariness and the poverty I saw every day never really got me down after that. Miss Van had given me a vision.

My Saturday and summer job at the paper unexpectedly turned full-time just before I was to graduate from Murphy High School in 1933. I was browsing through the back issues of the newspaper, reading such columnists as Dorothy Dix and O. O. McIntyre and catching up on Mobile history through the Sunday screed of an old editor-historian named Dr. Erwin Craighhead called, poetically enough, "Dropped Stitches from Mobile's Past" when the copy boy brought me a memo from the city editor. Memos were seldom pleasant, and I felt guilty to be wasting time in the files anyhow. They were probably firing me, I thought, fearfully delaying to unfold the memo.

"You've been a good part-timer," the city editor had written. "How would you like to join the staff full-time after graduation? We can pay you seven dollars a week."

I was dizzy with delight. The money didn't look too bad when you consider that it was more than some families had to spend for a week's groceries. I could live at home, pay a stipend for a ride to Mr. Huff, a mechanic who drove an ailing old truck to the Government Street Lumber Company every day, and eat lunch all for $1 a day. That left $1 I could give my mother toward the new living-room sofa she had been admiring in the Sears catalogue. I accepted with alacrity.

Later I was to ask Don Greenwood, my mentor and sometime city editor, how they came to hire me when I was plainly doping off in the old back issues of both our newspaper and our opposition, the *Register* and the *Item.*

"We liked it," he said. "A good newspaperman reads the papers. It looked like you were boning up on the stories of the past. Good foundation."

There were times as my graduation from Murphy approached when I feared I wasn't going to make it. I had been too wrapped up in my job at the *Press,* too engrossed in writing for *Hi Times* and our little quarterly magazine *The Ryan Review,* to pay a lot of attention to the rest of my subjects. Nearly everybody I knew was making better grades. They had already picked for the commencement program student speakers of high academic achievement. Then one day a couple of months before graduation my English teacher, Miss E. Lura Moore, announced to the class that I had won an essay contest sponsored by *Scholastic* magazine. I don't remember which prize it was, certainly not first, but because it was *national,* my teachers were impressed. I was pulled from the ranks of the near failures, the exam takers (you were exempt from exams if you were making a B average) to make a speech on the commencement program.

My mother was beside herself with joy and excitement. The *Scholastic* judges had echoed her sentiments exactly—write about what you know. My essay, written for *The Ryan Review,* was about a country road, a little woods trail that had been the route to Creola from the mill in the pre-truck and -car days. It certainly wasn't a spine tingler or a hair-raiser but it got me on the commencement program, and as a speaker I was allowed more tickets than the average student. Therefore, Muv was able to invite our Alford kinfolks, Aunt Babe, Aunt Dilly, and Sister, to come and rejoice with us in our triumph— the first member of the family to win a high school diploma.

I don't remember that they were particularly carried away with the triumph, but it may have been that the new linen pumps, dyed to match the long green organdy dress Muv made me, hurt so badly I couldn't notice the jubilation.

The next day I joined the staff of the *Press.*

By the end of summer I was making $10 a week and thinking about going to college. The university law school had been a fleeting dream. Pap had hoped to send me to Montevallo, a college for women up near Montgomery, to prepare me for a job as a schoolteacher. There was no money for either. About that time Spring Hill College, an ancient and beautiful Jesuit school for boys on a wooded eminence about ten miles from downtown Mobile, announced that it would take female day students for the duration of the Depression. (It has since gone coeducational.) Miss Emma Harris, the Mobile librarian, signed up. Student nurses from Providence and Mobile infirmaries, working toward a higher degree than the hospitals could offer, enrolled. Nuns from the local convents arrived in coveys to improve their teaching qualifications.

And I enrolled.

I had a problem sandwiching classes into my workday, but the men on the paper, many of whom had never been to college themselves, were challenged by the problem and determined to help me. They were willing to swap hours off, in fact entire days off, to make it possible for me to get to class, but they wanted the privilege of picking my courses. No journalism, they decreed scornfully, although I don't know if "The Hill," as Mobilians called their only college, even offered journalism them. They opted for English and history, skip the philosophy and who needs "social studies," for goodness' sake. When all of this had been worked out to their satisfaction, it became obvious that I needed to live in town, and one of the secretaries at the paper had a berth for me. She and two friends from her native Mississippi were taking an apartment in an old house on Broad Street. If I would bring a mattress from home and pay $5 a week toward the rent and groceries I was welcome.

Pap and Miss Evelyn were willing, even helpful in getting me settled there. Looking back, I marvel at their confidence, for my roommates, a changing group of older girls, were a great deal more sophisticated than I was. I had never had a date, not counting the young fellows I sat with to eat supper at Epworth League box socials and the high school tennis player who invited me to a High Y fête as compensation for writing a theme for him.

My roommates took pity on me and strove to remedy my deprived social dilemma by the age-old method of assuring their boyfriends that, although I wasn't pretty, I had a grand sense of humor and would be a lot of fun on a blind date. It practically never worked and I didn't care. I was very busy at the newspaper and at school. My colleagues at the paper, not the slightest bit interested in me romantically, were very good about trying to fill in the gaps in my education. They introduced me to bootleg whiskey by sneaking a bottle into the ubiquitous Greek's, a café such as every newspaper office used to have for a neighbor and reporters' hangout. They would pour a little hooch into my Coca-Cola and marvel at the way I sipped it, savoring it like fine old wine.

The accepted method of drinking in those days was to hold a jigger of whiskey in one hand and a glass of water at the ready in the other, choke down the whiskey as if it were fire, poison, or kerosene (it almost was), and with all possible speed chase it with the water. Sipping slowly, I thought the stuff tasted fine, not as good as a Van Antwerp's chocolate ice-cream soda but not virulent. I liked the

66

grownupness of being offered whiskey and, fortunately, didn't tax the resources of my benefactors by drinking much of it. After all, they paid fifty or seventy-five cents a bottle for it and I was a co-worker, not a high-priced date. I sipped and enjoyed the talk and sometimes we would take in a movie together—on passes, of course. But I didn't mind being dateless.

One of my roommates did mind. She had come from a farm in Tennessee and she craved popularity so much that she unwittingly plunged me into a mindless, meddlesome, presumptuous piece of do-gooding that only an ignorant teenager would have the effrontery to attempt.

I found her sitting at the kitchen table crying when I got home from work one afternoon. She had had a date with the handsome son of a prominent Mobile family and she had done the unthinkable—"gone all the way" with him. One date and she was pregnant!

She was a beautiful girl, even red-eyed from weeping. Her long dark hair was in a tangle around her face and half hid the blush of shame from the confession she had to make. She would have to kill herself. There was nothing else to be done. Her old parents on a farm in Tennessee could not survive the scandal.

"Don't be silly," I said briskly. "We'll think of something."

From books and movies I thought a shotgun wedding was called for, but she wouldn't even consider that. She hardly knew the boy and she couldn't bear the embarrassment of ever seeing him again. Besides, he was too grand and stylish to even think of marrying the likes of her, she said humbly.

If she was going to be such a mealy-mouthed dope, I told her, I washed my hands of her troubles.

"Oh, no!" she cried. "You've got to help me! Nobody else can."

She considered that my job on the newspaper empowered me to change lives and I agreed with her. After all, I knew about the Florence Crittenton Home for unwed mothers and the whole procedure for getting illegitimate babies born and placed for adoption.

She didn't balk at giving up her unborn baby then, but she did later and gave me no end of trouble.

Getting her into the home was fairly easy. I most certainly must have enlisted the help of my social-worker friends. But first she had to go home to the farm and tell her parents that she was in love, planning marriage. I equipped her with a photograph I picked up at the office. (I never knew if the macho face belonged to some civic leader or some obscure actor. It was in a trash basket.) Naturally it was ardently autographed to Stella (by me) and for a week or two Stella was home on the farm receiving daily love letters from the imaginary suitor. I drew on the best poetry and love notes I could find at the library.

Back at the Florence Crittenton Home, Stella prepared for her confinement, and I prepared a marriage announcement, accompanied by her photograph, for her parents to take to their hometown paper.

The baby, named Junior for his mythical father, had to have come prematurely, but that bit of timing didn't seem to bother Stella's parents. He was a darling little boy, and they were very proud of him and of her for having him.

Almost immediately, of course, we had to shuck old what's-his-name, the father. I can't remember what grounds we used for divorcing him but it was good riddance. I had wearied of writing earnest husbandly-fatherly missives every time Stella went home and had run out of excuses for his not showing up there himself. So it was divorce, although Stella's parents, good church people, opposed that with every fiber of their religious beings. Once or twice I thought of killing him off or having him simply disappear, but that would bring law-enforcement officers into it and I wasn't that daring.

So Stella regretfully divorced him. I think by this time she might have fallen a little bit in love with his handsome photograph and all those poetic letters. But she did as I advised, and six months later she married a perfectly charming young Mobilian who could give her and the baby a good home and membership in the country club.

A friend of mine reported seeing her and her husband at a dance. She was the loveliest-looking woman in the room, he said, and her husband obviously adored her.

By that time I was less self-confident about my ability to run other people's lives and I wondered at the teen-age effrontery that had made me feel invincible when I tackled Stella's.

At the office my education advanced apace. Frances Ruffin Durham, member of a distinguished southern family, was the society editor and clearly a gentlewoman of the old school. Only she had served a hitch as police reporter on the New Orleans *States* and she was no sheltered magnolia. Any time my youthful ignorance of the facts of life baffled the men on the paper they would send me to Mrs. Durham for instruction.

I took a story over the phone from the police reporter about a man who had been arrested for "carnal knowledge." Knowledge was always desirable, I thought, so what was this "carnal" bit?

"Remember your Latin, Celestine," Mrs. Durham said patiently. "Carnal . . . flesh . . . bodily knowledge. Sex . . . sexual intercourse."

One of those unspeakable things, I thought to myself and went back to my desk.

On another day Bill Longgrear, who was covering police at the time, phoned in a story about a man who was charged with a "crime against nature."

"What's that, Bill, something like setting the woods on fire?" I asked.

Bill choked and then rallied. "Not . . . *precisely,*" he said slowly. "Go ask Mrs. Durham."

Mrs. Durham did not turn a hair. A crime against nature, she said placidly, is sex with an animal.

Oh, me, I thought, there's no end to the ramifications of sex. I went back and sat down.

My first brush with a mysterious four-letter word that begins with "f" and is sometimes expanded to include an "er," did give Mrs. Durham pause. Country-reared, I had been sheltered from back fences and the obscenities they have scrawled on them. I had never encountered that word and, liking new words, I was interested when I picked up a police report on the city editor's desk one day and read that an officer had shot a man who called him a "mother f——er."

Don Greenwood, then city editor, was on the other side of the newsroom at the water fountain.

"Don," I called out, "what's a mother f——er?"

Reporters and editors froze at their typewriters. Don spewed water all over the floor and collapsed against the cooler. A dead silence fell. After a long moment Don wiped his face and said in a strangled voice, "Go ask Mrs. Durham."

The very idea of the word in those days was abhorrent and shocking to even the least-conventional people. And for it to come out of the mouth of a young girl was horrifying. Mrs. Durham paled visibly but she came through.

"Sit down," she said. "I'll try to explain."

She explained so well that I don't think I have spoken the word since and, as you have seen, I have to spell it with blanks.

The *Press,* with its circulation gimmicks, its contests and cartoons, its strident editorial policy, and perhaps just its liveliness, soon wore down the weary old *Register* and *Item.* We heard that Frederick I. Thompson, the publisher, had agreed to sell out. The afternoon *Item* was to fold. The old *Register* with its stately marble building down near Bienville Square was to move in with us. Some of its staff would survive the merger, some would not.

We were prone to detest, sight unseen, those who had been our opposition, but we turned out to be very lucky in the few who joined us. The Misses Nettie and Mary Chandler, old Mobilians and old-school society editors, were elderly ladies very like *Gone With the Wind*'s Aunt Pittypat. For so many years they had served as social arbiters in Mobile that, without them, nobody would have known who *was* Mobile society. They decided whose weddings and parties were important and snubbed those they considered unworthy. Miss Nettie, the older and more dominant of the pair, scorned the typewriter and wrote everything in longhand. Miss Mary was never comfortable with the machine but she tried to master it. And to help them they had a gifted young woman named Ann Battle, who had been Mrs. Durham's lieutenant.

For a month every year the Chandler sisters went to New York to see the new Broadway plays and to be entertained by expatriate Alabamians who lived there. Miss Nettie wrote back her celebrated "Betty letters," long screeds in the form of gossipy letters to a mythical character named Betty Bienville. Those letters, running in the Sunday paper, were celebrated at home and abroad, for Miss Nettie never said anything straight out if she could think of a literary way of putting it.

Babies were not babies and they were never just born. They were "bundles of joy," which arrived by different means according to the seasons. Santa dropped them down the chimney or the Easter bunny left them or St. Patrick brought them. Guests at a stylish luncheon at somebody's summer home down on Dog River did not walk in the woods after the meal. They "answered the call of Nature." As far away as California people were heard to quote the story about the elderly Mobile man who married a young girl and surprised her on their wedding night with "a magnificent antique pendant."

That may have been after Miss Nettie and Miss Mary took up Hollywood.

After being faithful to New York every fall of their lives, they suddenly switched to Hollywood. The reason was Robert Taylor. Both ladies fell madly in love with him. I never heard if they actually met him or if he returned their adulation but they persevered in their Hollywood vacations until their deaths, convinced that he was the finest actor the stage and screen had ever produced and clearly of "good breeding." They did not, unfortunately, care for his then wife, Barbara Stanwyck, who was, they felt, "a very common person."

Marion Toulmin Gaines, the *Register*'s managing editor, was another acquisition we liked, a short, plump, good-humored man who knew the newspaper business frontward and backward. He joined the *Press* staff as a deskman but he was promptly promoted to managing editor because of his ability and probably his old family knowledge of Mobile, valuable to the young editors who came from other places. One day a new copy boy showed up at the paper, the biggest and oldest copy "boy" we had ever seen. He was six feet tall, twenty-five years old, and incredibly handsome.

"Who's that?" I asked Mr. Gaines.

"His name is James Little. He prefers to be called Jim. He's my cousin," he said. "He wanted a newspaper job, said he would take anything. I'm trying him out."

"But as a copy boy? Isn't he old for that?"

"We'll see," Marion said, grinning.

The new "boy" was very quiet and diligent, apparently not above the menial business of running to answer the clarion call of "Copy! *Copee now!*" when a reporter on deadline wanted him to pick up a story and hand it to the city editor or take it to the composing room. He sharpened pencils and distributed mail and one day he caught the eye of Miss Nettie.

"Aren't you Mary Henry's boy?" she cooed, her knowledge of antecedents making her use his mother's maiden name.

"Yes, ma'am," said Jim.

"Ah, Mary was a belle!" she chirped. "I went to her wedding. And

71

I remember when you arrived from heaven. An adorable baby!"

Jim blushed and hurried by, but as he passed Ann Battle's desk she whispered, "You little devil, you!"

Right away we got the rundown on the new man. He came from an old Mobile family. On his mother's side were lawyers and Confederate heroes and an eighteenth-century mayor. On his father's side his grandfather was president of a bank, he had an uncle in some high place in Washington, and his girl cousins were always among the season's prettiest debutantes. No money, but he owned his own white tie and tails. He had invitations to all the Mardi Gras balls, having been in time a member of the exalted carnival court. Several rich girls in his set were believed to yearn after him. ("D.D.," Ann told me. "Deb's delight.") If only he had a real job . . .

He took on several jobs. The newly blended newspapers built a modern plant on St. Louis Street, and when moving day came they gave strong-backed staffers a chance to earn extra money hauling in and arranging the century-old accumulation of bound newspaper files. Jim and Tom Wainwright, a reporter, stripped to the waist, labored every night.

A prize was offered for animal stories. Jim wrote so many they found it more expedient to raise his pay and put him on the news staff than to give him the prize money. Charlie Leanman, the waterfront reporter, had a chance to go to England on a freight boat, and he was such a thoroughgoing Dickens fan he took it, never to return. Jim Little had shipped out of Mobile as a cabin boy when he finished Barton Academy, advancing to able-bodied seaman and traveling the world. He knew more about boats and shipping than most reporters ever learned. They gave him the waterfront beat.

I saw him come and go but I didn't think much about him. He was very quiet and he looked rather haughty. Later he was to tell me that he got reprimanded many times by teachers for "looking like that"— and he never knew what they were talking about.

Chapter Four

After work one afternoon I borrowed a typewriter in the quiet and empty society department to write a letter. Jim came in and sat at a desk across the room to use the phone. He was trying to get a date for that evening.

He made half a dozen calls with no apparent luck, and then he slammed down the phone and scowled at me.

"They all have dates—or pretend they do," he said. "How about you? Are you doing anything tonight?"

"Me?" I said, startled. "Not a thing."

"Then how about coming out with me?"

"Sure," I said and closed the typewriter.

It was the beginning of a courtship that surprised and baffled everybody. That this handsome, socially prominent, although dead broke, young man should be interested in a gangling, countrified girl who was eight years younger than he was, gauche and irrevocably plain, was unbelievable. On my side the wonderment came from, of all people, Jim's cousin Marion Gaines. He called me over for a talk.

"Don't waste your time with James," he said, calling him that out of family habit. "He'll never marry you and you shouldn't marry him anyhow. You can go somewhere in the newspaper business. Don't let marriage and a family stop you. Do you suppose I'd be working here for the little money they pay if I didn't have a wife and four children? Why, I could be in New York or London or Paris. Don't you make that mistake."

Aw, marriage wasn't even a consideration, I said, thanking him for his interest and rushing out to meet Jim at the Saenger Theatre. (We

73

did a lot of hand-holding in the movies.)

Actually, I didn't really want to marry Jim. I was profoundly jealous when he put on evening clothes and took some debutante to a ball. Never having been to one myself, I had no idea what it would be like to be in a grand march or to dance to the music of a name band. I would have kept him from all that if I could, but it really wasn't much fun to take him home with me to Creola.

He and Pap liked one another fine. Pap's Uncle Lyles, who had borrowed money from Jim's late grandfather, was very respectful of him. But he made my mother uneasy. She knew that his family lived in a big white house and, although they had to get an FHA loan to repair the roof and his brother worked for a filling station and his sister for the WPA, she figured they wouldn't think much of our little sawmill house. It wasn't pleasant for her to have what we valued diminished by comparing it with what they had.

There was also the matter of our speech. Jim was irritated by the way my mother and I pronounced "I" words. Pap, a Mobilian, spoke satisfactorily. Miss Evelyn and I had her native south Georgia way of saving "ri-us" for rice, "nigh-ut" for night and so on. He would correct me in her presence. She considered it snobbery but I think it was just a lack of tact.

His mother seemed to like me and we had a good time together when he took me to their house to visit. She was a bright, charming woman and I think she had long since given up on the friends' daughters she once considered potential daughters-in-law. The Depression had destroyed or shifted most people's fortunes, and she realized a canny girl might not want to marry a threadbare newspaperman.

"I don't care," she said of one post-deb who was busy with the Junior League. "She looks like an alligator gar anyhow."

Meanwhile, Jim and I found we had a bond in newspapering. We read Stanley Walker's *City Editor* together and we wanted to be the best on the biggest papers. He had read a great deal more than I had and, of course, had all that foreign travel, which he was ripe to appreciate. I read the diary he kept as a teenage cabin boy, and I saw many of the wonders of the world through his eyes, moved to tears by his feeling for them and the poetry he wrote.

He was friends with many captains of foreign ships that came into the port of Mobile, and one of our favorite dates was to be invited to an elegant European dinner in the cabin of some French or German, Greek or Italian ship's master. We didn't realize until some time later that one of our best evenings had been spent eating and drinking with a Nazi.

If Marion Gaines had not resigned to take a job as editor of the Pensacola *News-Journal,* I might have been deterred from marriage. In fact, I'm sure now I wouldn't have done it at all if Jim hadn't slapped the switchboard operator and got fired.

It was the custom in those benighted days for newspapermen to drink a lot, particularly on Christmas Eve. Jim, being oddly shy anyhow, apparently had to fortify himself before he could dress up in a red flannel suit and go out to Editor Ewald's house and play Santa Claus to his little boy. By the time that joyous caper was over, he and the colonel had had a few more drinks, and he returned to the newspaper in a great happy glow.

I was not there, having gone to cover a big fire that was destroying the Dauphin Street Baptist church. But, the way it was told to me, Jim, in an abundance of Christmas spirit, kissed the switchboard operator. She slapped him and it seemed totally reasonable to him to slap her back.

The next day he sent her a dozen red roses and abject apologies, but he got fired anyhow.

His cousin Marion, having tested him and found him worthy, promptly hired him for the Pensacola paper. The separation became a factor for us. He was seventy miles away and I missed him. He missed me, too, because he came home one weekend, drove us out Cedar Point Road and proposed to me.

He seemed so sad and vulnerable to be doing it my heart went out to him. The wit, the humor, the gallantry were oddly missing. He just stared at the gray sky and the gray water of Mobile Bay and said, like it was a painful admission of weakness, "I want to marry you."

There were many things about me that he wanted to change, including my south Georgia accent, but the one I found insuperable was that he wanted me to shuck some of my friends. They were interesting, attractive people to me but not presentable by his standards. Loyalty, I regret to say, had nothing to do with my refusal. I was young, impressed by and in love with him, but the people he found, for some silly artificial reason I could not fathom, objectionable, had been good to me. I enjoyed and needed them. I said, No deal.

For years I was to ponder the inconsistency of his attitude. As a

75

reporter he seemed to enjoy all kinds of people. He did not make friends easily but he kept the ones he made and he valued them. We once traveled hundreds of miles to visit a seedy old night watchman, who had been his pal when they were shipmates on a freighter. I think now it was a hometown thing. He wanted me to look better than I was to old Mobilians, to family friends who operated in a kind of closed circle.

Being from the country was all right. Being poor was acceptable. Even formerly wealthy Mobilians were closing off rooms of their big houses, putting up ugly little heaters before their marble mantels, and camping out in chilly drawing rooms. I even took loads of mill ends, small heater-sized boards, from home to his mother, who was having an uncomfortable time of it back of the big sliding doors in her double parlor.

Pap's family would have done, but I didn't really know the rich and social Mobile relatives, especially not well enough to expect them to provide me with a suitable background. I think he felt that my chances of moving into the magic circle depended on my coming without the baggage of wrong friends. I never could determine what their wrongness was.

It really didn't matter because as the months passed he was enjoying his work in Pensacola, fascinated by his co-workers, and seemed to have forgotten the conditions he laid down for a bride-to-be. He wrote me wonderful letters, talked to me, toll free, on the office phone when there was a business call between the two papers, and urged me to come for a visit.

My mother insisted that I either have a written invitation from his cousins the Gaineses, or a chaperone. I seized the chaperone—a jolly friend from the office named Kathleen Stimpson, who was a little older than I was but experienced in the ways of men, humorous and tolerant and full of fun. She and I checked into the wonderful old San Carlos Hotel, and went forth with Jim and a young man he rounded up for her to play on the beach, dance at the beach casino, and feast on seafood. Jim and I agreed that if we could ever live and work in the same town again we'd be able to afford marriage.

The chance came that summer. My mother had gone to Springfield, Missouri, to visit Aunt Ida and Uncle J. C. Pumphrey, the friends from 219 South Jackson Street, who had taken us in before we met Pap. Uncle J. C., a veteran of the Spanish-American War, had given up policing and taken a job as sexton in the U.S. National Cemetery there. Two friends from the office and I took our vacations, and, after stopping off for a weekend in New Orleans, drove up to the Ozark Mountains to get Muv. On the way back home we stopped in Mobile to drop off my friends, and one of them, Kathleen, found a message at her house for me to call Jim. I ran in and made the call and came out and told my mother I had been offered a job on the Pensacola *News-Journal.*

"Why would you want a job there?" she asked.

"Then Jim and I could get married."

"Oh, for goodness' sake!" she snapped with the irritation she might have shown if I let the puppy in the house to wet the floor.

Naturally I had to marry him then.

Sometimes on our dates we had gone to Jim's house, a wide-verandahed white two-story frame house on Montauk Avenue on a lot adjoining in the back the beautiful wooded Government Street grounds of his mother's cousins Stewart and Stella Brooks. Mary Little had lost her mother, the former Martha Brooks, when she was seven years old. Her father, a Meridian, Mississippi, lawyer, had sent her to live with the Brookses in Mobile, her sister Augusta to a cousin in St. Louis, and their brother, Crawford, to other cousins, the Irwins, in Mobile.

Her children, James, Ervin, and Mary Everitt (called Everitt), had spent their childhood trailing through the Brookses' yard with their nurse, Janie, on the way to the Government Street trolley and playing under the Brookses' trees. The two families shared a yardman named Willie, who lived in the Brookses' servant house, milked the in-residence cows of each, and took them to pasture in a field a few blocks away.

Mr. Little had been in the hardware business but when the Florida boom loomed big on the horizon he sold out and moved his family to Jacksonville, where he launched a big construction company. The Depression cost him his business and probably his life. He died of a stroke at the age of fifty-two.

All that was left to his widow and grown children was the house in Mobile, and they returned to it, glad that one of the alphabet agencies was the FHA, Federal Housing Administration, from which they could get a loan for a badly needed roof.

77

James got the job with his Aunt Augusta's son, Marion, on the paper; Everitt went to work for the WPA; and Ervin, who had secretly married while he was at the University of Alabama, quit school and came home, bringing his young pregnant wife with him. The only job he could find was at a filling station. They all lived in the big Montauk Avenue house, and so did a handful of boarders Mrs. Little had decided to take in.

I loved to go there mainly because of Mrs. Little (I would later call her Mamie, as did all her friends). She was a funny, spunky little woman totally undaunted by their new poverty and the loss of the staff of cook, maid, laundress, who had once kept the house going. She learned to cook, and they were the first people I ever knew who called their evening meal dinner (pure movie stuff to one who always called it supper). All meals were served in the graceful, long-windowed dining room, with its sideboard loaded with handsome family silver serving pieces and a big Tiffany shade casting jewel-tone colors on the table. Sometimes the fare was plebeian but Mamie could serve grits and canned corned-beef hash with a flair.

Afterward they always adjourned to the parlor, where in winter Mamie insisted on the comfort of a fire in the grate. She was resigned to a fuel-saving little heater in front of the beautiful fireplace in the dining room and had long since given up on heating the bedrooms or the big front hall and stairwell. I remember pulling my coat closer and shivering when we walked in the front door. But the living room, furnished with old family pieces and a worn, soft-colored old rug, was warm and welcoming, and Mamie kept the conversation brisk and amusing. Poor as she was, she didn't miss many parties given by her old friends.

I had heard of her before I met her. A friend in the society department at the paper had seen her at a luncheon or a cocktail party given for the debutante daughter of one of her friends.

"Mrs. Little was the most delightful woman there," my friend said, "and she had a run in her stocking."

She could not give the usual party a close friend was expected to give a girl making her debut but she did what she could without apology.

"You know I'd love to give little Ida a luncheon or a tea," she told her lifelong friend Miss Ida (Mrs. Stuart LeBlanc). "I can't. But I can make new curtains for her room."

It was enough.

She remained close and involved with what she called "our crowd." Once we talked about different members of that group, those she had gone through grammar school with, those she had made mudpies with, those who had been in her wedding and she in theirs. She came to a lady I knew as Miss Donnie.

"Oh, Donnie's new in our crowd," Mamie said. "She moved here from Virginia. We've only known Donnie thirty-eight years."

She was capable of a jolly prank. Her sister Augusta's husband, Dr. Toulmin Gaines, was an erudite gentleman who was knowledgeable not only about his field of dermatology (I think he was the first skin specialist in Mobile) but about the world of books and the theatre. He was a wonderful raconteur and often dropped in at mealtime, pulled up a chair, and took over the table talk. Once it became necessary for Mamie to invite some former business associate of her husband's from out of town to dinner. She wanted it to be nice but she hadn't thought to deceive the guest about her diminished lifestyle until her feisty sister-in-law Theo (Mrs. Ervin) Little took a hand. Theo insisted on "maiding," borrowing a uniform from some friend's maid and serving the meal with verve and style, except for two things. Her performance, of which he had not been apprised, rendered Uncle Toulmin, the raconteur, speechless, convulsing him with laughter. And Aunt Theo got so interested in what the guest of honor was saying she put down her tray, pulled up a chair, and joined the conversation.

It is not recorded what the guest thought.

Jim's mother and my mother would have been natural friends, independent spirits that they were, but the distance between their backgrounds was great and their acquaintance was slight. Jim and I went one Sunday night, when he was home from Pensacola for the weekend, to tell Mamie that we were engaged. We picked up her and Everitt and drove out to the airport for that much-admired nightly event—seeing the mail plane come in. On the way we told them that we planned to be married.

Unsurprised, Mamie assured us that she was delighted and promptly invited me to lunch the next day. Jim was back in Pensacola at the *News-Journal* and Everitt would be at work, so it would be just the two of us. We ate a festive little lunch in the dining room and then retired to the hall closet under the stairs, where Mamie pulled out family pictures and Jim's baby silver and gave them to me. I sat on the floor and admired the baby Jim in leggings and a big beaver hat at the age of two. I fingered the toothmarks on his silver napkin ring and traced his name and birthdate and his father's name and birthdate on the silver baby cup.

Mamie told me funny stories about her family, the Everitts and Brookses of Mobile and the Henrys of Mississippi, but really more about her husband's family, the Littles. Grandpa, also named James William, had grown up on a farm at Plateau just north of Mobile city limits. The dock from which they shipped their cotton was at a place called Magazine Point, almost directly in front of their house, and I had passed it many times on my way to and from Creola. Mr. Little left the farm early to get a job as a runner in a Mobile bank, advancing in due course to the presidency.

He must have been a domineering gentleman because all of his sons and their wives and children, no matter their religious preference (Mamie was an Episcopalian), were required to be in the family pew at the First Baptist Church on Sunday morning. Here, wearing striped trousers and a cutaway coat, Mr. Little passed the collection plate. He was said to have owned one of the first automobiles in Mobile—a contraption he never learned to drive but required his son Jim and his family to take out on Sunday-afternoon "motor trips."

"I sat in the back with the children," Mamie recalled, "and we all hated it. Mr. Little was in front with Jim, and he chewed tobacco and spat into the wind, which blew right back in our faces."

Before we quit that session in the hall closet, Mamie passed on to me some handsome silver serving pieces that had belonged to her mother, Martha, and to her grandmother, the first Mary Everitt, given to Mamie when she was married in 1900.

It was a lovely way to be admitted to the family and not too different in spirit from the way Muv and Pap welcomed Jim. I had made him ask for my hand in marriage, a chore he had performed when we had come back from swimming in the millpond and had eaten a cold supper on the screened porch. While I was putting my little cousin Jerry to bed, he cornered Muv and Pap and asked the question.

I was terribly nervous, trying to overhear, and poked three-year-old Jerry under the sheet before he had finished his prayers.

"Wait a minute, Westine!" he said. "I wanted to say, 'God bless you,' too."

"Oh, please do!" I cried. "I need it."

When I got back to the porch Muv had brought out a bottle of scuppernong wine, normally reserved for Christmas and New Year's, and she and Pap and Jim were sipping and smiling benignly on one another.

We were set to get married, but there was an unexpected delay caused by the fact that the Mobile *Press-Register* offered me a $5 raise (by then I was up to $20 a week) to stay and asked Jim to come back. The *News-Journal* countered by giving Jim a raise and upping their offer to me. We seesawed between the two papers for a couple of weeks, awed that our pooled income would come to unheard-of affluence—$55 a week!

"That's a lot of money," marveled Jim's mother.

"You'll be rich," said my mother, mollified at the prospect of the marriage.

We settled on Pensacola and were married on August 31, 1936, in the parsonage of Grandpa Little's beloved First Baptist Church. At his death his children and grandchildren had felt free to return to the churches of their choice, and Mamie and her children were back in old Christ Episcopal Church, in which she had been christened in infancy. But Jim and I both knew and admired the First Baptist pastor, Dr. John W. Phillips, a delightfully literary Englishman, whose witty lectures on Dickens and Shakespeare I had attended. We asked him to perform the ceremony in his study at home.

It was a hot, bright afternoon and the wedding guests waited in the shade of a tree in the front yard while Jim and I, late for the ceremony, drove to the courthouse, arguing angrily. We hadn't known that my presence was essential to getting the marriage license and I had dawdled at home, sitting in the kitchen in my slip eating rutabagas and drinking buttermilk. Pap had gone ahead with his cousin Clayton Haines from West Virginia, and Muv and I were to drive into town together. She was dressed and waiting and very impatient with my leisurely prenuptial meal.

"I'm gon leave you," she threatened.

"Ha!" I jeered smugly. "This one time the show can't go on without me."

Finally I got into my brown lace dress and broad-brimmed brown hat (I know now it must have been a hideous costume but it had the fall look we thought important then) and we headed for the Littles' house. There was Jim pacing the sidewalk.

I had to go back with him to the courthouse to get the license, supplying names like that of my natural father, Henry Colley, whose existence I had kept secret up until then.

Jim was furious with me. I was ready to call off the wedding. But there under Dr. Phillips's trees were our mothers; his sister, Everitt, who was to be my attendant; his lifelong friend, Alfred Dumont, who was to be best man; Pap and Cousin Clayton and four or five friends from the office.

Herbert Lyons, a newspaper colleague who was one of the first Neiman fellows and later went to the *New York Times,* wrote in his column saying farewell to me that they were all in a state of full-blown hysterics by the time the principals arrived.

Jim and I weren't speaking.

It might have been a tipoff on the marriage, which was to have some stormy weather. In fact, the song by that name became a sort of theme song for us. We kissed and made up after the ceremony, had a glamorous Tom Collins with our friends at a new place in town—a drive-in bar down by the G. M. & O railroad station—and embarked on a honeymoon drive to Jacksonville.

On the road Jim kept me giggling and urging him on as he composed Ogden Nashian lyrics to go with the "Stormy Weather" tune.

"Inclement meteorological conditions," he caroled, substituting for "I can't go on, everything I have is gone," the words "I find it impossible to proceed, I have been divested of my possessions."

I decided he was not only the handsomest man I had ever seen but the funniest and cleverest.

We spent the first night of our honeymoon at a charming old-fashioned hotel in DeFuniak Springs, Florida. Our bedroom overlooked a lake. The bathroom was down the hall, to which I went wearing Jim's brown suede size 12 shoes because my trousseau money hadn't stretched to bedroom slippers.

We wrote postcards to our family and friends at breakfast the next morning, and when I flippantly wrote my pal Herbert Lyons, "Cheer up, divorce is inevitable," Jim acted hurt and made me tear it up.

We had a week at the Seminole Hotel in Jacksonville on a newspaper duebill. In those days, short on paying guests, hotels swapped accommodations to newspaper employees for advertising. The business-office friend who had given Jim the duebill had appended a note introducing us as employees and adding, "They are on their honeymoon." Jim pulled up by the roadside outside of town and painstakingly erased those words.

That night we went out to the beach and feasted on chili and hot tamales and Jim came down with acute stomach cramps. The next morning I had to call a doctor, who gave him something to ease his pain and caused him to sleep. I took the $10 I had borrowed from Kathleen as honeymoon "mad money" and went to investigate Jacksonville stores.

Back in Pensacola we spent our second free week finding a place to live. I felt bridey and eager to feather my nest, as Muv put it, and I would have settled for any kind of housekeeping rooms in any part of town. Jim would not. Before I came he had lived in a boardinghouse in a fairly seedy part of town and had made friends with all kinds of people—fishermen, shrimpers, policemen, wrestlers, and even undertakers.

One of his first acquaintances was a proofreader, who invited him to an after-work session at Lloyd's Funeral Home, where "viewing the body" was apparently staple diversion for the night-shift crowd in the composing room.

"You want to go down to Red Lloyd's and take a look at that fisherman they brought in today?" the proofreader would invite. Reluctant but not wanting to seem unappreciative of hospitality, Jim went.

One of his fishing buddies was a constable who once asked him to serve as a guard for a prisoner they were transferring to Jacksonville. It would be a chance for a little expense-paid trip to his once home and Jim went. But the constable, in the city for the first time, couldn't be persuaded out of the hotel room. He looked out on the Greyhound bus terminal across the street, lost in admiration for the blue neon greyhound racing across the sign.

"Look a yonder!" he cried in wonderment. "Look at that little sumbitch run!"

Jim enjoyed these people but he had in mind for us a place in a nicer section of town among people very like his transplanted Mobile cousins, the Gaineses at the newspaper, and his beautiful cousin Theodora, Aunt Theo and Uncle Ervin's daughter. Dodie, as she was called, had married a Navy flyer named Schemerhorn Van Matre and lived near the Naval Air Station. We found an impeccable place—a room and bath with a small sitting room in the home of the distinguished and once-affluent P. K. Yonge family. P. K. Yonge himself, for whom many things in Florida have been named, including the University of Florida library, was dead and his other children had married and established homes of their own. But Miss Marjorie, an unmarried daughter, and Mr. Julien, an unmarried son, continued to live in the big ivy-covered stucco mansion at 1400 East Jackson Street, and they took us to board.

For $25 a week we had their mother's old bedroom, with a view of Pensacola Bay on one side and of Bayou Texar on the other, and, of course, all our meals. Three times a day we sat at a refectory table in the big dining room and ate simple, beautifully served meals, which Mr. Julien planned and shopped for and their long-time cook, Isabelle, executed.

Mr. Julien, in his sixties then, I suppose, was a slender, quick-moving, boyish-looking man, who elected to be a near recluse because of a bad stammer and severe deafness. He had started in his youth a collection of Florida histories, including complete files of all the area's newspapers, and it had grown to be one of the most valuable and sought-after collections in the state. His father had built a vault in the backyard in a stand of trees near the tennis court to house and safeguard the collection. Adjoining it was a small study, where students of Florida history from all over the country often came to do research. Many of them, including such popular writers as Marjorie Kinnan Rawlings, became Mr. Julien's friends, deeply indebted to him for his knowledge and archives, despite the disabling stammer and deafness.

We adored him and planned someday to name a child for him. (We never did.) But newlyweds are restless and venturesome and we didn't stay anywhere long, moving within our five years in Pensacola to four other places, with an interim return to the Yonges'. There was a garage apartment overlooking the bay in East Pensacola Heights with a scrap of lawn and a spot for my first garden. Then there was a green-stained cottage on the bayou, an apartment in the big barn of a house next door, and finally a pretty, newly painted and papered two-bedroom apartment a young couple had for rent in an old house down the street from the Yonges'. We must have had our reasons for traipsing around like that, but they seem unimportant now. The Yonges were welcoming even when we returned to them with a baby and a nursemaid, and it was a beautiful, shabby, wonderful place to live.

Miss Marjorie had little to do with running the house, probably because she was so busy as a volunteer at the big Christ Episcopal Church downtown. She and Marion Gaines's wife, also named Marion, were co-workers, almost totally engrossed in the church. (Uncle Toulmin called his daughter-in-law Marion Positive and his son Marion Negative. The rest of the family referred to them as "the Marions.") Probably because of these two women and the fact that we lived in the Yonge house we were suddenly taken up by old-guard Pensacolians and Navy society—this to my surprise and chagrin.

The custom of afternoon calls almost threw me. I had a job on the newspaper and almost no interest in calling on or being called on by strangers, especially when the call amounted to catching the hostess out and leaving a card at the front door. I didn't even own a calling card. When some of the young matrons in town invited me to a tea I was unprepared for the amenities involved. It seemed that I had to have a presentable "dressy" outfit but, worse than that, calling cards to put in a silver tray in the front hall as I walked in, one for each of the hostesses and one for the honoree. I appealed to Mamie and she immediately sent me half a dozen of her cards and ordered Gwin Stationery Company in Mobile to make up some for me. (Hers still said "junior" and she didn't want to become "senior" so we tacked "III" on mine, although by actual count Jim was the fifth James William Little in line. I wonder whatever happened to those cards?)

Work at the paper was much more interesting and satisfying. The force was small. Jim was the entire reportorial staff of the morning *Journal;* I was it for the afternoon *News.* Besides us, each paper had only a city editor–deskman, a society editor, and a sports editor.

For that reason Sam Ellis, the editor-in-chief, asked me to keep my Sibley name so it wouldn't look as if the papers had such a plethora of Littles. We were few and close, and the social life we generated was far from the afternoon-call kind. There were Saturday-night shrimp boils with beer in somebody's kitchen, spicy Italian spaghetti served up almost every Sunday night by the beauty queen of her high school days, Jane Pericola, whose husband, Frank, was both managing editor and sports editor for the *Journal,* fish frys and picnics.

In the daytime at work I was having a good time. I covered the courthouse and city hall, all federal offices, the city and county jails, and anything else that came up like conventions and visiting celebrities. When Warner Brothers sent a crew into Pensacola to make a movie called *Wings of the Navy* we all became involved with the movie stars for several weeks. The first morning they were in town I went down to the San Carlos Hotel to check out the stars. George Brent, wearing a beret and an ascot and dark glasses, just like movie leading men of legend, was waiting outside the door for the bar to open.

He got in just as I arrived and took a table. I walked over, introduced myself, and asked to interview him.

"Go on," he said. "You can talk to me. I'm no better than you are."

Oddly enough, I had not considered that he might be, but his reassurance did give me pause.

More fun to interview was the comic Frank McHugh, who had undressed and gone to bed but was amiable about letting me in and talking to me in his pajamas. He was charming and full of humorous quotes and asked permission to go to police court with me. When I found him waiting on the steps of the police station that afternoon he waved at me and called out: "Hi, I'm here! Recognize me with my clothes on?"

The fantastically handsome romantic lead John Payne was new to movie making then, well-mannered, shy, and apparently grateful to the newspaper crew, who invited him out after hours to play on the beach or eat at our houses. However, he spent many nights alone in one of the darkened and empty San Carlos parlors playing the piano or talking over the phone to his then love, Ann Shirley, who was in Hollywood.

Naturally we had a more-enduring friendship with the unit press agent, a former Los Angeles newspaperman named George Schaeffer. We liked George enormously and stayed in touch with him for years. Half a dozen years later, when I went to Hollywood for the Atlanta *Constitution* to preview Walt Disney's Georgia-born film *Song of the South*, George took me to the San Pedro waterfront, introduced me to reporters who covered it, and fed me my first clam chowder in a dockside bar.

Pensacola, an old city, acquainted me with many different kinds of people—the old Spanish and French families who were, effectively, its aristocracy, the intellectual and civic leaders, the cosmopolitan Navy people, who had lived all over the world and maintained a

Muv's Alford kin and friends posing with pigs, ducks, and watermelons in front of their Alford, Florida, home, West View. (Left to right) Uncle Lon (Alonzo Kennedy) *and* Aunt Babe (Elizabeth Kennedy), "Uncle" Rufus, *and* Aunt Georgie Gilbert *(others unknown).*

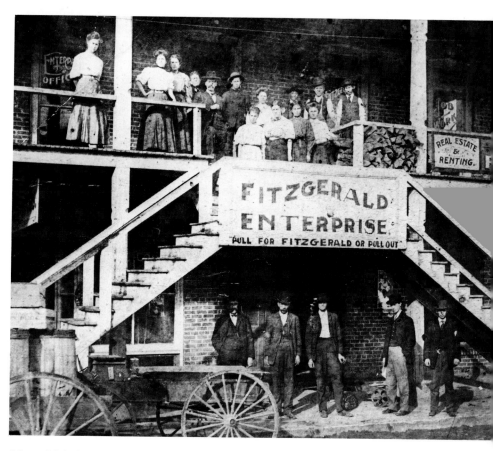

Muv—Dixie Barber—the smallest and youngest girl on the upstairs gallery worked for a season as a reporter and printer's devil on the Fitzgerald Enterprise.

Muv in her Nugget Nell costume the summer she was sixteen, playing with a stock company touring south Georgia.

Muv, with wrong foot in the mule's stirrup, clowning for her Cousin Sister, who came visiting the first year Muv was married to Henry Colley.

Family gathering at West View in Alford. I think Aunt Joy Crover (second from right) came in the Model T. *(L-R)* Cousin Roy Chapman (Sister's son), Aunt Babe, Cousin Woodrow (Aunt Joy's son), Sister (Mrs. Theda Chapman), and Muv, *seated on the running board. That's me leaning out of the front seat and* (standing at right) *Aunt Joy and Aunt Dilly. (Aunt Babe and Aunt Dilly were really my great-aunts.)*

Muv (fourth from left) *on an outing with her friends before her marriage. She and Ezella Gilbert* (to her right) *probably made all the hats in their millinery shop.*

Pap's family, rosy and affluent. (Left to right) *His sister Lillian, mother Ophelia Hatter Sibley, brother Clarence, and the baby, Pap, Wesley Reeder Sibley, on his mother's lap.*

Muv's kin—stringy and hard pressed. (Left to right) *Joy, Aunt Babe (Elizabeth Kennedy), Albert, and Sister (Theda) with children's curlers forgotten and still in her hair.*

*Postcard picture of Muv
sent to an aunt from
Dothan, Alabama,
in 1911.*

*First and only photograph
of Dixie and Henry Colley,
taken some months before
I was born.*

Pap—Wesley R. Sibley shortly before
we *married him*.

Pap—Wesley R. Sibley shortly before
we *married him*.

Pap as a young man—
before us.

Bob Sibley (Pap) and Muv taken
shortly after their marriage.

First photograph of baby Celestine after I got old enough for a trip to the photographer's studio.

After we married him— safe in Creola, Florida, and wearing a dress and hat Muv made from hand-me-downs.

Dressed up for Easter and a picnic with Mr. Sibley—my first outing with him.

First day of school at Creola.

"The Fairy Queen" in a crepe paper dress and silver crown and sandals Muv made. Got the role of Queen because I was the biggest girl in the third grade—too big to be a regular fairy.

Our first maid at Creola, Bessie, with me in a beautiful mail-order dress.

spirited social life. We knew many of them, like the commandant, then captain, later Admiral William (Bull) Halsey in line of duty.

Others became close personal friends. A young man named Harold Turner, who had gone to Hotchkiss and Yale with the publisher's son, John Perry, Jr., arrived unexpectedly one day with the word that he was to go to work there. He was in the Ivy League uniform, wrinkled seersucker jacket, worn gray flannel trousers, cordovan shoes, Brooks Brothers buttondown shirt, skinny tie pulled askew. Fearing that he had come to replace one of us, we greeted him uneasily.

We came to love him and virtually adopted him. He slept on our sofa as often as in the room he rented. We called him "The Childe Harold" and the three of us went everywhere together, when we could. Harold and I went by ourselves at night when Jim was working. He eventually started courting the *News* society editor, Hortensia Sublette, a sparkling little brunette from an old North Hill family. Then his mother and her German maid arrived in town from their Manhattan-Easthampton base. She had ostensibly come to get Florida sun and saltwater baths for her arthritis, but we suspected at the time that she meant to look over Tannie, as everybody called Hortensia, and break up the romance.

Mrs. Turner rented a furnished house, dispatched her maid to the market, and began a series of charming little dinner parties to which we were all bid. Harold, of course, brought Miss Sublette and, as any Pensacolian could have predicted, his mother was totally captivated by her. They did not marry. Harold went back to New York and met and married somebody else. We ourselves left Pensacola about the same time and lost track of him until his sister Martha moved to Atlanta a few years later and we picked up the Turner friendship again.

Country people from the still-backwoods farmlands and river bottoms north of Pensacola held most of the county and state offices. Sheriff H. E. Gandy was so colorful Jim took to hanging around the county jail just to hear him talk and watch him spin into action when somebody reported a drowning.

"Richard," he would call to his chief deputy, "git me my drags and my outdoor motor! I want my Evinruge! I'm gonna find that body!"

I liked a nice gray-haired man known as "Jedge" Kendrick, who presided over a commitment court. Practically uneducated, he was one of the gentlest, most courteous people I ever knew. He was meticulously suited and tied, always immaculate, and comported himself with great dignity. Once I went into his office when he was getting ready to perform a marriage ceremony for a country couple. The bride was turned out in lace and a veil and carried a newspaper-wrapped bouquet of wilting red rambler roses somebody had apparently handed her as she left home.

Judge Kendrick interrupted the proceedings to introduce me all around, coming finally to a chubby baby boy held by the bride's mother. "Ain't he a buster?" asked the judge exuberantly. "And ain't he lucky to be at his own mama and daddy's wedding?"

Another time I happened in while a commitment hearing was going on in his court. He stopped everything and made the usual introductions, coming at last to a gaunt, downcast fellow who sat with his head bowed.

". . . And this gintleman over here," said Judge Kendrick, waving at him, ". . . they got a li'l ole case of murder agin him."

With a night-working husband I had a lot of free evenings. I saw every movie that came to town and was a willing pupil when Miss Marjorie and a visiting cousin of hers sought to interest me in the domestic arts against the day when I would have a home of my own. The sum total of these sessions was a lumpy little rug, made out of dyed stocking loops, and candied grapefruit peel, which I never liked very much anyhow.

Among the young marrieds I met was a pretty girl from New Orleans named Clara Andrews. She had come to Pensacola with her sister Sara to demonstrate a dazzling new mayonnaise-making device put out by Wesson Oil. Instead of beating oil and eggs together in a shallow bowl with a fork, as Muv had always done, you dripped oil through a little hole in the cap of a tall glass bottle with a metal plunger to do the beating. So easy and effortless was the procedure said to be, the company hired as demonstrators stylish young women who wore hats and white gloves while they worked, the idea being that you could whip up a batch of mayonnaise on your way out the door to a party.

Clara and Sara were the daughters of a prominent New Orleans lumberman, and Sara, the elder, had been ready to make her debut the year the Depression struck. The Cooks lost their home and moved into an apartment, where they couldn't afford to have the electricity turned on or even buy much food.

It didn't slow down their social life.

"If I had a date with somebody I didn't know very well I would meet him at the door and rush him out on the pretext of getting a letter to the post office in a hurry," Clara said. "On our next date, if I liked him, I would tell him that we were having a quaint, old-time feast that night—biscuits and syrup! Also we just *loved* eating by firelight instead of electric light. You'd be surprised at how many men enjoyed it."

The Wesson Oil promoter apparently had friends in Pensacola because Clara and Sara were taken to parties when their stint at the grocery stores was over, and there they met their future husbands. Francis Andrews, the son of a Pensacola banker, was a struggling young insurance man. He and Clara were married in New Orleans with her three sisters in attendance, in a beautiful wedding for which they made every stitch they wore. (They were such skilled dressmakers that once Sara, needing a new outfit for a day-time party, cut up and dyed a wool union suit her mother had in a collection of old clothes to give her favorite seaman's charity. Sara turned it into an elegant sage-green frock, which garnered many compliments, particularly when she wore it with a velvet hat she had bought for ten cents at a thrift store and cleaned and blocked herself.)

When I met Clara and Francis they had a baby, a pretty little girl named Gayle, a silver service, and not much else. They lived in a scantily furnished rented bungalow, for which Clara cheerfully made curtains and planted flowers, and sometimes they had little to eat except eggs. A farmer who peddled his produce in town continued to bring them fresh eggs twice a week, even when they couldn't pay, and Clara learned to make more egg dishes than I ever heard of— eggs boiled, fried, baked, poached, eggs in creamed sauce, shirred, scrambled, in omelets.

She wasn't the slightest cast down by their financial problems, being absolutely certain that Francis would make them rich one day. (I think he did.) I didn't see why they couldn't call on his banker father, the donor of the magnificent Tiffany silver service. Clara shook her head ruefully.

Once Francis had told his father that he made only $18 that month and the banker had said placidly, "Well, son, you'll just have to sell more insurance."

I loved Clara and her sister Sara, who had things a little easier, a house of her own and a salaried husband, and I spent a lot of my free time with them.

Clothes were a passion with them and they were painstaking seamstresses, with concern for things my mother, who was also expert, wouldn't have considered important. The length of a sleeve could engross them in debate for long moments. Did it look "new" or was it deplorably "last year"? Would a dart or a gather here or there make it more becoming? My mother had been known to draw little sketches of a dress in a store and go home and copy it. Clara and Sara would try it on, turn it wrong side out, examine its seams, check the lining, ponder the matter of its color. Was it "right" for one of them or should they copy it in a lighter or darker shade?

Once their mother, who had taught them this urgent concern for clothes, was along when Clara found a simple pink silk dress with white braid on the collar, which she wanted desperately. They were able to buy matching fabric in a remnant at a bargain price but there wasn't enough of it for the collar. Mrs. Cook took infinitesimal scraps and carefully pieced them together, covering the seams with braid. The collar on the frock at the store was one piece, the one on Clara's new dress invisibly eight pieces.

It seemed worth the effort to them, and I caught enough of their zeal to devote many evenings to sewing at Clara's house and sometimes babysitting so she and Francis could make one of the many parties to which they were invited. On occasion the dress she meant to wear wasn't quite finished and I would help pin her into it as she walked out the door.

Some of this interest in clothes evaporated when I became friends with Rita Bogan, a stunning young woman with a great knot of chestnut curls in a disordered wad on top of her head, a run in her stocking, the hem falling out of her dress, and a marvelously exuberant way of throwing back her head and showing her flawless white teeth in a bellow of laughter. Rita had gone to the tea that had given me such anxious pangs over costume and calling cards, wearing one of her baby's diapers as a turban. Somebody had spotted it and blurted out the question: "Isn't that a *diaper?*"

"Unhuh," said Rita cheerfully. "But not birdseye, the new Curity kind."

It was a sensation at the party.

Rita was a sensation everywhere she went, funny, irreverent, totally original. She had grown up in Tallahassee, member of the big Cawthon family. Her father was state superintendent of education, her mother a teacher, and her sister and four brothers Phi Beta Kappas all. Rita reacted by loafing amiably through school and conning the system into a degree. She was teaching in a Pensacola junior high school when I met her, and it was her boast that she had managed a Bachelor of Arts degree and come close to obtaining her master's without reading. One book, a Lloyd C. Douglas novel, broke her clean no-read record. She couldn't remember why she had read that one.

Her husband, Leslie Bogan, had played football at the University of Florida and was working as an aide to a legislator at the state capitol in Tallahassee when he first saw Rita. The then Florida State College for Women, now Florida State University, was having its May festival and Rita, acclaimed May queen, presided over the ball.

"She was the prettiest thing I ever saw," Leslie recalled.

They dated some and he was additionally impressed by the elegant late suppers Rita would set out in the Cawthon dining room when her family had gone to bed. He didn't find out until years later that Rita made a deal with a cook at a downtown restaurant and smuggled the food in before Leslie picked her up.

A couple of years later, when she was a graduate student at the University of Texas, Rita decided to quit school and become a missionary to China. She took off for the Pacific Coast with a writer-lecturer who had come to Austin to speak. She hitched a ride with him, they camped out on the way, and when they arrived in Los Angeles she found lodging at her sorority's UCLA house. She had started making plans for China, when she learned that Leslie was in town. She looked him up and they were married.

Leslie had had little luck in getting a job in Los Angeles and they decided to make their way back to Pensacola, his hometown. He got a job selling hearing aids on commission, and with Rita as his assistant, carefully enunciating and mouthing the sales pitch, they made enough money for gas home.

They were living with Leslie's parents and had a little boy, called Geno for Leslie's middle name, Eugene, when I met them. Rita had returned to school, night classes held by the university's extension department, to shore up her teaching qualifications, and I decided to sign up for political science. It seemed more interesting than hemlines and collars.

All married couples, I suppose, exchange reminiscences in the middle of the night about former loves and earlier sexual experiences. Jim had to be the sole raconteur on these occasions because I had literally nothing to relate. He liked to talk about two women who had meant much to him—one I'll call Mimi, a totally fascinating Government Street girl he had known since babyhood, having helped her brother take off her diaper for a look when they were little more than toddlers. The mental picture I had of her was the way he described her when he enveloped her in a red velvet, hooded evening wrap, the first ever seen in Mobile, preparatory to leaving for a ball one evening. I seethed with jealousy. In my mind's eye she was Garbo in *Anna Karenina* all over again, and my only hope was that, since she had married a lawyer and gone to New York to live, she would never surface again in Jim's life.

The other was a girl I'll call Andrea. He met her in Florida and had visited at three of her family's several homes, Palm Beach, a Virginia plantation, and a Manhattan townhouse. This maiden was not only beautiful but a sexual entrepreneur, splendidly aggressive and original beyond my wildest imagining. Jim had gone so far as to buy an engagement ring to give her, and then, having no money left for railroad fare, started to hitchhike from Jacksonville to New York to present it. Luckily, somebody he knew fixed him up with a ride in exchange for driving one car in some rich man's cavalcade of family and servants back North after a season in Florida. The chauffeur drove the children; Jim drove the servants. Food and lodging were provided along the way.

He arrived with his ring and had a sensational reunion with his girl, who happened to be in her parents' Manhattan townhouse with only the servants at the time. It was Jim's first trip to New York. I had made one myself by Greyhound bus with three girls from the paper the summer before—total cost, with a duebill on the Barbizon Plaza, $100. But I found I couldn't compare notes with Jim about the Statue of Liberty or the Empire State Building because he and Andrea, surprisingly, did no sightseeing. They got out enough to dance to the music of Rudy Vallee and his Connecticut Yankees one night, either at a party or some nightclub, I don't remember which. Except for that it seemed to me that they must have had a dull, indoor time. No wonder they had started bickering, I thought. But I was horrified that one of their spats ended with the girl throwing the engagement ring in the East River. That sent Jim back South and the girl on to marriage with somebody else. The romance was dead but the memory of it lived on to haunt Jim—and me, to the extent that it was a reminder of my inadequacies. I wished Andrea in the East River with the lost diamond many a time when Jim spoke of her beauty and her sexual expertise.

The ghost of the first love, the one with the hooded velvet cape, was laid when Jim and I went to New York on a vacation the first year after our marriage. That time he did see the Statue of Liberty and the Empire State Building and the Aquarium and museums and anything else I could drag him forth to look at. He admitted to me that the big city overwhelmed and intimidated him, and all he wanted to do was stay in our room at the Roosevelt Hotel (this, too, on a duebill) and nip along at his bottle. But he had a cousin there, Olive Brooks, of the Government Street household where his mother had grown up. She worked in public relations for the Shell Oil Company at that time, but she had worked on newspapers and was later to become editor of a paper in the Canal Zone. She had a whole coterie of newspaper friends from Alabama, and she took us out to dinner with them and arranged for theatre tickets. One night we went down to Greenwich Village to have drinks with Mimi and her lawyer husband, who had heard by the Alabama old-friend network that we were in town. I was struck by the spaciousness and charm of their apartment, with its beautiful long windows and wood-burning fireplaces, and I was relieved and captivated by Mimi, a rangy, long-faced, long-legged woman who looked more like the movie character actress Edna May Oliver than Garbo. She was delightfully welcoming, very funny, and I loved her.

My meeting with Andrea was less felicitous. A Pensacola friend called to tell me that his college roommate and the roommate's wife had taken a cottage at the beach and were going to be around a few days.

"She knows Jim," he said. He mentioned her name.

"I'll *say* she knows Jim," I mumbled but dutifully wrote down the new name and beach-cottage address.

Then I went in search of Jim. He was covering a trial in federal court. I could have thrown away the name and address but my conscience wouldn't let me. I wrote a note for the bailiff to hand him telling him if he wanted to run out to the beach and see Andrea I would take over the trial for him, hoping, of course, that he would do no such thing.

His hands were shaking when he met me in the hall and took the car keys.

Well, she wasn't any beauty either. We all had dinner together and I thought she was very much my style—plain and gawky despite riding in all those Virginia hunts and crewing on her father's yacht in Florida. But Jim was mesmerized by her and hardly spoke all evening, except to say that the new green dress I had made myself looked like a waitress's uniform.

"Gimme a ham on rye!" he muttered nasally.

I *felt* like a ham on rye and fully expected Jim and Andrea to link arms and walk off into the moonlight singing "Ah, Sweet Mystery of Life," à la Nelson Eddy and Jeanette MacDonald, when the evening ended. As I recall, they exchanged pecks on the cheek and that was the end of Andrea.

Work at the paper and friends and after-hours activity kept me happy enough except for one thing. I had begun to worry that Jim was drinking too much.

After the *Journal* was put to bed at night the staff, led by Editor Ellis, who was not a drinking man himself but liked a late snack, adjourned to the B. & B. restaurant-bar down on Palifox Street and hoisted a few drinks. I had known that Jim liked to drink. He had introduced me to Coca-Cola bottles filled with half Coke, half bourbon, and passed hand to hand in the bleachers at football games. And it was inescapable that drinking had led to his being fired from the Mobile *Press-Register.* But I was unprepared for the regular, nightly drinking bouts, and I turned shrewish about them.

One night when we lived in the little garage apartment on the bay I had been wakeful listening to rain on the roof and the sound of Jim turning in the driveway. When he climbed the steps at 4 A.M. and opened the door I was there to greet him.

Smiling genially, if drunkenly, he handed me one of the B. & B.'s hot, fragrant oyster loaves, which we both had always found delectable. That night I grabbed it, hit him over the head with it and flung it out into the rainy yard.

Through the years I did many senseless things like that, first in the naïve belief that if he saw that I disapproved of his drinking he would forthwith cease and desist. Second, I thought that if I made it unpleasant enough he would realize that a happy home was better than booze.

Neither happened.

In time his mother, also worried about his drinking, saw an ad for a nostrum in the Mobile paper and clipped it out and sent it to him. It promised that Cravex cured the drinking habit.

"Dear Mother," wrote Jim. "Thank you for the remedy. I have stopped drinking whiskey. Now I crave Cravex."

Mamie thought it was funny, as she thought nearly everything her son said or did was amusing. They had the same kind of sense of humor. But she also worried until two years after our marriage I came up with what we both thought was a surefire remedy—a baby.

It seemed absolutely certain to both of us that a man with a child would be so ennobled, so inspired by the experience that he would never touch beer or whiskey again. Experiences like that really changed people, Mamie told me solemnly. Her own father was known, as Jim put it, to "take whiskey," but when her mother died he renounced it forever, she said.

That reformation seemed long deferred to me and I certainly didn't want to wait that long for Jim to see the light but I didn't say anything. Jim later told me that his Grandpa Henry fooled the family. He lived with his daughter and Mr. Little the last few years of his life when they were very social and spent many evenings going to balls and similar fêtes. Grandpa stayed home and drank.

One March day in 1938 I walked back to the *News* from my beat, climbed the stairs, and went to the bleak and smelly bathroom we all used and started retching. What Mamie and I thought might cure Jim was on the way. I was pregnant.

Jim was as thrilled as we were at the prospect of a baby and agreed that he shouldn't drink again. The responsibilities of parenthood were so monumental, so momentous, he was awed and inspired.

To celebrate both events, the approach of a baby and Jim's newly declared abstinence, we decided to take a long weekend for a second honeymoon in New Orleans. We stopped by her house in Mobile and picked up Mamie to go with us.

Naturally in New Orleans, one of the world's premier places for dining and drinking, Mamie I had a little wine with our meals. Jim was drunk the entire weekend.

Jim argued—and Mamie and I saw the logic in his argument—that New Orleans was no place to begin a drought. Pensacola wasn't either, it turned out.

Jim was working very hard, handling his job, and later when I became too pregnant to work, covering for me, too. This was an arrangement Sam Ellis thought up to keep my job for me and to preserve for us the grandiose double salary of $55 a week. We needed it because the baby was going to be expensive—$50 to the doctor and $100 to the hospital—and we had moved from the garage apartment to a bigger place, a five-room cottage in the woods on Bayou Texar, where the baby could have a room of his own, and there were porches and an open deck for wheeling him out into the sunshine and fresh air. There was even a big attic with an almost finished room, which we would assign to a nursemaid if we were lucky enough to get one willing to live in, after I went back to work.

None wanted to and I knew why. The bayou house was wonderful in the daytime, but at night when the neighbors, whose lights were barely visible through the trees, had gone to bed, it became spooky. Great golden hickory trees sheltered the roof, and there was a mammoth crop of nuts that year. When I was there by myself at night I seldom slept more than a few minutes at a time because hickory nuts kept falling off the trees and banging on the roof or against the green-stained walls of the house.

Reared by Muv to investigate noises rather than to cower fearfully indoors, wondering about them, I would take the flashlight and go out to make sure I had been awakened by falling nuts instead of some nefarious intruder. I never could be quite sure because once the nut had landed you didn't know where or when it had hit. The situation made me so jittery I sometimes fled the house, and one disgraceful night showed up on Palifox Street to wait in the car in front of the B. & B. for Jim to finish drinking and come out. I was monumentally pregnant, clad in a housecoat that didn't quite meet in front, and swamped in self-pity.

Jim didn't know I waited until some near-cousins of his, Barbara and John Ed Toulmin from Mobile and Toulminville, came out about dawn, saw me, and went back into the restaurant and told him. He was embarrassed and indignant, accusing me of making a spectacle of myself and exposing him to ridicule and criticism. He was right but I wasn't penitent. I wanted him to come straight home from work—sober. I wanted the money spent at the B. & B. to go to fixing up the house and buying things for the coming baby. I wanted, more than anything else, it seemed, a night's sleep.

A month before the baby came Muv provided that. She arrived with her trunk loaded with handmade baby dresses, dozens of everything, including ribbon-edged receiving blankets and embroidered sheets and pillow cases. She also brought a baked ham and roasted chickens and a chocolate cake, and we set to work furnishing the baby's room with secondhand furniture, white-painted, and frilly curtains for the time when he would outgrow the silk-and-lace-flounced bassinet Mamie's friend Miss Ida had lent us, and move out of our room.

We took long walks to strengthen my muscles for the delivery room, we went Christmas shopping and did Christmas sewing, and Muv told me wonderful tales of country births and country lore. Listening to music and reading poetry, studying the Bible and thinking beautiful thoughts were all calculated to "mark" the baby with beauty and intelligence and a good disposition. Under no circumstances was I to get angry or harbor hateful thoughts, even about Jim's drinking, and I was to avoid at all costs seeing ugly sights, such as frogs and snakes and alligators. She even knew of a swamp woman who had so marked her unborn baby by looking at alligators that he came into the world with a long tail and ferocious teeth and thrashed about and roared when it rained and he got wet. He was known as Shug Brown's "gator youngun."

Bayou Texar may have had alligators but I studiously avoided looking for them and approached delivery feeling happy and optimistic. It had been our hope to have Mamie's first male grandchild (first of either sex for Muv), but on the night of December 13, while I knelt on the floor cutting out Christmas pajamas for my little cousin Jerry, Mamie called. Ervin's wife, Jane, already the mother of a girl child, had come through that very day with a boy baby!

The news gave me pains in my middle. Jealousy, Muv said, or either the mincemeat pie we had eaten for lunch.

It turned out to be labor pains, of course. The next afternoon, December 14, 1938, James William Little V was born.

Poor as we considered ourselves to be, I realize now that Baby James and I were thoroughly pampered. We stayed in the hospital two weeks and went home for two weeks' more care from Muv and a practical nurse, and the drop-in attentions of Rita, who lived next door and came daily on her way home from school.

On Christmas Eve my doctor called to check and to remove stitches, but I was not allowed to put foot to floor for two weeks more. Then I moved around in my new housecoat, languid and looked after, with nothing much to do but admire and hold the new baby. On New Year's Eve Sam Ellis sent us a bottle of sparkling Burgundy, and we stood in the moonlight on the open deck sipping it, watching showers of stars exploding over the velvety black bayou from a fireworks display underway across the water, and toasting ourselves. It seemed to me that the world was almost unbearably beautiful, and I was overwhelmed with a sweeping sense of happiness.

Muv and the practical nurse, a half-black, half-Indian woman named Sarah Whitehead, left and we hired a girl from the German colony in Baldwin County, Alabama, to come and take care of the baby so I could go back to work. She was very efficient, but I ran home from the office one day to see how things were going and found that she had taken a damp nightgown and shirt off the clothesline and put them on Jimmy.

Maybe it wouldn't have hurt him. Babies usually wet themselves, even if they start off dry. But I thought she was trying to give him pneumonia and I grabbed up Jimmy to change him and howled for Jim, who was back on his old schedule of sleeping days and working nights. He promptly fired the nursemaid, who went under protest, crying, "I *vant* my money!" We got it for her, all $3 of it, and then went in search of Sarah Whitehead, who was expensive, $5 a week, but well worth it.

Before Jimmy was a year old we found our expenses were almost unmanageable and decided on a cheaper—and jollier—place to live: the big Garfield house next door, where Rita and Leslie had made camp in one room and were cleaning and painting and planning to rent out apartments. It was a splendid big one-story house with enormous oak trees encircling it and lining a walk down to a boat dock on the bayou. It had a central living room, which the original owner had built concert-hall size because he liked to sing and wanted room for his audiences. Big rooms surrounded three sides, and Rita and Leslie took three for themselves, and divided the rest of the rooms into two apartments, which they could rent out. We took the back one, two vast former Garfield bedrooms, a bathroom as big as a ballroom, and a glass-enclosed sun parlor, which would serve as a kitchen. For this we paid $22 a month.

The front apartment, including the concert hall, was rented to Angeline Levey, a marvelously witty schoolteacher friend of Rita's, who had left her husband and come with her little girl, determined to get a divorce. She was a collector of antiques, and by the time she had moved in her piano and arranged sofas and wing chairs, a handsome secretary, and a Hepplewhite sideboard in the living room, the house seemed warm and elegant. Best of all, any of us was free to use the big room for any occasion that warranted such magnificence.

Angie was also a good cook. (Rita avoided cooking at all costs and I liked to cook but was so inexperienced my idea of a green vegetable was a can of English peas.) When any of us lucked into anything bountiful in the food line, a mess of fish or a basket of vegetables, Angie would take charge and cook for the whole household. We had many such suppers on her big screened porch.

One night in September 1939 after we had been crabbing at Fort Barrancas and come home with a washtub of the big blue beauties, Angie was making a mammoth gumbo and the rest of us were deployed around the screened porch, putting together a salad, setting the table, watching our respective children. Charles Henry Levey, the big, good-looking man Angie intended to divorce, came often to see them, and he was there that night, sitting on the steps playing with their little girl, Charlene. Rita and Leslie had their five-year-old son, Geno, and Jim and I had Jimmy buckled into his high chair nearby. We were merry and talky and had paid no attention to the radio, which was playing softly in a corner of the porch.

Suddenly the music stopped. H. V. Kaltenborn came on with a special announcement: Germany had invaded Poland.

Angie turned off the gumbo and came to the door to listen. Charles Henry stood up and stepped inside the porch. The rest of us stopped what we were doing and stood mute and anxious.

What will it mean? we asked one another.

"It means," said Jim soberly, his eyes on the three children, "that we probably shouldn't have had them."

I don't remember that we ever ate the gumbo. We sat a long time talking about that strange and fearful man Adolf Hitler, who had become so powerful in Europe. Then we all returned to our own apartments to put our children to bed. Rita and Leslie had walked back across the big room to our living room and the four of us were sitting there waiting for more news over our radio when Angie knocked on the door.

She wouldn't come in, she said, when I went to greet her.

"I just wanted to tell you," she said, blushing a little, "there's a bride and groom in the house tonight!"

She had decided not to divorce Charles Henry. In such a precarious world, to loosen even fragile family bonds seemed frightening.

Angie and Charlene moved back to the pleasant house she and Charles Henry had built when they were first married. Leslie and Rita decided to take over an ugly little bungalow he had inherited on Pensacola's picturesque Seville Square in a then-shabby, now-restored downtown neighborhood. We took Jimmy and his nurse, Sarah Whitehead, back to the Yonges'.

The Seville Square house was on a corner, small and dark on one side, where it sat cheek by jowl with a snapper fisherman's cottage, but light and pleasant on the side running parallel to the sidewalk, and, of course, on the front, which faced the square.

The location of that house, downtown in a near-slum section, was what got me into another venture in amateur social work, which I had all but given up.

Rita happened to be looking out the window one day when she saw a beautiful dark-haired girl walking by with her hands clutched across her heavy, bulging stomach and tears streaming down her face. Rita was out the door and after her in a flash, catching her as she paused to rest in the shade of a tree in the square.

Her name was Brunette, she was expecting a baby any day, and she was crying because she had given it away. Rita led her into the house, served her a cup of coffee, and got the story.

Brunette came from a farm in the north end of Escambia County and worked in a bar down on Zaragossa Street, hangout of sailors. There she met and was seduced by a married seaman, whose solution to her problem, when she told him she was pregnant, was to take the baby home to his wife. At that stage Brunette willingly signed away the unborn child on condition that the couple pay for its delivery. But, as her time for *accouchement* approached, she had come to love the unborn child and was tormented by the thought of giving it up. She had appealed to her parents, who would have been glad to take her

100

and the baby home to the country, but didn't know what to do about her contract with the father and his wife.

Rita thought she knew. She called me. It was monstrous, she said, for that oafish, faithless fellow to have deflowered a pure little country girl and then to rob her of her child! We had to do something.

I agreed, but what? I knew enough from Miss Van Sickler in Mobile to realize that publicizing what in those innocent days we thought of as a young girl's "shame" was unacceptable. But what to do? Since I covered the courthouse I knew Judge L. L. Fabisinski of circuit court pretty well and I appealed to him. Judge Fab, as we called him, was a warm and friendly man, and he was, if anything, more moved by Brunette's story than Rita and I were. The proper path for recovering the child, he advised me, was a court order.

He would get, free of charge, a lawyer to petition for one and he would persuade the clerk of the court, Langley Bell, to waive court costs. Then the ethical step for him, already in the thing up to his neck, was to disqualify himself and let another judge handle it. The baby, a little girl, was born, and before the sailor and his wife could claim her Rita had snatched up mother and child and hidden them in her house.

While I was working out the legal course, she was working with her friends at Red Cross and the Public Health Service, assembling a baby bed, a layette, and cases of canned milk, and lining up infant and postnatal medical care.

The day of the hearing came and Rita and I, proud as godmothers, flanked Brunette as she stood before the judge, beautiful and madonnalike with the rosy baby girl in her arms. Her mother, wrinkled and bent from hard labor on the farm, kept her seat in the courtroom beside a cuspidor. She had a mouthful of snuff.

The sailor and his wife made a limp, ineffectual protest. Rita and I exchanged triumphant glances. Poor things, they didn't have the sense we had to get a free lawyer and a fee-less clerk and a sympathetic judge, as we had done. For it was foreordained when Judge Fab disqualified himself that his replacement would be sympathetic. He granted the order promptly, giving Brunette custody of her child and, flushed with success, Rita and I loaded the young mother, the baby, and the grandmother into the car, which was already pretty full of milk and baby clothes.

It seemed a long trip to the farm but we went happily. Brunette told us as we walked out of the courthouse that she had decided to name the little girl Margarita Celestine.

Our baby, we gloated—a peerless child with what we modestly felt was a gloriously matching name. Even when the baby's grandmother stopped us at a neighbor's house we were patient. We felt sure she wanted to show off the baby and tell its glamorous name.

But the grandmother did not get out of the car and she said nary a word about little Margarita Celestine. She rolled down the window, spat a brown stream of snuff and yelled, "Say, Essie, how 'bout sending me that receipt for them nine-day pickles?"

For years Rita and I could each induce hysterics in the other by saying, "How 'bout that receipt for them nine-day pickles?"

It wasn't long until we heard that Brunette had gone back to the Zaragossa Street Bar where she had been working and had returned the baby to its father and his wife.

"How is little Margarita Celestine?" Rita inquired.

"Okay," her informant said. "But they changed her name to Ouida Mae."

Subsequently we heard that Brunette had left her job at the bar and run off with a Marine. Some months later Rita was working as a volunteer in the prenatal clinic at the hospital and she saw Brunette, heavy with child again.

"What was she doing?" I asked.

"She was humming," Rita said. She hummed a sample. The tune: "I Don't Get Around Much Anymore."

Rita herself had a baby and then, as she put it, "seven months, three days, and ten minutes" later, another. My second child was on the way, scheduled to arrive a good two months before the Bogans' third child but Rita upstaged me with a preemie.

She was recovering from a bout with the flu and I went over to her house to take her to the grocery store.

"Will you take me to the hospital?" she pleaded piteously, glancing toward Leslie, who was leisurely shaving.

"Aw, Rita, don't be silly," I said. "It's not time. Let's go to the grocery store."

It was not time, Leslie agreed, and when the time came he would, of course, take her himself. He went on shaving and I pushed Rita toward the car and headed for the A. & P. A block later she was putting on a fair show of being in the throes of labor so I reluctantly turned toward the hospital. The admission people didn't know which of us was the patient and I had to fend them off to keep from being hauled to the delivery room.

Thirty minutes later Rita gave birth to her second daughter. Ten days later Muv, who was living in a house she and Pap had acquired at St. Andrews Bay down the coast, stopped by our apartment and saw Jimmy playing in the sandbox in the backyard.

Mommy, he told her, had "gone to the hospital to get a Susy."

I had, indeed, and that afternoon—January 28, 1941—a baby girl with swirls of red curls arrived. We named her Susan Sibley for all the Susans who preceded us (grandmothers Susan Broxson Colley and Susan Hinson Barber and great grandmother Susan Nix Hinson) and Sibley for Pap.

She was easily the most spectacular baby I ever saw, rosy and blue-eyed as nearly all babies are, but with a wonderful plump and dimpled little body and masses of coppery curls.

Before she could stand alone her father and I looked at the hills in Atlanta and wondered how she would ever learn to walk there. Her first steps, we decided, could plunge her down a steep driveway or over a bank. We had never seen such hilly country.

Jim had finally got what he wanted most—a job with the Associated Press in Atlanta.

Being a diligent reporter of the daily routine should bring you to the attention of the wider vineyard of wire services and the *New York Times,* but I doubt if it ever does. Jim got hired by AP because of his coverage of a shipwreck off the coast of Pensacola. The *Tarpon,* an old freight boat out of Mobile in the coastwise trade, was swept aground and battered to pieces in a storm. Its master and many members of its crew died. A few, clinging to floating timbers from the wreckage, managed to survive.

While I was at the hospital interviewing the survivors, Jim filed the first stories and then led a late-arriving AP reporter, Romney Wheeler, to the scene of the wreck and rescue. Jim had known the ship's captain, a crusty old veteran of schooner days, who didn't hold with modern weather-forecasting techniques and doggedly pursued his own course, gales be damned.

He was famous for a saying Jim was probably the first to report: "God makes the weather and I make the trips."

His wife, fearing that it sounded sacrilegious, kept telling people he was a pious man and did not tempt the Lord God with such talk. But it never sounded sacrilegious to me, and I've thought of it and been guided by it many times during the years when the weather has deterred other people from doing things they wanted to do. The weather is patently God's business and mine is often to get out in it.

The AP liked Jim's coverage of the story and invited him to Atlanta for an interview. He was hired, and three months later I took the babies, Jimmy and Susan, to Muv, who was remodeling and shoring up the old house at St. Andrews Bay, west of Panama City. In the midst of painting and carpentry and bouts with the septic-tank man, she took on keeping her two grandchildren while I drove to Atlanta to spend my vacation with Jim.

It wasn't strictly a vacation because I intended to use it to get a job. Once more, we knew that if we wanted to be together we had to have jobs in the same town.

The Atlanta *Constitution* was the paper I wanted to work for. It had been famous since the days of Joel Chandler Harris for its tri-weekly edition delivered by mail all through the South. Pap had admired it all his life, and we usually bought it on Sundays along with the New Orleans *Times-Picayune* when we went to town. Sunday evenings by the fire found us in a welter of newsprint, reading bits and pieces aloud and marveling at the news in Muv's native Georgia.

"The *Constitution* might not hire you," Jim said. "But you could probably start on the *Journal* and maybe Ralph McGill [editor of the *Constitution*], will see your work and give you a job."

So I dressed up, donning my best yellow linen with white gloves and a big cartwheel straw hat, and went down to see Mr. McGill. The old building, a red brick pile with cupolas, round and peaked like Hershey kisses jutting out from its corner, had an elevator, the first in Atlanta, I learned later, but I didn't know it was chronically slow and wheezy and assumed it wasn't working that day. I climbed the five flights of worn marble steps to the editor's office, somewhat wheezy myself when Mr. McGill offered me a chair and listened to my pitch for a job.

He didn't have much to do with hiring, Mr. McGill said. Even then he was traveling the world, covering international stories (he had been present at Hitler's beer hall putsch in Vienna) and beginning to be invited into the councils of the mighty. But he would take me in

104

to talk to the city editor, a bald-headed little man with the voice of a bandsaw named William R. (Pop) Hines. Mr. Hines wasn't bowled over by my presence or my qualifications, but he wrote down my name, and Jim's address and telephone number at the house in Morningside where he had a room, and said he would call me if anything turned up.

I was disconsolate. I loved the place on sight, a grimy old room with the ceiling sagging under the weight of the composing room on the floor above, the turgid air only slightly stirred by the perfunctory efforts of little electric fans attached to posts here and there, the smell of newsprint and glue pots and the heavy blue pall of cigarette smoke. It was too early in the day for all the morning-paper staff to be in evidence, but the room seemed full and pulsing with life.

While I was there Number One fire station, half a block down Alabama Street, got a call and sirens screeched and bells clanged and a big truck roared out.

"Catch that fire!" Pop Hines called.

"It's here," a reporter said, and a fireman in a tin hat climbed in the window.

"Here!" I cried, jumping up.

"Happens every day," the city editor said wearily. "Sit down."

That was a trash-basket fire. Somebody poured Coca-Cola on it and the fireman withdrew. Not all of them were that easy, I was to learn.

Mr. Hines dismissed me and I trudged up Forsyth Street, across a viaduct, which spanned railroad tracks, and into the *Journal* building. That was a cleaner, more spacious, more modern building—and they didn't want me either. The city editor, a man named Fred Moon, said he didn't like female reporters, they distracted the men and spread a kind of virus in the newsroom.

"A what?" I asked.

"Love," he said succinctly. "Where you have women you have *love.* It gets in the way."

It did no good to explain that I was twenty-four years old and past all that foolishness, having a husband and two children. He didn't want me.

It seemed it was going to be a vacation, after all. I went back to Jim's room and got out the portable typewriter he had given me for Christmas and started work on a series of pieces I planned to do on a massive analysis of the Escambia County, Florida, school system.

105

I had to do *something* while Jim slept out the daytime hours so he could work AP's lobster shift.

The first week's vacation was gone when Pop Hines called me. Could I come to work right away? He would pay me $35 a week.

As soon as I could work out a week's notice in Pensacola, I said eagerly. Looking back, I feel that my bosses at the *News-Journal* could have made it easier for me, letting me go right away with good wishes and godspeed. Instead, they claimed their pound of flesh. I worked like a dog that last week, up until late Saturday afternoon, the day I had to leave for Atlanta in order to start my new job on Monday. Muv had come and packed and called the moving van, and about dark with the babies loaded into the car and the baby bed tied onto the back, we embarked for Atlanta.

It should have been an easy six- or seven-hour trip. It was a horror. Muv brought a Thermos of coffee and kept pushing cups of it on me to keep me awake. She bottled and diapered Susan and fed Jimmy, and I was so tired I kept dozing at the wheel. When my head bobbed she would shake me and yell and I'd pull over to the side of the road and get out and walk briskly up and down until I was conscious again. Or we would stop at a filling station, where I would throw cold water into my face, refreshed and alert for half an hour maybe. Once when I got out of the car I bumped into the door and cut a gash across my nose, thinking as I mopped blood that it was going to be some adornment for meeting my new bosses.

Jim had rented us a temporary three-room apartment in College Park, a little town that adjoins Atlanta on the west and was on our route. I had the address and pulled into the driveway at 2 A.M. The landlady heard us and crawled out of bed to let us in. Muv, helping me to untie and haul in and set up the baby bed, tried to hold her tongue, but she couldn't quite make it. Where was he? Why wasn't he there to help us? she asked furiously.

It turned out there had been a Saturday bash at some AP staffer's house and Jim had gone, deciding to spend the night.

"But look what he left us," I said placatingly, opening the refrigerator door to a temptingly arranged bowl of fruit.

Muv sniffed and found a bed and I was glad she wasn't looking the next morning when the landlady's son came to claim the fruit, which they had stored in the tenant's refrigerator temporarily.

Muv stayed to help with the children until we could find a maid, and

I reported at the *Constitution* at 10 A.M. Monday with a Band-aid across my nose. The man who hired me, Pop Hines, had left the paper and taken a job with the Army Quartermaster Corps while I was working out my notice in Pensacola. As I approached his desk a giant fellow, young Lee Rogers, unfolded his six-feet-four-inches length and stood up.

"Miss Sibley?" he said. "I'm the city editor. I've been expecting you."

Part Two

Chapter Five

No Jason seeking the golden fleece, no Ponce de León on trail of the fountain of youth was more charmed with the exotic and magical places they found than I was with Atlanta. The old *Constitution* newsroom seemed to me to be exactly what a newspaper newsroom should be—crowded and noisy, first, its splintery wooden floors caked with almost three-quarters of a century of old crankcase oil and dirt, its windows clouded from without by smoke from railroad trains and from within by the blue fumes of burning tobacco. AP and UP teletype machines clattered out news from distant places, old manual typewriters under the touch of hunt-and-peck two-fingered virtuosos alternately sputtered and fizzed with local and state news.

The walls were plastered with yellowed news pictures going back to the days of Jack Dempsey, Man Mountain Dean, Clara Bow, and Marie, the Queen of Roumania. Mixed in the curling and dusty gallery was a picture of a typical movie-version reporter—snap-brim hat, trenchcoat, cigarette smoke curling up artfully from a butt caught in the corner of his mouth. "Don't Talk About Him," said the hand-lettered caption glued to the bottom. "He Works Here Now." I knew he must be the new Lee Tracy–type hot-shot reporter and I couldn't wait to meet him, but he must have come and gone pretty speedily because I never saw him or anybody in the motley assembly around the city desk who remotely resembled that glamorous photograph.

The city desk was the heart of the newsroom in those days. It's hard to find it nowadays. No green eye shades, no baskets brimming with glued-together sheets of copy, no lethal copy spikes or long-bladed scissors and, above all, no bellowing Simon Legree. City editors now are often soft-voiced pretty girls.

The *Constitution,* founded in the days after the Civil War when the region cried for the return of constitutional government to the South, was singular in many ways, not the least in its name, of course. I found in my travels for it years later that the name alone, unique among newspaper names throughout the country, opened doors for me. It was so unmistakably Atlanta, the bailiwick of such famous editors as Joel Chandler Harris, Henry Grady, and, contemporarily, Ralph McGill. Less impressive to most members of the newspaper fraternity was the fact that the heavy machinery of the composing room, instead of being consigned to the first floor or basement, was situated on the floor above the newsroom, where it must have constituted a hazard to reporters and editors working below it with only a frail and peeling ceiling and a splintery floor between.

We didn't notice it particularly, as I recall. We were too fond of another *Constitution* original, the old department-store change carrier, which ran on a track through the ceiling and transmitted copy to the composing room.

The gadget, lopsided and lumbering, moved at the stately pace of a resigned old crab caught in a tideline pool. Visitors were mesmerized by it. Reporters, striving for a lead, mindlessly followed its progress with their eyes. Half the time the contraption reached the ceiling and let go of its load, sending a carefully folded wad of news story and headline plummeting. I had been on the staff but a day when I found myself joining the general cry that went up when this happened.

"Copy on the floor!" chorused the staff, and Leroy Noles, even then a veteran copy boy, rushed, limping a little, to pick up the paper and restore it to the metal jaws on their next passage.

Oh, I loved that old newsroom, as did almost everybody who ever worked there. A decade later, when they would move into a new building, the members of the staff put on black armbands and grieved actively. Clean walls were an affront to us, for the management had issued a memo saying nothing was to be pasted, nailed, or strung to these pristine spaces. No pictures, no clippings, no sassy and irreverent comments about ourselves or our superiors. "The stuff we pasted on the walls is what held them up," protested one aggrieved staffer.

Ralph McGill, sensitive to the mourning, wrote a column saying that even in a new building the staff would be the same flesh and blood, erring and achieving human beings. "You can't put out a paper with turnips," he observed.

Nobody ever felt more turnipy. Losing the old copy carrier symbolized our bereavement. The new building had a pneumatic tube to whisk copy to the composing room, a bloodless, turnipy device if we ever saw one. We hated it.

Every night when the pace slowed down and the paper had been put to bed, Jim Furniss, a brilliant and phenomenally handsome reporter who had been a track star at Yale, would take up an on-your-mark-get-set stance by that pneumatic tube. Somebody would stuff a piece of paper in it and yell, "Go!" Jim would be off like a shot, racing it to the composing room. Night after night he lost. Technology won.

We grew sadder, listless and pallid in our grief. Then one night by some fluke something went wrong in the mysterious airy innards of that tube and Jim won.

A cheer went up in the composing room. Pandemonium broke out in the newsroom. Our side had won. Our flesh-and-blood colleague had triumphed over the turnip!

We all felt better and settled down to accept, if not to love, the new quarters.

But the day I arrived to begin work there I only sensed that the old paper was going to latch onto my heart, that it would in its way become as dear to me as home and mother. I sensed it, I think, going up in the elevator in my broad-brimmed hat and Band-aid. There was a young woman photographer with her Graflex camera in hand and her photograph gear strung to her shoulder. She smiled at me but looked anxiously upward, in a hurry, I could tell, to get back from some important assignment. She works here, I thought enviously. She *belongs.* And then I thought, Me too, I'm going to belong.

Lee Rogers, the new city editor, told me that I was to replace a colorful little man named Lee Fuhrman on the federal beat. He was sending a veteran reporter named Frank Drake, who had covered every beat in town, to show me the ropes. Frank, tall, slender, thin-faced, humorous, with curly black hair and dark, sad eyes, took a Thermos of milk and some antacid potion with him. He had ulcers. But I would never have guessed it that day as we walked through the shady canyons of downtown streets with the August sun knifing

113

through the interstices of buildings, the smells of Forsyth Street restaurants and bars and little shoe-repair shops and dry cleaners and fruit stands rising in the air.

I had felt a certain pride in and allegiance to Mobile, that beautiful old seaport city. I had enjoyed Pensacola and the friends we made there. But Atlanta seemed to me to be the most vibrant, richly alive place I had ever seen. I wouldn't have called it beautiful that day, with its high incidence of cold gray Stone Mountain granite in building and street, its garbage trucks rumbling by, the jackhammers and bulldozers tearing it up, the riveters, moving grand and lordly overhead, putting more steel beams together. I would come to believe it beautiful as a mother may believe her knock-kneed, pigeon-toed, buck-toothed son is handsome. But that day I just knew it *felt* right, that there was some electric magic in the air that filled my heart with excitement. I had come home.

My mother had never been to Atlanta, but, as a south Georgian, she felt about Atlanta as ancient Egyptians must have felt about their old capital, Memphis, called "a place of good abode." In that day Georgians invariably put the state's name after the town's when they told you where they were from—"Valdosta, Georgia," or "Rossville, Georgia"—and then almost always added how many miles it was from Atlanta. I was within sight of Mile Zero, the little marker on Peachtree Street that marked the beginning of Atlanta, and I felt a surge of pure joy.

With the day my pleasure and content grew. The people on the federal beat were the friendliest people I had encountered in line of duty. In every office in the big granite-and-marble building clerks and stenographers stopped their work to shake hands and make me welcome. Off the bench the federal judges, Marvin Underwood and Richard Russell, greeted me cordially and inquired about my background, as if they really cared where a new reporter came from or was going. Judge Samuel Hale Sibley, the eminent U.S. Circuit Court of Appeals jurist, swore he recognized a family resemblance in me, and I didn't have the nerve to tell him that Pap gave me my Sibley name and I had no blood-kin right to it.

All day long I visited offices from which federal news emanated and met people who could tell me about it, and in each place I felt that I had a friend. Part of this was due to my mentor, Frank Drake. He was a good reporter, fast, accurate, fair, and he commanded the respect of the town. But part of it was bone-natural with the people.

Toward the end of the day we returned to the office of the U.S. District Attorney, a handsome gray-haired gentleman named Lawrence Camp, who had been groomed by President Roosevelt to wrest the post of U.S. Senator from Walter George, intended to have been purged for his opposition to packing the Supreme Court. The purge fizzled; Senator George held on for nineteen years more. (I was to cover his last illness and funeral in 1957.) President Roosevelt consoled Mr. Camp with an appointment to the job of DA. It was lucky for me because Mr. Camp and I hit it off right away, and if he had a good story, which didn't happen every day, of course, he gave me a break on it.

Several people in his office were to be sustaining friends but that day my most memorable and impudent welcome came from a stocky assistant DA named Raymond Martin, for easily apparent reasons called "Chatty." He was a LaGrange lawyer, homely, untidy in his dress, the back of his head shaved high in a country-style haircut, with a raucous sense of humor.

Frank introduced us.

"Celes . . . what's that name?" demanded Mr. Martin, looking up at me.

We told him and he scoffed. "I can't remember no name like that!" he cried. He looked up into my face from a distance about six or eight inches below it. "Ain't she tall?" he demanded irrelevantly. And then: "Celest . . . Celestine . . . heavenly. Means heavenly. I'm gon call you 'Heavenly Heights'!" And he did for all the years I knew him.

Judge Underwood maintained an atmosphere almost churchlike in his courtroom, so decorous, so dignified no voice was ever raised in there, no flippancy uttered—except by Chatty Martin. The irrepressible Chatty was almost always good for what city editors used to call a "bright," a short, humorous story. And, if he saw me slip into a bench in the back of the courtroom while a trial was in progress, he would bow his back to Judge Underwood ceremoniously and mouth an inaudible welcome: "Miss Heavenly Heights!"

It was easy to learn the federal beat and I counted the people there my best friends, exchanging family news with them, even as I poked about in their court records looking for news. Frederick Beers, Jr., a deputy clerk of the court and son of the clerk, was a young man who had wanted to be a pediatrician, but the Depression, marriage, and a couple of children sidetracked him. He ended up working for his father, which may not have been altogether easy, but he was sunny-natured and had a wry sense of humor and professed to enjoy hearing about everybody's children and examining their photos. When I approached his desk every day he invariably grinned up at me and said, "How are the Gracchi?," pretending to believe that my two youngsters were like Cornelia's of ancient Rome: jewels.

They were—almost. We moved from the cramped quarters in College Park to a two-bedroom apartment in an old building across from the prestigious Piedmont Driving Club. Jim Furniss, the handsome ex-Yale runner, also lived there, sharing an apartment with a poet named Daniel Whitehead Hickey. I thought it a delicious irony, typical of Atlanta, that the two bachelors could not afford a telephone but they could afford membership in the Piedmont Driving Club, and they had Julius Gaines, the headwaiter, taking messages for them and sending white-coated minions across the street to summon them to the phone.

As the newest reporter on the staff, I had to work most Sundays and nearly all holidays. I happened to be off Sunday afternoon, December 7, and was sitting on the floor holding my arms out to Susan, who at eleven months was standing alone and trying to take her first tentative steps. Jim had the radio going in the bedroom and suddenly he turned it up and yelled: "Listen!"

Pearl Harbor had been bombed!

The details came pouring out. A surprise attack by the Japanese forces at 7:55 A.M. in Honolulu—18 ships sunk, 174 planes destroyed, more than 3,000 people killed or wounded.

It meant war, we told one another, as the horror story rattled out. Pearl Harbor, where so many of our Pensacola Navy friends were assigned, crippled, all but destroyed. The attack had gone on for two hours, and the roll of lost battleships—*Arizona, California, Oklahoma, West Virginia*—was especially shocking to Jim, who had an acquaintance with some of them.

We sat by the radio all night, and the next day I learned that as federal-beat reporter I was to cover the military, which suddenly became very big and very active in Atlanta. Recruiting offices were jammed, lines of would-be volunteers flowed out into the street and around the block. Fort McPherson, the Third Army headquarters, became a reception center for enlistees. Colonel Stacy Knopf, the

Third Army intelligence officer, who had an office in the old federal building and had been an amiable source of little stories about a pet cemetery he was establishing, suddenly became very hard to see.

Back at the office the staff collected around the teletype machines, whose bells jangled and whose keys clicked out President Roosevelt's speech to Congress asking for a declaration of war against Japan. He called December 7 "a date which will live in infamy."

When I got home, late and exhausted from the most frightening, exhilarating, world-shaking story I had ever participated in, I found Jim already there, a drink in hand—surprisingly hovering over the steam radiator, a man who was never cold.

He, too, was exhausted, his face gray and drawn, his eyes evasively sliding away from my face when I tried to talk to him.

Finally he told me. He had not gone to work that day but had spent it going from recruiting office to recruiting office, starting with the Marines but trying to join any branch of the service that would have him. None would. He had a heart murmur. At thirty-four years he had been rejected and classified as 4-F.

I didn't know how serious a heart murmur was but I was to find out.

Men at the office were rushing to join up. Lee Rogers, the city editor; Luke Greene, the political editor; Johnny Bradbury of sports, all showed up in Navy whites. Half the photographic staff was gone. Jim Furniss went in the Army to become General Mark Clark's aide in Italy. Harold Martin, the star reporter-columnist, was traveling the state by Greyhound bus because rationing was on the land and staff cars were among the first casualties on the homefront. And, while he traveled, Harold, father of three children with another on the way, was trying desperately to get a commission in the Marine Corps. The day it came, he wrote, was not an occasion for trumpets sounding, and flags flying, but Mittie, "the lady who comes to iron," called him at the office to say, "Mist' Martin, yo' permission done come."

The staff suddenly looked like what Parker Lowell, a member of the copy desk, called "the Camisole & Casserole department"—all women. Pint-sized Lee Fuhrman, the reporter I had succeeded on the federal beat, was moved up to city editor, and, on the theory that he might also be called into the service, they made me assistant city editor. I needed to learn it all, they kept saying, because I might be the next city editor.

117

Fortunately, Lee lasted out the war and years afterward—a funny fellow much given to alcohol and whimsy. He had grown up on a Philadelphia newspaper and covered such big stories as the Lindbergh kidnaping, and was well-versed in all the lore that made newspapering a caper, an escapade, a jolly adventure, instead of a cold-eyed business operation. Schoolchildren often tour newspaper offices, and Lee, wanting to give them their money's worth, donned a green eyeshade, signaled to the few men reporters who were left to grab their hats and stick their press cards in the bands, and began yelling, *"Flash! Stop the press!* Get me Joe Stalin on the telephone! Get me Eleanor Roosevelt!"

One of those schoolchildren, when grown up, told me that the *Constitution* was the only bona-fide *newspapery* newspaper left in the country. He had worked on a few and visited many.

Because the staff was depleted I got to cover a remarkable range of assignments, while filling that onerous gaping hole, assistant city editor's slot. There was a trunk murder and I asked to go. A sailor had reported his wife missing. I handled the picture, suspecting, as did the police, that the young woman had left home voluntarily and would show up. Her body did—in a trunk in a rain-flooded basement after some days of evil and mysterious smell. A little widow, suspecting the sailor's wife of being after her handsome son-in-law, had done her in with a sash weight and pushed her into the trunk.

The afternoon a black man hired to clean the basement came upon the body and called the police, the little widow was coming home on the bus from shopping downtown and saw the police cars in her yard. She rode past her stop, wondering what to do, and then apparently making up her mind in the space of a block, she got off the bus and walked back home and confessed.

I went to see her at the jail—a neat little old lady who looked lonely and bewildered. I began by asking her if I could do anything for her and she smiled on me warmly.

"Yes!" she said. "Would you bring me some bananas?"

While I fed her bananas through the bars of her cell, she told me how she had been persuaded that it was necessary to eliminate the buxom girl named Mildred she suspected of breaking up her daughter's marriage. Later her defense attorney got her life sentence commuted to the state mental hospital with a device I, when I became a columnist, found offensive. She had a "plunder room" filled with stacks and stacks of boxes jammed with clippings of Dorothy Dix's columns. Proof, said the famed defense counsel and former congressman William Schley Howard, that the poor woman was mentally incompetent.

There was a lot to do—other murders and fires; a daily military column; a weekly Victory Garden page, which I wrote, edited, and made up; politics; air-raid alarms and blackouts; vicissitudes of rationing; bond-selling campaigns by such luminaries as Bob Hope, Dorothy Lamour, and our own Margaret Mitchell. Fortunately, it took some of the onus off assistant city editing, which I loathed. Not a piece of copy passed through my hands that I didn't tackle it with the wistful notion that I could have written it better, and why wasn't I out there covering the story instead of being office and deskbound? I think it became clear to everybody then that I was not made for command but was by instinct and inclination a member of the ground troops.

As much as I liked my job, Jim hated his. We both had been bedazzled by the Associated Press. Today Atlanta, tomorrow London or Paris or Berlin, we had said confidently. But in Jim's case it looked like today the Atlanta bureau, tomorrow unemployment. The man who headed the bureau was a genial gentleman who was said to be the image of actor Henry Travers, humorous and benign. He may have been to everybody else. He rode Jim to the extent that his self-confidence was shattered and he approached his job every night trembling with hideous foreboding. There was no getting around on assignments, fraternizing with policemen and court officials, no seeing the other facets of the town and the state for Jim. He was deskbound and sentenced to filing a wire so complicated that he sat up in bed when he should have been sleeping, trying to memorize the needs of AP members around the state. This town wanted Catholic news, that one a certain kind of sports coverage. The deadlines of all the small papers had to be ever-present in his mind. It was tedious, it was boring, and eventually Jim flunked it.

I had an inkling that it was going to be that way when Romney Wheeler, a friend who had been hired from the Mobile *Press-Register* by AP, asked me to meet him for a cup of coffee one afternoon. He was on a mission from his boss. The AP wanted to know if I would be willing to swap jobs with Jim if the *Constitution* agreed to it.

Why? I asked. Jim wasn't working out with AP, Romney told me. They figured the pressure of the wire service might be too much for him. He had been good on the staff of newspapers and might be again. On the other hand I was flexible, adaptable, a wire-service natural.

I was outraged. No matter how tactfully Romney tried to present it to save our jobs, it still struck me as a stinking, humiliating trick on Jim. I said, "No." A few weeks later Jim was fired.

We had moved to a bigger but cheaper apartment in Decatur on the five-cent carline. It had the advantage of a big playground next to the apartment building and the disadvantage of some neighbors that I remember to this day with a twinge of pain. There were two or three who sat in the yard in the afternoon watching their children play. I would see them there when I came home from work and would speak. They nodded cooly, if at all.

We found out why. They had complained to the management about our children. We went down one Saturday morning to face the rental agent in fear and trembling because after all it was cheap—$27 a month and spacious, with big windows overlooking the playground, nice trees, and that five-cent carfare to town. The complaint was (1) that our three-year-old son, Jimmy, had been running down the hall naked; (2) that our one-year-old daughter, Susan, cried all night.

The first was true. Jimmy had escaped from his bath one day and dashed down the hall with the nursemaid, Mary, in full pursuit. She scooped him up and covered his shocking exposure with a towel as soon as she could—but not before the neighbors had seen him.

The second was untrue. The crying baby the neighbors found so offensive was a block down the street, a newborn baby said to be very ill. Our Susan was red-headed and furious most of the time, but she conked out early at night.

The agent laughed at these indictments but I didn't. Jim was out of a job and we weren't among friends. I found myself hurrying home from work in the afternoon to get the children indoors and tranquilized with food and stories and songs so they would go to bed early. To make sure they wouldn't cry out, I went to bed with them. I skulked by the women sitting on the playground, examining their faces timorously. Is it you? I wondered. Are you the one who hates us?

Jim got a job on the Jacksonville *Journal,* and I took my vacation and drove him halfway there, veering off at Tallahassee to go to Muv's house on St. Andrews Bay. It was a blessed respite from life among our neighbors, but it wasn't easy at that. Mindful that they

120

didn't own a foot of land in Creola, Muv had persuaded Pap to buy an old house at St. Andrews against the day when he would want to retire or business already slow would expire entirely. T. A. Hatter & Son would close down and no longer need him. The old house had been pretty in its youth, an L-shaped two-story white clapboard with big porches upstairs and down, fine shade trees, and a view of the water. But, by the time Muv found it, it had the infirmities of old age, including an overflowing septic tank, which caused Muv to call it privately "Stinky" or "Old Stinkpot." By working hard herself and spending every cent she could get her hands on, she had it repaired and painted and at least antiseptic-smelling by the time the children and I arrived for our vacation.

She also had it stuffed to the gunwales with shipyard workers. There was no room for a woman with a black maid and two little children, but Muv made room. She put a bed in the kitchen for the children and me and a cot in the pantry for Mary, the maid. By getting out and to the beach as early as possible every day, we were able to stay a week without too much strain on ourselves or Muv's tenants. If the noise of children disturbed them, she said staunchly, let the tenants move. Her grandchildren were welcome.

We got back to the apartment in Decatur to find the lights off—not sabotage by the unfriendly neighbors but failure to pay the power bill. I borrowed the money and the children and I jogged along for months, missing Jim, going to bed at sundown every day out of fear of the neighbors. Then I heard of a little house a few blocks away. The owner had joined the Army and his wife had gone home to her parents. They rented the house furnished.

I called the secondhand man down on DeKalb Avenue and he came and looked over our possessions—a new mattress and springs, a bed we had paid for on the installment plan, a couple of funny-shaped chairs (Jim said one of them looked like a monkey with a dress on it). There was the lumpy studio couch, our first purchase after we were married, a plastic-and-chrome dinette set we had bought at $5 a week from Romney and Beth Wheeler. It seemed like a wondrous stock of house fixings to me as I stood in the middle of the living room and looked at it. The only things I held back were the children's beds, some bookshelves, and a big double mahogany desk we had bought from the U.S. marshal in Pensacola, a basement left-behind when the federal government moved out and sold its building to the county.

The secondhand man looked it over and gave me his price: $18.

It was robbery but I took it, eager to move into the shiny new FHA–Sears Roebuck bungalow down the street. I had settled in when Jim called to say I had a job at the Jacksonville *Journal* if I wanted it. Again, we could be together if we had jobs in the same town. I didn't want to leave the *Constitution* but it was lonely with just the children and me, and a new paper and a new town might be fun. I had that affliction Elinor Wylie, the poet, claimed was hers—"a reprehensible nature to welcome excitement and change." I went to Lee Rogers in the office and quit. Mr. McGill called me into his office.

The *Constitution* would like to have Jim come back to Atlanta and cover politics if we could persuade ourselves to give up Jacksonville, he said. And me? They wanted me to stay on and there would be $5 a week more for me if I did. I was jubilant and Jim seemed to like the idea, too. He had found out that there was a movement to start a Newspaper Guild in Jacksonville, and the publisher, an old friend from Pensacola, assumed that we would be on management's side. With that in prospect a reporter named Keeler McCartney departed, showing up in Atlanta with the word for me that we were going to be scabs.

"But we're not!" I cried happily. "We don't want to get in a labor fight and we don't want to leave Atlanta!"

Keeler was glad to be back in his old hometown, too, and he stayed for thirty years, gaining considerable renown as one of the best police reporters in the country.

Jim arrived and it was lovely having him back. The house was all new and not very big, but there was a field behind it and a barn where a neighbor kept a horse. I remember standing with Jim at the kitchen window watching Jimmy and Susan going through the field grass to take apples to the horse. The sun gilded their young heads and they looked like beautiful little voyagers trudging through the waving grass. It seemed to me with Jim standing beside me shoulder to shoulder that it was a scene of poignant beauty, and a wave of happiness swept over me. I had my husband with me; I had my children. I was fortunate among women.

Such euphoria never lasts, of course. The young couple who owned the house wanted it back and we had to move again. A friend at the paper, Eugenia Bridges Harty, knew about a house in an old close-to-town neighborhood a block from her parents' home, to which she had returned with her two children, waiting out a divorce. It was bigger than anything we had ever had—four bedrooms and three baths, two of which we could rent out to help pay the stiff $70 rent. We took it.

Shortly afterward I discovered that I was pregnant again and I had to quit my job, because in those days there was no maternity leave and pregnant women did not go on with their jobs, heavy-bodied but confident, until delivery-room time, as they do today. I was careful to quit before I was "showing," as the expression had it, and I, of course, did not explain the reason for my resignation. Maybe if they had known at the paper they wouldn't have fired Jim the following week.

To this day I don't know why they dismissed him. He was hurt and bewildered. He had thought he was doing a good job. I thought he was the best reporter they had—and he wasn't drinking. At least no more than any other reporter who got around to the places where legislators met at night and tossed off a few. I always meant to ask why he was expendable, but my pride wouldn't let me. My friend Eugenia gave me the opportunity. She had a group of executives from the paper for dinner up at her mother's house one night and she knew of our plight.

"You come, too," she said. "When they know the situation they'll take Jim back."

I couldn't do it, I told her. Jim would be furious to have me making myself an object of pity because of him. But the night of Eugenia's party I put Jimmy and Susan to bed early and left Jim to sit with them. He was in the kitchen, easing his distress with a drink. I told him I was going for a walk and I did walk purposefully up to the Bridges house. Lights blazed at all the windows, somebody was playing the piano, and I heard a fine tenor voice take up the melody of the then-popular "Yours."

Eugenia had good parties. Jim had always enjoyed them even more than I did. He would love to be there singing with them.

I got as far as the front steps and turned back. For an hour I walked the dimly-lit sidewalks of Penn Avenue and Myrtle Street and finally went home to sit on the front porch and fight the urge to cry. The next morning I took my typewriter and wristwatch and pawned them for the rent money.

Jim eventually got a job editing the house organs of the new bomber plant out at Marietta, then Bell Aircraft, now Lockheed. It

123

was better paid than any job either of us had ever had, and we had the additional bonanza of paying tenants. A delightful old lady, a spinster named Miss Eloise Pittman, rented a bedroom and bath from us, and for the other spare bedroom and bath we lucked into a very quiet traveling man. He needed a room because his wife was divorcing him, he said, and that was very nearly the only thing he ever told us about himself. He came and went quietly, usually at night, insisted on caring for his room himself, changing the bed with his own sheets, using his own towels, so we seldom knew if he was there or not.

Miss Pittman was a delight, a member of an old Atlanta family whose home had been the base of General William T. Sherman during the battle of Atlanta. She began by asking me if she might have a hot plate in her room to prepare tea and light snacks on the days when she didn't go out for her meals. Cooking in the room by Jim's standard was a very low-class and slummy thing to do (bound to attract mice and roaches). He told me not to allow it, but since most of my early childhood was nourished by meals cooked on an oil stove in the corner of a rented bedroom and since we needed the money, I countermanded his order. Miss Pittman moved in with a few beautiful antiques and turned the bedroom into an exquisite little sitting room, with a handsome daybed for sleeping and an elegant old screen to shield the small marble-topped dresser where she kept her hot plate and a canister of tea and her eggshell-thin teacups and plates. She was comfortable financially. Her father had bought some stock in a small, struggling telephone company when telephones were a freakish novelty for a few people with more money than sense. He had been more cautious about buying in on a soft drink that an Atlanta druggist had brewed as a headache remedy and Asa Candler had turned into a phenomenal financial success.

"If Papa had only believed enough in Coca-Cola to buy more stock," Miss Pittman mourned.

But I didn't regret Papa's lack of vision. She was comfortable. She had pretty clothes and went out every day to lunch or dinner at a tearoom or the home of friends. She contributed generously to her church, worked as a volunteer for the Red Cross, and went regularly to the meetings of her beloved Daughters of the American Revolution. If she had been a Coca-Cola heiress she wouldn't have rented our room.

And we would have missed her. Many an afternoon a cup of hot tea in Miss Pitt's little parlor was the only thing that saved me from a day of humdrum drudgery and backache. I rested my swollen ankles on her little footstool, sipped her good tea, and was soothed and comforted by her friendship and the peace and order of her room. Some days she invited Jimmy and Susan to join her, and it was a revelation to me how well-behaved they could be when they went, scrubbed and combed, to sit on her delicate Victorian chairs and enjoy cookies and chocolate from her tiny flower-sprigged cups.

She expected them to be civilized and they were. Later, when the house was sold and we had to move, Miss Pitt prepared to transfer to a small apartment owned by a lifelong friend and fellow DAR member, and the question this time was not about cooking in the room but if she proposed to have "those children" visiting her.

"Certainly," she said with some spirit. "If it's my home, my friends will be welcome."

"I don't want children here," her friend said. "Children are noisy and destructive and I don't want them on the premises."

"Then keep your apartment," said Miss Pitt.

Her friend relented and Jimmy and Susan did visit Miss Pitt once or twice, but the feeling of high privilege and grownup sociability had somehow evaporated.

Meanwhile, our male tenant had become a problem.

"I think he must *drink,*" Miss Pitt whispered to me one night.

Her room was closer to his than ours, and she heard him making strange noises in the night. She knocked on his door to inquire if he was ill and he came staggering out, passing her in the hall, and went to the telephone, where he called up a man named Hubert, who was apparently his ex-wife's new love. This time I heard him.

"I bet she didn't tell you I had a husband!" he shouted into the telephone. "I mean I bet she didn't tell you she had a wife!" he tried again. Then he collapsed on the floor, weeping.

Jim, late coming home from the bomber plant, was in time to pick him up and comfort him with a drink in our kitchen. I heard the heretofore silent tenant and Jim lifting their voices in song as I drifted off to sleep before dawn. At sunup I asked him to move.

We considered not renting that room again but moving Jimmy into it when the new baby arrived. Then a young couple came to the door with their baby one afternoon. He was in uniform and terribly anxious to have his family with him while he underwent treatment at the

125

Army's Lawson General Hospital out on the edge of town. I was about to tell him we had decided not to rent the room when I saw his hands—mutilated with most of his fingers missing.

Horrified, I could but stand there staring.

"Land mines," he said briefly. "They're going to fit me with artificial hands."

"Oh, please come in!" I cried. "This is the room. You can have it *free!*"

They didn't take it free. They had money and wanted to pay but they also wanted what landlords in those days called "kitchen privileges," which meant that the young wife and I bumped into each other constantly at stove and refrigerator, trying to prepare our separate meals. They took to using the dining room and inviting in guests, and the soldier liked the chair that Jim regarded as his own in the living room, unthinkably, and he dismantled the newspaper when he read it. Worse yet for my period of peace and quiet in the afternoon, the wife's favorite radio program conflicted with Jimmy's *Terry and the Pilots* and *Little Orphan Annie.* Out of politeness he had to forgo his programs for hers, but it was bitter deprivation and he didn't take it quietly when she sat down before the old Philco radio in the living room and tuned in a soap opera.

It certainly wasn't my intention to run those tenants off. I felt guilty that I had no one in the war, and every time I looked at that young soldier's hands I wanted to cry. It just happened that mosquitoes were bad that summer and there was a new product called DDT, which was guaranteed to wipe them out. There was also something new called Clorox for bleaching dingy clothes. We acquired a bottle of each, and late one afternoon, about mosquito time, I began spraying the front porch and progressing to the back porch, hitting bedrooms and clothes closets along the way. I didn't know until the young wife set up a howl the next day that I had sprayed with Clorox instead of DDT. Every garment in her closet, many of them precious holdovers from her trousseau, was splotched with white!

They packed their possessions and moved immediately.

Mixed with my fierce feeling of guilt was one of relief. The new baby was due and our friends Rita and Leslie Bogan had decided to move to Atlanta from Pensacola and they were going to stay with us until they found a place.

"I'm coming to midwife for you!" Rita told me, and it turned out to be true.

Leslie went to work at Bell Aircraft, and he and Rita and their three children moved in with us and stayed to be with Jimmy and Susan while I was in the hospital and to take care of what Susan called "Oo Baby" and me when we came home. Rita determinedly put me through the exercise routine that Muv had instigated when Jimmy was born. On the hot August nights when the other five children were safe in bed she would make me walk up to Piedmont Park and then, sweating and itching from heat, back aching and ankles swollen, through the park and around the lake.

It was her delight one night to find a young couple in a heavy clinch in a swing by the lake. She marched me up to them and, shaking an admonitory finger, cried, "Un-uh! Un-uh! Doing *that* will get you *this!*" and pointed to me, a miserable outsized atrocity of a woman.

The young couple sprang apart guiltily.

I went home and cried.

But the next day that last-minute energy that seems to be a part of the birthing pattern gripped me. I cleaned the house, washed curtains and slipcovers, mended and washed and pressed one of the two maternity dresses I owned, and read fast in Lloyd C. Douglas's *The Robe,* which I hoped to finish before I left for the hospital. I didn't quite because at daybreak the pains started and I had to get my one maternity slip off the clothesline and press it while Jim walked around the corner to our friend Mary Gash's and borrowed her car. She had offered it and all she had to do was walk out on her upstairs porch and toss him the keys.

I finished *The Robe* two days later because all that day I was involved in getting Mary Everitt, my third and last child, into the world. It was August 18, 1943, and we named her for her Grandmother Little and all the Mary Everitts before her, going back four generations.

Jim stood by, pacing and waiting during the long delivery-room session, and saw me a moment after I was transferred to my room, long enough to give me a dozen of my favorite yellow roses and to tell me that he was delighted with another girl and very happy that I wanted to name her for Mamie.

He did not return to the hospital that night, and the next day I

127

understood why. He came in bringing me a Bible, which I had asked for to check the facts in *The Robe.* He was limping painfully.

"What's the matter with your foot?" I asked.

He looked sheepish. His friends at the bomber plant had given him a party to celebrate the baby's birth, and in a burst of alcoholic exuberance he had danced one of the girls off the deck, a drop of a couple of feet, skinning her knee and spraining his ankle.

I expressed sympathy, which I did not feel. I was in some pain myself.

Muv waited until I got home from the hospital to plan her trip to see the new baby. She had received a good offer for "old Stinkpot" from an oil company, which seemed interested in tearing down the St. Andrews house and putting a filling station on the corner. Mary was born while they were negotiating and Muv, eager to see it through, waited a while and then caught the bus for Atlanta. Less than fifty miles from home she looked out the bus window and saw a sign on a pine tree reading: "Repent or Burn in Hell." She woke up in Dothan Hospital.

The bus had gone off the road, landing in a ditch, and Muv's injuries, which were extensive and painful, came not so much from the impact as from her fellow passengers. She had been thrown to the floor of the aisle, and in their panic to get out they trampled over her, breaking ribs, wrists, and collarbone. She was in the hospital nine weeks.

Looking back, I now know I could have gone to her, but Mary was so new and was nursing and I was uneasy about leaving the other two. So I stayed at home and worried. Pap had been in Creola at the time of the accident, but he went straight to Dothan and stayed for the duration except for a run down to St. Andrews to close the sale of the house. He asked only one thing of me, that I send Muv some nightgowns. I'll never forget what a problem that presented. We were more broke than usual, and friends I could borrow from were broke, too. Finally one of them notified me that her charge account was in good enough order for me to charge some things, and together we got the gowns in the mail.

When Muv was able to leave the hospital the medical chief, who was also the bus line's doctor, sent her and Pap to the little house they owned in Alford in his chauffeur-driven car. They stopped on the way for Pap to buy some groceries and they arrived to find the furniture Pap had moved there, after the Stinkpot sale, piled high in the front room.

Pap built a fire in the fireplace and Muv sat beside it and planned what she was going to do with the house. The next day she started tearing down walls. She was to spend the rest of her life in that house.

When spring came I took the children down for Muv to see her newest grandchild. Aunt Babe was standing at her gate to greet us as we passed and she looked Mary over carefully.

"I'll be John Brown," she said, "if she ain't the spit of John Barber!"

As soon as I was on my feet I went back to work. The Bogans found an apartment in a complex near the bomber plant in Marietta and moved. I hated to leave the children, but it seemed that we truly had to have the money. Although Jim was making a warplant salary, considerably more than either of us made at the paper, he didn't get home with all of it.

Winter came and we ran out of coal for the furnace. I called him at work and he was cheerful and reassuring. Don't worry, he said; it was payday and he would get home with money in time to order a ton of coal.

It was a great old house, snug and well-built many years before, and it held the residual heat long enough for me to bathe the children and give them supper and put them to bed. Then it started cooling off.

I wrapped myself in a quilt and sat down with a book to wait. Sometime around midnight Jim got there—with a drunk stranger, a supply of whiskey, and a *sack*, not a ton, of coal. He had missed his carpool ride by hours, so he and his friend had grandly taken a taxi—all the way from the bomber plant twenty-five miles away.

The crowning insult to me at that time was that they had stopped for dinner on the way—with the meter running!

It was obvious that I had to go back to work and I was glad. When I got off the bus downtown and walked toward that old building, my heart lifted. Problems I couldn't handle were behind me. The problems ahead of me in that old newspaper building were ones I knew I could manage, maybe not magnificently, but adequately—or even a little better than. I walked cheerfully, optimistically, glad that there was work I could do and that they wanted me to do it.

One of the first stories I covered after my maternity absence was a fire south of town in which an old house and its entire contents were

129

burned. The family narrowly escaped with their lives. The father was badly burned rescuing the little children. He was in Grady Hospital in need of blood transfusions. At home that night I got to worrying that there would not be enough donors. Rita and Leslie came by and I told them about the family's plight.

"Come on, we'll go give blood," said Rita, ever generous.

Jim had been drinking and was asleep but Leslie said he would keep an eye on all six children.

Rita and I caught the bus for the hospital. On the way she told me that Jim was having an affair with a woman at the bomber plant.

I was stunned. I don't know what I said, if anything, but after we were in the hospital and lying on the little stretcher carts with tubes in our veins she looked at me curiously.

"You really mind, don't you?" she said.

Mind? I was devastated. I thought I would die there in the hospital. I hoped I would die.

Rita sighed. She had thought things had come to such a sorry pass between Jim and me that I might be relieved to have him turning to somebody else. The woman, somebody she knew, most certainly didn't want him permanently, but she felt that he was a troubled man in need of something he wasn't getting—something to shore up his confidence and renew his self-esteem. There was no use pretending that he didn't know he was a failure. I shamed him with every well-meaning act, keeping a job, paying bills, the brave, uncomplaining helpmate who made it possible for him to drink, because, as he put it sometimes, I had my "little career."

There was truth in what she said but it didn't ease my agony. I went home too numb to cry, gripped by a sense of paralysis. When I rode to town on the bus I would look at my fellow passengers and wonder if they could see that beneath my sweater or my suit jacket my heart was a bloody mess, actually physically broken. It's an expression, I thought, nobody believes it. But it's true, the heart breaks.

When I told Jim I knew he was nearly as upset as I was. He didn't deny it. He didn't excuse it. He simply said the woman was beautiful and available, usually at lunchtime. He didn't love her. The sheets on her bed were dirty. He loved me and the children and would die if we left him.

And, like Miniver Cheever, he went on drinking.

For a time I went into a desperate act to win him back. I tried to make myself more attractive, resorting to such feeble and absurd devices as mascara and new clothes, which I bought with money I borrowed from Muv.

I read magazine pieces and books on how to keep your man, and, hating myself, I tried every silly strategy. Jim had immediately disclaimed any further interest in the woman and vowed that he would never see her again, and I don't think he did, although it wasn't because I had become what the magazines called a Desirable Woman. So far as I could tell he hadn't noticed that. I watched him sleep at night and it seemed to me that even if he stayed I had lost him. The love I thought he had for me hadn't withstood the negligible test of a beautiful woman's "availability." The fidelity I had believed in wasn't there.

Perversely, I seemed to love him more. The shape of his dark head on the pillow moved me terribly. The big square hands, empty and curled in his sleep, seemed inexpressibly dear. I wanted to hold them and kiss them, but instead I would slip out of bed and roam over the house, checking on the sleeping children and choking on my own misery.

Sometimes I sat on the front porch and looked at the leaves of the old Penn Avenue trees stirring under the street light. I remembered one rainy night Muv and I had sat there mulling over some problem— a problem I now knew was minor because all else was reduced to nothingness by this one. Muv had sighed and said, "Well, we can't count on getting out of anything by dying because the women in our family live forever."

Forever? I couldn't bear the thought of it. Obviously I had to keep on living. The three little beds in there held reason enough. But how to go on in such pain was beyond me.

Unexpectedly an escape was offered.

131

Chapter Six

Harry Lee, a bright and successful young novelist, who wrote two books, *Fox in the Cloak* and *No Measure Danced,* before he was twenty-five years old, had come to work at the paper. He was courting a young woman reporter named Martha Summer, who rented our back room for a time, and between the office and our kitchen, where we spent a lot of time drinking coffee and talking, he became my dear and valued friend.

He wasn't any great shakes as a news reporter, having no taste for setting down the facts in an orderly fashion and withholding his personal views, and he was a terrible speller. But obviously he could write, and he was the most *literary* person most of us knew. Almost totally self-educated, he had read everything in the world during the intermittent periods when he was unemployed. Even the older members of the staff, like our editor, Ralph McGill, who had been a student at Vanderbilt and knew John Crowe Ransom, Robert Penn Warren, and the other Fugitives, hadn't been privileged to sit over a coffee or a beer at the Greek's and discuss Trollope and Schopenhauer in the late afternoon. Harry offered that.

He was only a few years older than I was but eons beyond me in wisdom and knowledge. He was the first person to suggest to me that segregation was wicked and immoral. He had the kind of black friends I had never met, college professors and lawyers and writers. He read aloud the works of Richard Wright and Countee Cullen to show me that feeling and quality writing were not confined to the white race. He was unique in my experience in that he criticized, really criticized, *Gone With the Wind,* held sacrosanct by everybody else in Atlanta except Margaret Mitchell herself, who once told me that she couldn't be paid to reread some of it. Harry agreed that she had done what she set out to do—told a good story—but that it was not a flawless piece of writing. I was dumfounded.

Harry encouraged us all to write, obviously aware that everybody who worked for a newspaper had a novel in the bottom drawer. He asked to see mine and he read it with care, critically, sensitively, pointing out its flaws and making suggestions but giving it so much praise my sore and battered spirits moved upward a little.

Then one afternoon he showed up at my house with an editor from Doubleday named Bucklin Moon.

"Show Bucklin your novel," he directed.

I was barefoot and had Mary on one hip and Jimmy and Susan eddying around me. The manuscript was messy and dog-eared but Mr. Moon took it and left, promising to read it right away and let me know.

He left town that night, and I got a telegram from him the next day saying he liked what he read and offering me a contract with $1,000 advance, to be paid in ten monthly installments.

It seemed a fortune at the time—enough for the children and me to live on . . . somewhere. Not there in that $70-a-month house. But suddenly I knew I was not going to stay there anyhow. I was leaving that house and Jim.

The opportunity to change my mind—then—was denied me by the owner of the house. He had a sale for it and we had to vacate anyhow.

Rita and Leslie also had a house for sale—one they had built in the country at the head of Bayou Texar in Pensacola. Rita was going down to spend a few weeks packing up and preparing to move while Leslie looked for a house to buy in Atlanta. She invited me to go with her, and I packed my typewriter (I was then doing a twice-a-week column only for the *Constitution*) and my manuscript, gathered up a few sunsuits for the children, and took off.

Rita was good for me. Pregnant with their fourth child, she relaxed and left the housekeeping up to me. We pooled our resources and bought a beat-up old car for $50. It had FOR SALE CHEAP painted on its windows in black enamel, a sign we didn't bother to remove, and we were able to get around to see old friends and take the children to the beach, picking up strangers from time to time because in those war years any kind of car for sale had instant appeal. (To this day our children refer to that vehicle as "the For Sale car.")

Mamie came by to see us, on her way home from Jacksonville, where she had visited Ervin and Jane. We sat in the yard until a late hour and talked. She hoped there would be no divorce, but, typically, her sympathies were with me.

"I used to say the Little men had their faults," she confessed wryly. "Some of them drank and some of them gambled, but they were never, never unfaithful to their wives. Constancy you could count on."

She made a face and we both were able to laugh.

Bucklin Moon came down and spent the night. We took a picnic and went to the beach and he talked a little about my book. It needed more conflict, he said, and Rita and I whooped derisively. We thought conflict was one thing in life that came unsought and unplanned-for and the prudent avoided it at all costs.

"Not in a book," said Mr. Moon and went back to New York.

I went back to the typewriter, writing my column and a little on the book, but more often than not just sitting and reading and rereading the charming, funny, loverlike letters Jim wrote me every day.

Then one afternoon he called from the bus station. He had come for the weekend. Joyfully the children and I drove the "For Sale" car in to pick him up, and that night he and I walked for hours along the sandy paths by the bayou talking. He was desolate without us, he said. Life was arid and pointless. He ached for the pain he had caused me but it had its purpose, he felt sure. It had strengthened a momentous resolve to give up drinking. He was trying very hard to save money to buy us a house, where we could be happily and steadfastly married forever.

Would I come back?

"Yes!" I said and fell into his arms so fast that he toppled over in the sand from the bank where we had been sitting.

Jim went back to Atlanta, the movers were coming for the Bogans' furniture, and I prepared to go to Muv's house in Alford to wait out the place he was going to find for us. I was ironing the children's clothes and, although it was April, it was summertime hot there on the bayou. I moved the ironing board to the back porch, where I could catch a breeze and talk to Rita, who, heavily pregnant, sat in the shade in the backyard.

Suddenly the young sailor and his wife who lived across the road

134

came out on their porch waving and yelling at us. President Roosevelt was dead!

The ironing forgotten, we gathered in the road, all the people who lived at that end of the bayou, going over the details and weeping. I should be there, I thought. I had never been to Warm Springs. Jim had once, to interview the Canadian prime minister, who was visiting in the absence of the Roosevelts. But if I had been in Atlanta now the *Constitution* would most certainly have sent me to Warm Springs to cover the President's death. I wept for the man who had been President since long before I was old enough to vote, but mixed with my tears for him were tears of homesickness for Atlanta and my job.

Life at Muv's house wasn't altogether easy. She was glad to have us, but it's not exactly auspicious to have a married daughter come home with three little children to stay. Besides, she had projects of her own going.

A troop train had broken down in Alford on its way to the coast. Stalled there for hours the young soldiers had roamed the little town restlessly, bored, and, worst of all, hungry. When they had demolished the supply of cheese and crackers and soft drinks at the town's one filling station and drugstore and gobbled up the sardines and canned beans at the town's one grocery store, they were out of food. Muv and her friends, the other women in town, saw the problem, and in a rush of patriotic fervor they hurried to their kitchens and got to work. Sugar was in short supply but they made cakes somehow with what they had, also biscuits and hoecakes of cornbread. Meat was rationed, but those who had farms had hams and they brought them forth. Everybody had a few chickens, even in town in those days, and some had cows. They fried the chickens and boiled eggs and made platters of potato salad. Grabbing up their best tablecloths they spread them over the splintery freight platform of the railroad depot and set out their food.

It may not have been enough. I never knew for sure. But the effort produced a grateful letter from the commandant at the military base where the train was headed, and now and then through the years an ex-serviceman has dropped by to visit in Alford, mindful of the time when he and his fellows needed friends and found them there.

To Muv the incident proved that Alford needed a restaurant, and she determined to open one. Pap had bought a lot on the only highway through town, and Muv visualized a small, four-table restaurant, where she would serve vegetables and one main dish a day.

It was in full swing when the children and I arrived. Muv manned the wood-fired cookstove. A plump, amiable country woman named Bertie Lou arrived daily by oxcart, driven by her father, to wait on tables. And my assignment was to stay at the house and write on my book, if I could, but mainly keep the children out of the way.

Muv thought she wanted them around. She had us come down for our dinner every day, usually eaten under the big oak tree in the backyard to free a table for paying customers. She even had a carpenter build a sandbox under the tree so the children could play there on occasion. But they bothered her when she was busy. Jimmy wanted to put nickels in the jukebox and play "Chattanooga Choo-Choo" endlessly. Susan was easier, content to play with imaginary friends by herself for hours on end, but Mary was a toddler and into things.

Besides that, we were tacky. Muv had ever been one to want to put up a good appearance. And in Alford, her almost hometown, she especially wanted her child and her grandchildren to be presentable. The other little children in town were bathed and dressed in sandals and frilly pinafores and sunsuits every afternoon. I thought it was all right for my children to play in their underpants, unwashed unless we turned the hose on them. The other young mothers put on crisp summery dresses, took their parasols, and walked out to visit or to see and be seen at the drugstore or post office after dinner. I was comfortable in ragged shorts and sneakers.

"Oh, I wish you had something better to put on!" Muv cried one day. "I hate for my neighbors to see you wearing tennis shoes."

"Ha!" I hooted. "Mrs. Roosevelt had on tennis shoes when she entertained the King and Queen of England."

Once to appease Muv I took a check that came for columns and caught the bus into Dothan to buy myself some shoes. The ones I found were green canvas—not sneakers but so close that when Muv saw them she broke down and laughed helplessly—at herself and at me.

It was a hot summer in Alford and typhoid fever broke out in a neighboring county. The Public Health Department sent teams out to inoculate us all, and the children and I went up to the community house for shots. They suffered no ill effects but my arm swelled up and turned blue-black and I had a raging fever for a day or two. All

I wanted to do was lie in bed and sleep, but child care and household chores went on, and one afternoon, when I had somewhat recovered, I was at the clothesline, taking down the washing I had done that day, and I saw the man who lived across the street coming home from work.

His children were yelping joyfully, "Daddy! Daddy's home!" and rushing to meet him. His wife stood in the doorway, smiling and aproned, and I thought I smelled good food cooking in their kitchen.

The little domestic scene seemed more than I could bear. I went in the house and wrote Jim not to wait until he could get us a house of our own but to find us an apartment or rooms or anything. I was ready to come home.

He sent us bus fare and we lovingly took leave of Muv and Alford and embarked for Atlanta. As the bus lumbered down Spring Street toward the terminal I caught a glimpse of the *Constitution* building, familiar and dear and, in a way, home. I felt a rush of affection for it and Atlanta and gladness in coming back.

But Jim was not at the bus station to meet us.

He had written that he had rented an apartment in Pine Forest, a new complex in Marietta not far from the bomber plant, but I had no idea where it was or how to get there. So we sat. Or rather I sat and the children romped around the bus station. They were hungry and dirty from the day-long trip but excited to be in such a busy place, alive with its wartime crowds, and keyed up to meet their father.

I wasn't sure that he was coming. As the hours passed I was sure he wasn't coming. He had known the time of our arrival but maybe he had forgotten. Or didn't care. Or had abandoned his resolve and was drinking again.

The last was true. A couple of car-owning friends brought him to meet us—eventually—but they had all stopped on the way to have a celebratory drink. They were that glad that we were coming.

The apartment Jim had rented for us was not available yet, but we were to spend the night at a hospitable printer's house. His wife and children were out-of-town and there would be plenty of room for us. I don't remember the man's name. I'm sure I never thanked him. But it was a lot for him to do, to take us all in that night, and I know I didn't appear grateful when I declined the festive drinks he and Jim and some other men were sharing at the kitchen table and groped my way tiredly to his wife's bed.

We did get the apartment the next day, and our things, which we had stored in a friend's basement, looked good to me—beds all around and the old mahogany desk, which served as our only living room, dining room furniture. I put a cloth over it and we ate from it. I put my typewriter on it and wrote columns. The children climbed on it and stored their things in its pigeonholes.

It was our best-loved possession and would serve in all capacities until we could do better. People were moving in and out of the apartment complex as the war seemed to wind down, and there were many chances to buy furniture. I had my eye on a sofa that was going to be for sale, when Jim came home with a case of beer and the news that his job had just ended.

A few days later the atomic bomb was dropped on Hiroshima and a few weeks later Jimmy and all the other little boys in the apartment were marching around the playground whamming garbage-can lids and yelling in jubilation. September 2, 1945—V-J Day, Victory Over Japan, three years eight months and twenty-two days after Pearl Harbor.

It seemed a long time to have been at war, and although none of us knew the details of the Hiroshima bombing then, President Truman's voice seemed very sad when he announced it over the radio. I was sad and worried about the future. Jim was out of a job and drinking. The rent would be due again on the apartment. The small check I got for my columns would barely feed us. The payments from Doubleday were long since exhausted and the book itself was something I couldn't bear to think about. Henry Volkening, the agent Bucklin Moon got for me, had written that the manuscript was "of course, perfectly publishable but, as you know, it's not great literature." I hadn't known that. I'd had to assume that it was or I couldn't have kept plugging along on it in other people's houses in the midst of self-doubts bordering sometimes on despair.

Jim received the news philosophically.

"Just drop it in the first cornerstone laying you come to and forget it," he advised.

Years later at a happier time I was to pay Doubleday back that $1,000 with another book.

One of my primary concerns at that time was starting Jimmy to school. It was September, time to enroll him in the first grade, and he was very excited about it. Pine Forest was fast emptying out. My favorite neighbors, wartime workers from the mountains of Tennessee, had already borrowed a truck and were loading up to go home to the hill country. My least-favorite neighbor, a woman who washed her garbage can with Lysol every day and set her shoes out to air, had already told me that her husband was "seeking a position" in downtown Atlanta, and she expected to return to the pleasant social life they had known there.

Jim made a daily trip up to the pay telephone on the corner to check out job applications he had sent to several newspapers, came home his shoulders sagging, his face glum with defeat, and started drinking. The most I told Muv was that the war's ending had cost Jim his job and we were again unsettled. The next mail from her brought two war bonds she had signed over to me and a reminder about the crazy old lady at the mill in Creola who used to go down the road crying for everybody to "be happy in the name of God."

"Be happy in the name of God," Muv reiterated and that very day I saw where it was going to be possible. Jim came back from the telephone booth with word that he had a job! He was to leave immediately for Orlando (Florida) and the *Sentinel Star*!

He would get there and find a place to live, and the children and I would follow as soon as we could again store our belongings with somebody, clean out the apartment, and catch a bus. Mindful of school's starting, we did it with all possible speed, arriving in Orlando late one night after a horrendous trip on hot, crowded buses, for if they had express buses in those days we never managed to catch one. We would travel awhile on one bus, a decrepit old vehicle, get off and wait a couple of hours, catch another, and travel awhile and get off and wait again. It took nearly two days of this zigzag, on-and-off progress, and when we got there Jim had rented connecting rooms at the hotel where he had been staying.

"Hotel!" I cried. "We can't stay in a hotel. It'll cost a fortune!"

I was saving one of Muv's war bonds to rent a house—and where was the house? There weren't any, Jim said. Orlando was filled up. But the paper did furnish him a car (he was the citrus, livestock, and political editor) and he was going to take a little time off so we could look. A hurricane was brewing and he would probably have to work that night, but we had the morning and we used it. We found a tourist cabin, which would serve until we could do better. It had a kitchen and I hurried by a grocery store to stock up on cheap food we could fix there. The morning's breakfast at a restaurant delighted the children but cost enough to feed us all a week.

The little tourist cabin was on one of the small clear, sand-bottomed lakes that abound in Orlando and as soon as we checked in I took the children swimming. By late afternoon wind and rain swept in and I knew from experience the hurricane was close. About dark the proprietor of the cabins was distributing candles to his guests with the prediction that the electricity would go off soon.

Remembering one of the canons from hurricane season in my own childhood, I kept the children dressed and awake in case we had to get out of a falling house. To keep them from getting drowsy I stripped sheets from one of the beds to make curtains for an improvised stage where we could act out stories and plays. The little cabin trembled and lurched under the force of the wind. The electricity did go off and I lit the candles. We went on with our show by candlelight, taking turns reciting and singing until finally a dead calm told me the storm had passed.

The candles burned down and guttered out. The little actor and actresses tumbled into bed, exhausted. But I sat on, waiting for Jim to come. He didn't come that night or the next.

He had been so exhausted, he said, he went on back to the hotel, where he had been staying, for a little rest. Whatever hurt or feelings of neglect I might have been nurturing were melted when he added that he had run into a girl from Atlanta, who had married an Army officer, and knew of a house we could rent.

It was a wonderful house in an orange grove on a lake near the little suburban community of Lockhart. A Chicago hotel man had built it as a retreat for his daughter and her family when they came South for the winter. He had gone broke, lost or sold the hotel, and died, and now his daughter lived year-round with her mother in the big house at the other end of the lake and the smaller house had passed to her married son, who was in the Army. We could have it until the son and his wife came home.

Right away I enrolled Jimmy in the first grade in Lockhart School. The girls and I walked him halfway to school every morning and wandered home in a kind of idyll through the groves heavy with the fragrance of orange blossoms, to the sandbox under an avocado tree, to the lake where we would swim most of the afternoon. Jim was away a lot, traveling over central Florida for the paper, but the house

140

was comfortable and interesting. It had great boggy leather chairs, which had been in the lobby of the Chicago hotel, and boxes of dusty old novels in the attic, some of them quite good. In fact I first read *Jane Eyre* and *Wuthering Heights* there.

But the idyll was short-lived. Before the month was out the owner of the house wired his mother that he and his bride were coming home and would like their house by the end of the month. Muv arrived to help me find another place. After days of fruitless looking we finally settled for a little shack on another lake, the weekend camp house of some fishermen. It had no electricity, no plumbing, a privy, and a two-burner oil stove, which blew up every time I approached it. I hauled water from the lake to bathe the children at night, for by that time we were having a touch of weather too chilly for swimming, and we brought drinking water in bottles from the filling station a mile or so away.

Jimmy could still walk to Lockhart School, and despite my struggles with the smoking, smelling little oil stove and the children's fear of spiders in the privy, we were reasonably content. Jim was working hard and apparently pleasing the publisher, Martin Anderson, very well because Mr. Anderson took him along to meetings and invited us to a large party at his house. I couldn't find a sitter for the children so I didn't go, but I was fascinated by Jim's report that white-coated minions on motorscooters handled guest parking.

One afternoon some new friend at the office took Jim fishing on Lake Apopka and he came back with word that there were places to rent at Johnson's fishing camp. They were intended for fishermen, many of whom flocked there in wintertime from colder climes, and they were considered pretty primitive. But not by us. Lights and indoor plumbing had become the height of luxury to us.

The little apartment we rented was on the second floor of a big frame building, set back from the boathouses and fishing dock. It had two tiny bedrooms, one bigger central room with a long table, a two-burner gas plate, which had to be fed quarters to keep going, and a sink. Our refrigerator—a very small one—was in the hall, shared with the people in the apartment across the hall. We also shared a toilet in a little cubicle in the hall with that apartment and a shower in the yard with *everybody*. Once at the height of the winter season I counted up seventy-five people using that shower, waiting to use it, or maneuvering to use it. We limited ourselves to one hot shower

141

a week, using a dishpan and a quarter's worth of hot water for daily ablutions. Even once a week made showering with three children a traffic-fraught experience. We developed a method. I would take soap and washcloths into the shower, Jim would wait outside with towels. After I had bathed he would hand me a child to be scrubbed and handed back for him to dry. Then he would hand me another and so on until the family was clean, taking the last shower himself. It tied up the shower longer than the fishing-camp crowd liked but it was the only sure way we knew to get use of it while there was still hot water.

"There they go," we heard one grumpy old fisherman cry. "Watch that pass—Tinker to Evers to Chance!"

It was not a bad life, living at a fishing camp. Jimmy was enrolled in the first grade at Apopka School and could walk up the hill by himself to catch the school bus. Mary would fall in the lake occasionally and get fished out and hauled back to me, dripping, by some fisherman. Somehow I never worried particularly, assuming, I suppose, that she would float until somebody spotted her. Susan, a dreamy little five-year-old, seemed to live in the world of the imagination, playing with a whole raft of make-believe friends.

A doctor and his wife from Black Rock, North Carolina, moved into an apartment downstairs and became our mentors and friends. Dr. Prichard had heart trouble and regularly took a winter vacation at Apopka, so they knew how to make themselves comfortable in the bare little apartment and became acquainted with many of the local people. One couple, who owned an orange grove, became our friends, too, and invited us to help ourselves to the golden fruit on their trees. We kept a washtub on the little screened porch off our big room filled with sweet, tree-ripened oranges and grapefruit.

Maria Prichard, a plump, gray-haired lady, was considerably older than I was but buoyant and sunny and full of projects for celebrating the Christmas holidays, which were approaching. It was her idea that we have a joint tree in the hall, decorated with anything we could put our hands on. There was no chance of buying lights or ornaments in that postwar year, and nobody had thought to bring them from home. So we made cookies in the little tin ovens Maria taught me to use on the gas plates. The children drew and crayoned birds and bells and blobby Santa Clauses. And then I thought of Christmas cards.

We didn't get many but every one that came was like the hand of a friend reaching out to us, and I hung them all on the tree with love and gratitude.

Half a dozen fishermen who stayed on at the camp during the holidays had not thought of and probably didn't want a celebration, but Maria wouldn't let Christmas go by unobserved. She decreed that we all get together for dinner, pooling our resources. We wanted a turkey but how to roast one in a tin oven no bigger than a bread box?

Jim solved the problem by buying the turkey and taking it to a baker in Orlando to cook for us.

The children's toys were simple and cheap, except for a bicycle we got for Jimmy—his first—and the dinner with the turkey *and* platters of fried fish and cakes and ambrosia was a feast. Afterward we walked over to visit the Prichards' friends in the orange grove, and I had a fleeting feeling of discontent. The sun was too hot for the children to wear the clothes Muv had sent them for Christmas. They were back to sunsuits and bare feet. The smell of orange blossoms suddenly seemed unctuous and overpowering. Hibiscus was blooming madly everywhere. I wanted to yell, "Stop it! This is no way to behave at Christmas!" But what I really felt was a small and unacknowledged twinge of homesickness.

Jim had been having some problems with his back, necessitating staying home and calling in sick at the office. There was a little store down by the dock, which had a telephone and a small stock of canned goods and beer and soft drinks for the fishermen. One day Jim went down to call the office and make his excuses and stayed to drink a beer. It seemed immoral to me to skip work and spend the day drinking, if you were able to be on your feet at all, and I went down to the store to see if I could persuade him to at least treat his backache with bedrest.

He followed me out the door and said quietly but distinctly: "Go away for God's sake! You are *nagging* me!"

I went but I was seething. That night after the children were in bed I prepared to have it out with him—the drinking, the job-losing absences. But he beat me to it.

We were sitting on the little screened porch and he looked unutterably sad. He had to talk to me, he said. He had something to say that had been on his mind for a long time. He hated it but there it was: He simply could not be responsible for supporting the children and

143

me. He loved us. He would like to take care of us. But it was more than he could manage.

It wasn't that we were expensive. My $15-a-week check for columns kept the grocery bill within reason. And our standard of living was anything but extravagant. It wasn't the money. It was responsibility.

I listened and believed, feeling only sadness for him and sympathy. He was a good person, a man who really cared about us, I knew. It was not his fault that he had this flaw, this weakness. There were probably a great many men who had it or I wouldn't have seen so many cases of abandonment when I covered the courthouse. Those husbands and fathers simply left. Jim had been honest with me. I was forewarned.

I reached for his hand and held it and told him it was all right.

The next day Maria Prichard drove me to the Western Union office in the little town of Winter Garden. I sent three telegrams, one to Josh Skinner, managing editor of the *Constitution,* asking for my job back; one to my mother, asking if she would keep Jimmy and Mary for me, a little boy and a baby—the two children who were the most trouble at the time; and a third to Mamie, asking if she would keep Susan, a docile little girl best suited to the ways of an elderly woman in a city apartment.

The answers came back within twenty-four hours. Josh Skinner, bless his heart, wired: "Yes! Yes! Yes! Come at once. Do you need any money?"

Mamie wired that she deeply regretted her inability to take on the care of a child, but she was old and had no suitable place. Muv wired, "Don't separate the children. Bring them all to me."

The following day I was packed and Maria drove us to the bus, where I discovered I didn't have quite enough money for our tickets. She lent the balance to me, and we were on the bus and ready to pull out when Jim rushed up and jumped aboard.

He didn't want us to leave, he said. He wouldn't let us leave. He started unloading our bags and grabbed my portable typewriter and hurried down the steps outside the bus, smiling up at us, undoubtedly certain that he had scotched the trip, for without clothes or typewriter how could we go? Or maybe experience had taught him that any sign that he wanted me would cause me to capitulate.

Instead I said to the driver, "Please go on. We've got to go!"

Muv asked no questions but served us a good supper by the fireplace and tucked us all into beds, which seemed always at her house to smell of fields and flowers. She got out a suitcase for me and laid out underwear and blouses and a new suit and yellow tweed coat, which she had just ordered for herself from Burdine's in Miami. And she counted out $30, which would take me to Atlanta and keep me until I could make a payday.

The trip from Alford to Atlanta, although only a little more than 250 miles, took all day by bus, which digressed into little towns off the main highway, picking up people waiting by gates or mailboxes in front of their farm homes—sometimes with a crate of chickens or a bushel basket of vegetables—and taking them into the county seat to shop or go to the doctor or to attend a session of Big Court. I loved those bus trips usually and, like my mother who talked to everybody, I often made friends with my fellow travelers.

That day I didn't. I turned my back on my seatmate and leaned my forehead against the window, staring out at the red clay hills, the pine woods, the fields of broomsedge brushed with gold. I had come to a time for decision—a decision long overdue. I was going to Atlanta and get to work and make a home for my children, somehow somewhere. My dreams of going on to New York, Paris, London were a girl's dream with no substance to them. My dream of writing a book, a good book, which would bring fame and fortune was patently silly. My hope of a good marriage had proven even less attainable.

I thought of people I knew at the *Constitution* who had been there many years. Hacks, I thought, with little talent and no ambition. They would be there until they died, doing the mundane jobs somebody had to do on a newspaper. Not for them stardom, travel, glamorous assignments, fat paychecks. They worked hours nobody else wanted to work. In personnel shifts they uncomplainingly took demotions. In some way they were indispensable but always undistinguished. I had felt sorry for them but now I envied them. They stayed put, they owned their own homes, their children went to the same schools term after term, they belonged to churches, they had hospital insurance, usually a car of some kind, and they knew their next-door neighbors and the people at the corner drugstore and grocery store.

In my borrowed suit with the remains of the borrowed $30 in my purse (I had to pay $8 for a bus ticket), not knowing where I would go when I arrived in Atlanta, the idea of a stay-put house and neigh-

145

bors and acquaintance with the people at the drugstore and the grocery store suddenly seemed to me to be the finest things life had to offer. It would be foolhardy to look for more, and I vowed I never would wander off that course again.

I hadn't thought to worry about what Muv would do about clothes for the children. I knew she would manage. Anyhow, before the week was out Jim drove to Alford in the *Sentinel Star*'s staff car with their suitcases and toys and Jimmy's Christmas bicycle. The children were very glad to see him.

Within a month he called me from the Atlanta bus station to say he had quit the *Sentinel Star* and come to be with his family. I had a room with kitchen privileges with a widow and her daughter in a neat, pretty apartment overlooking Piedmont Park, having inherited it from another reporter, who was being transferred to our Washington bureau. I turned from the phone to ask if my husband might come there, and my landlady, a sweet, white-haired woman, said graciously, "Of course, my dear. Tell him to take a taxi."

Jim arrived and, like the children, I was very glad to see him. I hurried to cook him some breakfast and was telling him my big news. I had *two* jobs, instead of one. From 10 A.M. to 7 P.M. I worked for the *Constitution,* and then I caught the bus for Buckhead, where I worked till midnight on the weekly *Northside News.* So far I had sent the extra money to Muv for the children, but in time I would have enough for a down payment on a house—our own house. Rita was looking hard for one and had enlisted the help of several real-estate agents. It seemed perfectly possible that we'd find a place with a small down payment and monthly payments that I could manage.

Jim seemed only mildly interested. In fact, it was clear that he was thinking about something else. He walked restlessly around the small kitchen and living room and then he slumped down on the bed.

He was having chest pains.

The problem the recruiters had seen on the day after Pearl Harbor, when he tried to join the Army, the Navy, the Marines, and the Coast Guard, had increased in gravity and he was truly ill.

I called a doctor, who came and sat by his bed and listened to his heart and finally ordered him to bed for a month.

Before the month was out Rita found us a house. It was a deep-eaved, slanting-roofed white clapboard with Stone Mountain granite foundations; it was situated at the west end of Thirteeth Street, a close-to-town neighborhood of unbelievable convenience in these drive-everywhere days. The West Peachtree trackless trolley between Buckhead and downtown ran a block away, the Peachtree streetcar two blocks. Stores, restaurants, banks, the post office, a branch of the library were all three or four blocks away. A big oak tree in the tiny front yard filtered the street light, which illumined the interior like moonlight. The backyard was weed-grown but of a good size and had the biggest sweetgum tree I had ever seen. The house, the real-estate man told us, was the first one built when the street was opened up in 1914 and so soundly constructed the builder chose it for himself. His name, carved into a granite block, was half hidden by ivy at the edge of the front steps.

Without Rita I would have thought buying a house impossible—$10,500 the asking price, $1,000 down, $97.90 a month! How could I hope to do it?

Easy, said Rita. Wasn't I making $35 at the *Constitution* and $15 a week at the *Northside News*? That came to over $200 a month. Everybody knew that budgeting half your income for shelter was the tried and true, acceptable way of managing. (I didn't find out for years that the formula is one-fourth your income.)

Rita had a chunk of the down payment to lend me and I borrowed the rest from the *Constitution*. I don't remember the sale-closing ceremony but I do remember that the real-estate agent's wife brought me a pink African violet, the first I had ever owned. And the memory of moving day makes me tired even now. I had my two jobs to do but somehow I scrounged enough time to borrow an old car belonging to Bill Boring, a fellow reporter. I drove it out to Rita's basement and loaded the cheap fake maple bed with mattress and springs, which we had stored there when we left Marietta. I hauled it back to Thirteenth Street and set it up in one of the two big bedrooms, put sheets and pillows on it, and drove over to Tenth Street to the apartment by the park and got Jim.

He was weak and shaky from pain and inactivity and leaned on me to take the few steps to the car. He had not seen the house and he was too exhausted to look it over. Besides, I had forgotten to get the electricity turned on so the only light came from that blessed street light on the sidewalk. He went straight to bed and I went to return the car and look in on my two jobs.

By midnight I was home but too excited to sleep. I roamed through

147

the house, looking at the leaf shadow playing on the walls and ceilings, admiring the space—two bedrooms and a sun parlor and a sleeping porch, in addition to living room, dining room, kitchen, and breakfast room. It seemed a palace.

So restless I knew I would awaken Jim, I spread a pallet on the little screened porch off the other bedroom and lay down there. A wind sprang up in the night and I heard it in the branches of the sweetgum tree, sighing and turning and brushing the screen. The wonder of owning a house and a tree filled me with such awe, such exultation, I couldn't sleep.

Gradually, with the help of friends raiding their attics and basements and Salvation Army and Goodwill finds Rita kept turning up, we got the house habitable, if not stylish. I bought a $10 gas range with a high side oven from our state-news editor, Stiles Martin, and it worked splendidly as long as you kept the broom propped against the oven door so it wouldn't flop open. Rita found an electric refrigerator—almost impossible to come by in those postwar years—and except for the fact that it sounded like Gene Krupa on the drums and kept our next-door neighbor, Louise Garmon, awake, it functioned fine.

We had beds all around and Muv came and brought the children and their belongings and helped us get clothes ready for school, which was opening soon. Jim recovered and took over my job at the *Northside News*—with such pleasure and such competence that the publisher Matt Perkins was to write later that he was the finest newspaperman he knew and one of the funniest people, but, as Jim himself put it, he was prone to "take whiskey."

Meeting those monthly payments on the house was not the snap Rita had envisioned. I was late so often foreclosure was always imminent. I took on any job of writing that came up, doing pieces for trade papers on the opening of dairies or drugstores. I wrote torrid adventures for confession magazines. I rented out rooms. We had a Georgia Tech cheerleader who seized his megaphone and practiced in his bedroom till we thought we'd go crazy. We had a Tech freshman from Hershey, Pennsylvania, who brought us silver-bell chocolates, almost unobtainable, after Christmas holidays, but who was so homesick he ran up a $32 phone bill. Neither he nor I could pay, so we were without a phone for months. I put up beds in the dining room for Jimmy and Susan and rented out every other inch of space we could spare. Some of our tenants became enduring friends. Amelia Smith, who rented the bigger bedroom for a time, became deputy clerk of the Georgia House of Representatives and both a news source and an unfaltering friend. Ann Wood, youth editor at the paper, made a cute little bed-sitting room of the sun parlor and cheered and comforted us all when groceries dwindled and I was short on the house payment.

Once when I was stitching up a curtain for our only bathroom and worrying about the house payment, Ann remarked cheerfully, "This house is going to look good—when you lose it."

My children stuffed Ann's dates and hauled some of her cherished belongings to the sandbox, and when she decided to marry Martin O. Waldron, called Mow, a fellow reporter, we all went by bus to Birmingham to have a hand in the wedding. Mow went on to win a Pulitzer Prize for the Tampa *Tribune* and later worked for the *New York Times* until his death a few years ago. (He and I were to meet now and then on national stories, such as the James Earl Ray trial for the murder of Dr. Martin Luther King, Jr.) Ann works for Princeton University and writes books and our paths happily cross from time to time.

We were poor, of course, but not in the oppressive, spirit-killing, demeaning way some people were poor. Sometimes the lights or gas was cut off and groceries ran thin before payday, but we nearly always had tickets to the Metropolitan Opera, to all concerts, circuses, movies, and the ballet—courtesy of my job. Leslie, who had an eye for bargains, steered us to an Edgewood Avenue emporium we called "the bent-can store" because the cut-rate goods we got there nearly always came in dented cans, and sometimes the labels slipped off before we could identify and use the contents. If I had been picky about such things it would have upset me to depend on the last can in the pantry to be corned-beef hash for supper and to open up rich red cranberry sauce instead. We congratulated ourselves on having an out-of-season Christmas treat and ate the cranberry sauce.

Muv came and we took up the Municipal Market, where country people brought in beautiful cheap vegetables and what we had regarded as the "odd" parts of animals sold prodigiously. Oxtails were cheap and made good soup. Pigs' feet and the bony parts of chickens, kidneys, and livers were nourishing and far less expensive than even that old standby hamburger. Once Muv bought a rabbit and took him

149

home and marinated him overnight in a vinegar mixture. By morning he gave off a peculiarly unpleasant odor, but Muv cooked the little beast anyhow and fed it to my children's friends, who frequently hit our kitchen at mealtime.

"Freeloaders," said Muv maliciously. "It's better than they deserve."

With the help of friends, who brought their hammers and saws and their sometimes sketchy knowhow, we walled in a couple of old servants' rooms, which were open to the basement—aboveground because the slope of the lot made the house two-story in back. There was also a servants' toilet and we turned it into a full bath with contributions of plumbing fixtures from Leslie, who had opened a secondhand store on Decatur Street. I went to the bank for a loan, and we hired a little black carpenter named Johnny Hunt for a time. He was a totally dedicated workman, who went at a full gallop all the time and would tackle any project. Presently, with nights of working down there myself, papering and painting, we had a presentable apartment to offer for rent. It was called a terrace apartment and it had a neat entrance in the side yard with a small porch.

A deaf-mute couple with two children were the first applicants and I grabbed them gratefully. It seemed a godsend to have tenants beneath us who wouldn't be disturbed by the turmoil in our part of the house, and the rent was the princely sum of $65!

It turned out to be a less-felicitous arrangement than I had anticipated. The tenants decided the whole backyard was theirs, and they attempted to run my children out of it, and just as I was beginning to feel that we could breathe and meet those house payments with their princely $65 they complained to the federal housing agency regulating such things and got the price cut to $45.

At the office I was deep in the problems of a man named Floyd Woodward. The paper had had a big story about him when I first started to work there. He had been involved in the bunco racket in Atlanta back in the twenties and had killed a man. He was not arrested and brought to trial right away, and he disappeared, but not before he had written the rector of the Episcopal church where his family were long-time parishioners a shocking account of how many Atlanta police and court officials were also involved in the racket.

The state prosecutor in a Javert–*Les Misérables* turn became obsessed with the idea of finding him and bringing him back to stand trial. But he miraculously eluded capture until a postal inspector recognized him on a golf course in Monrovia, California, twenty years later. He was arrested and returned. The day he arrived in town Harold Martin boarded the train at the suburban Brookwood station to ride into town with him and interview him.

He said very little about himself and I had not been particularly interested in the story even when he was tried and convicted, until one day months later he tried to commit suicide in his jail cell. The city editor sent me down to talk to him, and I was surprised and overwhelmed with pity for the convict. He was a white-haired, blue-eyed man then in his fifties and one of the gentlest, most-courteous people I ever met. Weakened by his suicide attempt and ill, he still got to his feet when I entered his cell and greeted me in a courtly, deferential manner.

He did not want to be interviewed but he seemed to feel that objecting was pointless, perhaps a little rude to a young woman who had gone to the trouble to look him up. He let me ask the usual run of questions and answered them politely, if briefly. He had been reading a letter when I went into his cell and I asked him about it.

He smiled and picked it up and turned it in his hand thoughtfully.

"It's from my wife, Blanche," he said after a moment. "Would you care to read it?"

Of course, I'd care to read it! It wasn't every day in the week a convicted murderer's letters were available to me. What I read to "Dear Tommy" (her name for him) was the kind of letter any good woman, any loving wife and mother might have written. She had been notified that he was ill—not precisely why—and expressed regret that she couldn't have been there to move a cot into his hospital room, as they always did for one another. She sent him tender admonitions about his health and then she got to family news. Their little girl, also called Blanche, had joined the Girl Scouts and was loving the experience. They had gone to choir practice the night before and she mentioned some of the songs they had sung. A man came to give them an estimate on repairing the roof . . . the roses were doing beautifully this year . . . she had to stop and put little Blanche to bed. They loved him, they missed him . . . do write.

I think I had tears in my eyes when I handed the letter back to Mr.

151

Woodward, and he looked unspeakably sad.

"She deserves so much better than this," he said, looking at the narrow prison cell.

I asked him if I could do anything for him, get a minister or somebody to talk to him. He nodded. "I'd like that," he said. "Blanche and I are regular church members back home."

I thought about that letter all the way back to the office and for days to come. A man whose wife wrote him such simple homely things— choir practice, Girl Scouts, repairs to the roof, roses—couldn't be a criminal. My first impression of him had been that he was a good man, a gentleman. His wife's letter had confirmed it.

I went back to the jail again and again to see him, and I started digging into his case. He had shot, in self-defense he said, another gambler who was looking for him with a gun in the corridor of a downtown hotel. The coroner's jury had held it was self-defense and he was free to go. Unfortunately, he wrote a letter back to the pastor of his family's church implicating police officers and the solicitor general's staff in gambling operations. The minister made the letter public and the solicitor general angrily reopened the case and launched a nationwide search for Mr. Woodward. Naturally, Mr. Woodward acquired an alias and by the time I got interested in the case I found that the coroner's jury report was mysteriously missing. I began trying to track down the jurors. In twenty years some of them had died, some had moved away. I could only find one or two but they said it was true; they had held that Floyd Woodward shot Ed Mills in self-defense.

I called and wrote to people in the little town of Monrovia, California, and what he and Blanche had indicated about their life was also true. He had changed his name to Tommy Thomas when he left Atlanta and changed his way of living. He met Blanche on a ferryboat, they fell in love and were married, and she never knew that he had a background of gambling or that he was wanted for murder. They bought a home and adopted little Blanche and became well-liked, well-respected citizens in the community, church members, active in civic affairs. One man I talked to said, "Our town had no more valued citizen than Tommy Thomas." He had a woodworking shop in his backyard and he invited in troubled and erring kids and taught them to use the tools and to make things of value.

I had begun to think of getting him a parole, and it was necessary to talk to him often. In the peculiar hierarchy of the imprisoned, he rated very high at the jail both with the other inmates and with the jailers. He was allowed trusty-like freedom and often called me at night after I got home.

One night we had as a houseguest the wife of a friend of Jim's. Jim had accompanied the husband on a business trip and they had asked me if the wife, who had been ill, could come and stay with the children and me. I had put her to bed, but she was acting strange, turning restlessly and babbling senselessly, and I kept going in to see if she needed something or if I could somehow calm her down. The last time I went in the room she had hitched up her pajama coat and was trying to get something out of the fingers of a kid glove she had tied on a string around her waist.

Was it dope? I had heard that she was an addict. I was rocked with fear and consternation. Alcoholics I knew about. But dope addicts were an unknown quantity. I didn't know what she would do next and if it could possibly be dangerous to the children. While I stood in the hall puzzling over it the phone rang.

Mr. Woodward had a couple of things he wanted to talk to me about. And at that moment the basement door popped open and the deaf mutes came filing up with soap and towels. Their hot water was off!

I sagged weakly against the wall.

For the first time it occurred to me that my ménage might not be quite normal. A dope addict in the bedroom, deaf mutes erupting from the basement, a murderer pal on the phone . . . did other people live like that?

Mr. Woodward, the alleged murderer, was, of course, my favorite of the lot. His soft-voiced observations, his wry humor, delighted me, and, of course, I was determined to get him out of jail.

There were other stories to work on at the paper and major domestic distractions all along the way. Jim had lost the job at *Northside News*. I've forgotten why if I ever knew. He got another at the St. Petersburg *Evening Independent,* so congenial a job and so pleasant a place to live he began by urging me to pack up and come on down. I missed him and I thought about it, but not after Jimmy had gone down to spend a few weeks with him in the summer.

Jimmy came back with wondrous tales of the proximity of the beach and how daddy got off work in the early afternoon and they went swimming or fishing. Daddy, he told me solemnly, with a little-boy earnestness that broke my heart, "doesn't drink whiskey anymore, he just drinks vodka."

My brief and transient thoughts of a reunion in Florida went a-glimmering. So shortly did Jim's job in St. Petersburg.

Back home, having nothing else much to do, Jim drank. With the ingenuity and imagination of the parched and suffering drunk, he always seemed to find the money, raiding my purse of the grocery allowance, filching the money I had put aside for the mortgage payment, once even taking the check the tenants left in the mailbox and forging my name to it. Torn between guilt and remorse, and consumed by defeat and some inner pain I could not fathom, he turned abusive. Not to the children, except that he would grow lonely in the night and wake Jimmy up to talk to him and travel around the dark and deserted streets of Atlanta with him, but to me. The random slap, the brandished fist saddened and infuriated me, but I wouldn't have done anything about it, I'm afraid, except that one night, after a daylong bout with the bottle, he came at me uttering obscenities and threatening to beat me. I know now that he must have been in some unspeakable agony himself.

All I knew then was that I was standing by the fireplace and the poker was handy. I picked it up and waved it at him.

"Come one step closer," I hissed, "and I'll kill you!"

He backed away and I saw the little girls were there in the hall behind him, white-faced and trembling.

The next day I dropped by the office of the clerk of a minor criminal court I visited regularly and took out a peace warrant. That night a deputy sheriff came and got Jim and put him in jail.

Then I got in bed with all the children and shook in anguish and self-abasement. I had never put anybody in jail before. And Jim was no criminal. How could I do it?

Fortunately, before the evening was gone Mr. Woodward called me.

"You have someone down here," he said. "Don't worry, I'm looking after him. I got him a blanket and a sandwich and some cigarettes and he's asleep now. Don't worry."

Thank God for friends in jail, I thought, and went to sleep myself. The next day the judge released Jim under a bond signed by an old friend of his from his youth in Florida. Jack Fant and his wife, Elizabeth, ran a little variety store in the south part of town, and Jim had called them. They signed his bond, which assured that he would neither telephone nor appear at my house for thirty days. And they gave him a job.

He called Rita and she found him a cheap room, lent him the money to rent it, and came by the house and picked up a suitcase for him. In defiance of the court's instructions, he did call that night.

"You don't have to worry about me bothering you again," he said. "I'll never bother you again."

"Jail . . . ?" I jabbered.

"The worst thing that ever happened to me," he said and hung up.

Judge Quincy Arnold, who had placed him under the peace bond, called me into his office when I passed in the courthouse corridor the next day.

"I don't know what kind of trouble you're having," he said, "and I hope a peace bond helps. But your husband is a gentleman. I get a lot of drunks and wife beaters in here but he's a different breed. When they read the charges in the warrant you signed, all he said was that if you made that statement it was true and he was sorry. He's a gentleman."

I bowed my head in contrition. I hated being the kind of woman who would put a gentleman in jail—Mamie's son, Ervin's and Everitt's brother, my children's father. I hated myself and I grieved for Jim in his tacky little room across town with his job selling thirty-five-cent drawers and rayon underpants to poor whites and even poorer blacks in a slum neighborhood. All that lovely intelligence, the humor, the poetry, the voice lifted in song . . . wasted.

But I had made up my mind to get a divorce. I got a lawyer, a friend who wouldn't charge me, and went to court. It was "Split Day" in Superior Court and the halls and corridors teemed with women of all ages and descriptions intent on getting out of bad marriages.

There was a sort of holiday mood about it, but I wasn't happy. I believed in marriage. I believed in the marriage vows I had taken. I couldn't forgive myself for promising to stick "in sickness and in health till death do us part."

I prowled the halls in distress, and then my lawyer came out of the courtroom and told me my case would be called soon and I was to take a seat near the front of the room. Ahead of me there was a skinny little black girl named Pinky.

155

She took the witness stand and was sworn and then the questions: "Was your husband a drinking man, who got drunk frequently? Was he abusive? Did he threaten you with bodily harm?"

She kept bobbing her head and saying yes and I got up and tiptoed out of the courtroom. The questions and answers for Pinky and me were identical. There was nothing unique about my situation. It was common and tacky and graceless. I was about to be one more "Split Day" statistic. I fled the courthouse and went back to the office.

When the court-imposed thirty days were up Jim did come back home. It was Saturday night before Easter and he came bearing gifts for the children—baskets and candy he had bought at the Fants' store. He was so humble and self-effacing and diffident I couldn't believe it, and when he brought out socks he had bought for each child I thought I'd cry. They didn't fit but he had selected them with loving care—the first garments he had ever bought for them that I could remember. I held the socks in my hand and choked up when he said he had a favor to ask. Could he go to church with us the next day?

Of course, he could, I cried, of course! He worried that his one suit was so shabby that it would embarrass us, but I hurried to sponge it off and press it and to round up a shirt and a tie. I had only old, shabby clothes myself and I didn't regard it as important, not so long as the children could go with a touch of Easter splendor. Besides, wanting to go to church . . . didn't that mean a momentous change in his attitude? Didn't that mean that he was seeking, really seeking, to change?

People don't change, my friend Harry Lee had told me. That was nonsense, I told him. The basis of the Christian religion is that people can make a new start, have a rebirth, a regeneration.

Maybe . . . just maybe . . . it had happened to Jim.

Mr. Woodward's case was shaping up. I had found some of the old coroner's jury members and had assembled some of the trial jurymen, who were sympathetic to the defendant and would be glad to have the parole board undo the life sentence. The prosecutor had died but the judge made no objection to a parole. The minister I had asked to visit him after his suicide attempt was Dr. Stuart Oglesby of the old Central Presbyterian Church a few blocks from the jail. He had become Mr. Woodward's friend and counselor, taking him books and newspapers and spending part of almost every day visiting him. He would be a witness before the parole board.

Ralph McGill, our editor, had followed the case as I wrote about it and worked on it, and he agreed to emcee the show I had lined up.

I had letters from people of Monrovia saying that Mr. Woodward had led an exemplary life there and my plea was to be that he had done what the prison system could not do, rehabilitate himself after a bad youthful start as a gambler, which had led almost inevitably to that shooting.

The hearing was quick and easy; the parole was granted without a dissenting vote. Mr. McGill and I walked back to the office together, and in my excitement and triumph I felt my stockings slip their moorings and start sliding down my legs.

I pushed my notebook and my purse into Mr. McGill's hands.

"Will you be embarrassed," I asked anxiously, "if my stockings fall off?"

"No," said our editor, courteously averting his eyes and examining the sunlit skyline. "But once I was dancing with a young lady and her underpants fell off. That *did* embarrass me."

There was a day's delay in Mr. Woodward's departure, and I found out later that he and his lawyer, my old friend Lawrence Camp, formerly U.S. district attorney, had arranged it so it would happen on my time and after the *Journal*'s deadline. They had a private plane waiting at the Atlanta airport to transport him to Memphis, where he would board an airliner for California, something the *Journal* never suspected. The whispered invitation to me to meet them at the jail came half an hour before takeoff time.

I waited in the car in the prison yard with Mr. Woodward's friends, who had supplied the plane, and watched as he came out into the light fall of rain. He stood a moment, feeling the drops on his head and shoulders. He was smiling.

"You forget what it's like in *there*," he said to me, nodding toward the gray walls of old Fulton Tower.

At the Memphis airport he called Blanche in Monrovia, and when he came out of the phone booth he had a puzzled look on his face.

"She cried," he said wonderingly. "Do women always cry when they're happy?"

I nodded. I was crying, too.

Sometime later a policewoman friend, Frances Lykes, nominated me for the Pall Mall Big Story award for the Woodward case. The

157

cash prize—$500—came in handy, and later when they turned it into a television show there was another $500 emolument.

I was thrilled with the money. We needed it. But our police reporter, Keeler McCartney, echoed my sentiments when he said, "They give you all that money because they're going to embarrass you." The whole pitch toward making me out a Brenda Starr–type reporter was embarrassing. The television crew was the most confounding of all. The facts in the case did not suit them and they rearranged things to conform to their ideas of what the story should be, including such small details as picking Christ the King Catholic Church as the church of Dr. Oglesby the Presbyterian minister.

"It *looks* more like a Presbyterian church," a cameraman explained to me.

For years my children could amuse themselves by doing imitations of the little dark-haired actress who played me, wearing ankle-strap shoes and purple lipstick. (I didn't see it. I took Mary and went to the movies.) But Susan and Jimmy watched, and they loved to lean against a wall with cigarettes hanging out of their mouths, smoke curling upward (it was, after all, sponsored by a cigarette company), saying huskily, "My name is Celestine Sibley. My friends call me Sib."

Some of them did, after that.

Several years later Walt Disney invited both Atlanta papers to send two people each to Hollywood to preview the film *Song of the South,* which was made from the Uncle Remus stories written by the *Constitution's* editor Joel Chandler Harris, and which was going to be premiered in Atlanta. Paul Jones, the movie editor, and I went from the *Constitution.* Rebecca Franklin and Fred Moon represented the *Journal.* It was a gala week, with visits to all the big studios and their stars, lunch at the commissaries, an interview with Mr. Disney, who took us to his personal screening room to see the picture. We went to a Saturday-afternoon football game, were driven by limousine to Tijuana on Sunday, with a luncheon stop at the elegant old Coronado Hotel, and had dinner every night at such Hollywood spots of legend as the Coconut Grove, Chassen's, the Brown Derby.

The only free afternoon and evening we had I slipped off by myself and went to Monrovia to visit Floyd Woodward and his family. They lived in a little apartment in a new building. Blanche had a job in an office nearby, little Blanche, a dimpled teenager, was in high school, and Mr. Woodward, looking frailer and older than when he was in jail

158

in Atlanta, worked a bit in their tiny yard and played checkers with the fireman up the street.

They seemed happy and they treated me like a royal visitor. But when I left Mr. Woodward said softly, "I hope there won't be any more Big Stories about us?"

It was a question and I shook my head, knowing guiltily that I had already exploited him too much and really for personal gain. When he shook my hand in goodbye he said, "I probably won't see you again. I have cancer, it seems."

I never saw him again but I think about him often—a gentle, kind man who taught me much about the goodness and the generosity that may be found in prisons and prisoners.

As determined as I was to hang on to my job even if it meant doing hack work to the point of boredom, I have never been bored. I covered every beat in town, caught the best of the general assignments, and gradually became a regular at murder-trial coverage. There were others who could do it as well but none enjoyed a good trial as much as I did. A murder trial was to me the purest form of drama: Shakespearean tragedy played out on the small stage of a courtroom with a couple of differences. The principals were playing for keeps, often for their lives, and far from being theatrical types made up to star they were frequently sad, sick, desperate men and women, whose stories opened doors on lives I had never known and could not visualize.

Sometimes going to a country courtroom was like going back to another century. There would be a water bucket and dipper instead of drinking fountains, spittoons for all the tobacco chewers (and they were numerous), the festivity of country-come-to-town for Big Court. An entrepreneur named Dock sold spring lizards to fishermen on the Blairsville courthouse lawn in the mountains, local church ladies offered gingerbread and cider for sale, there was a spirited traffic in coonhound trading, and in the courtroom an audience pitifully, acutely vulnerable to judgment and punishment, the real commodities of the day. I saw young mothers nursing babies, and one teenage boy, who had helped his mother kill his father, sit stoically at the defense table staring vacantly at the sunlight on the scarred old table top. He had good reason to want his father dead. The man was a drunkard who abused his wife and children monstrously. But I found that out by chance. Like his mountain forebears, the young fellow could kill, if he

159

felt that he had to, but he stubbornly refused to say anything against his father. It created quite a problem for the court-appointed defense attorney.

Once I was covering a mountain trial in which an elderly man with Old Testament vengeance in mind had killed his daughter's suitor, a young wastrel who hung around the town's pool hall. The murder weapon, poetically, was a billiard cue, wielded with deadly accuracy. That trial went on for several days, and I began to notice that a regular, front-row spectator was an old lady who looked like Grant Wood's American gothic. She wore a neat cotton-print dress with a little white collar pinned by a small gold wishbone, cotton stockings and lace-up oxfords, and a rusty old straw sailor hat set primly in the middle of her head, with her thin gray hair pulled back tight and skewered in a hard little knot. She was in the same seat, early and late, and she impartially fixed stern and unloving eyes on the witnesses and court attendants, listening intently to every word that was spoken. Puritan conscience, I thought, here to see evil get its comeuppance, here to will punishment for the guilty.

A local friend slipped into the seat beside me during one morning's session and I pointed out the old lady to her.

"Carved out of hickory," I said. "Straight-laced, unbending, righteous."

My friend laughed back of her hand and whispered, "I'll tell you at recess."

The austere-looking old lady, she told me, had had a beautiful, buxom daughter years ago. She came home from cleaning one of the town's more prosperous homes and found her daughter in bed with a city official. The man, a respected deacon in the church and a devoted husband and father, by all accounts, was distraught. He leaped into his pants, jabbering out apologies.

"I'll do anything on earth that I can do to make this all right," he promised the straight-laced mother. "If money would help, I'll pay whatever you ask."

The old mother took off her prim little sailor hat and skewered it with a hatpin before she answered.

"Just tell me what you want," pleaded the cornered adulterer. "I'll pay whatever you ask."

The mother fixed him with a gimlet eye.

"How does four bits strike you?" she inquired coldly.

160

That incident convinced me that I'd make a poor juror judging people by their courtroom appearance.

Once I did encounter relentless hatred of sin in a courtroom. It was not a murder case or even a trial I meant to cover. I was in the country courthouse to cover the case of a state official charged with some road-building impropriety. Before that case was called the clerk called a misdemeanor case involving a dwarf-sized little man called Hop John.

The complainants were a couple who went out on their front porch after Sunday dinner, and most assuredly after church, for a little peaceful—and pious—relaxation. What disturbed them and brought them to court was the spectacle of Hop John and a woman identified as Mandy having sex in the old barn across the road. They reported this iniquitous behavior to the sheriff's office and the principals were summarily hauled to jail.

But they were released on bond before the day of the trial, and it appeared that Mandy was not going to make it to court. Hop John sheepishly prepared to admit to the whole shabby affair when a state trooper arrived with Mandy. He had found her drunk in a ditch by the roadside. She had recovered sufficiently to take the witness stand, but she had difficulty taking much interest in the proceedings. She was at that stage of sobering up where she felt that flies were attacking her, and she kept slapping herself in the face.

The good citizens who had complained had not expected a full complement of city-newspaper and wire-service reporters on hand to hear their testimony, and the wife was nearly as undone as Mandy when the prosecutor forced her to tell in burning detail just what she had witnessed in the barn that afternoon. Her righteous wrath came and went in waves, her hatred for the Sunday-afternoon practitioners of illicit sex was so palpable I think the judge couldn't bear to do her a favor and find the miscreants guilty. He dismissed the case.

That night, Muv, who was visiting us, asked how the trial of the state official had gone.

"Oh, it was postponed," I said. "But I did sit in on another trial. A man named Hop John and a woman named Mandy were tried for adultery in the barn."

"Oh," said Muv, surprised. "Is *that* against the law?"

The murder trials sometimes took weeks, and for assignments like that Muv would come and stay with the children or, if it was summertime, have them visit her in Alford. After years of now and then, hit-or-miss help, who might or might not come, we lucked into Bessie Galloway, a little black woman, who stuttered when she was excited, sang when she was blue, was an indifferent housecleaner and a terrible cook, but faithful to the job. She came. No longer did I have to stand on the front steps, my carfare in my hand, looking anxiously up the street for the day's caretaker of my young. Bessie might be late. She might be ill. She had terribly high blood pressure. But she would be there, scolding and laughing with the children, threatening to "board" them if they didn't mind her, singing her doleful funeral songs.

We knew her three children by reputation as well as she knew us, and we fretted with Bessie when her son was drafted and, as she put it, "sent over sea."

"Where, Bessie? Where did they send him?" we asked.

"Oh—oh—over sea," said Bessie. "Wichita."

Somebody in her family gave Bessie a trip to New York City, and she came back with dazzling reports of her ride on the subway. As close as we were, sharing our most intimate concerns, we marveled when Bessie reported that she had sat "up front with the white folks" on the New York train.

"I didn't want 'em to think I was g-g-green," she said.

I rejoiced in her daring in those pre-integration days, but the children were spellbound by the notion that anybody, even disadvantaged New Yorkers, could be confused about Bessie's color.

Money was a problem for both of us. Sometimes I had to borrow carfare from Bessie and more than once I had to co-sign a note for her at the bank. We had not had a car since our first years in Atlanta— the war years (I can't remember what happened to that vehicle!)— but Paul Jones, a friend at the office, got to talking to me one day about the ineffable joys of owning a car. Like most of us, he rode the bus or walked until he found that he could buy a car for $25 a month. It had been a great pleasure to him and he could foresee the possibility of trips and maybe even cross-the-country junkets, camping out along the roadside. In fact, he knew a man who could be persuaded to sell me a car cheap.

It wasn't exactly a giveaway, that car I bought. It cost $300—$30 a month—but everything else Paul had said about it was true. We were liberated. We could drive out in the country on picnics. We could even load up the car and travel down to Muv's for the weekend. On more than one occasion we set out without a spare tire and with only $8 to buy gas along the way, confident that Muv would insist on filling the tank at the Alford general store for the return trip. Even then we sometimes ran out on the outskirts of Atlanta and had to scrounge for nickels and dimes to put a gallon in the tank.

Jim had no hand in choosing the car—a faded-blue vintage Plymouth the children named Miss Guided for a Dick Tracy character—and he resented that. But he enjoyed driving it and he would frequently take Bessie home at the end of the day, loading up the children, teaching them sassy lyrics to old songs to spring on me when they would pick me up at the office. Bessie liked him and would occasionally shell out fifty or seventy-five cents to make up the price of a pint of Century Club for him, for, of course, his resolve not to drink crumbled pretty soon after he came back home. I was too busy or too tired to enforce my ultimatum that if he drank he moved.

But then Bessie called me from a neighbor's house one day and said Mr. Little was chasing her with the butcher knife. He was pulling out of a twenty-four-hour drunk and was in a murderous mood. I sent Bessie home and then hurried to the school and got the children.

By the time we got back to the house Jim was asleep again but I knew it would be a short nap and he could be back to butcher knives when he awoke. We had used up our friends on similar occasions, refugeeing to first one and then another, and I was pretty weary of that, too. I tiptoed into the house and called a little neighborhood hotel.

The weather was cold and our furnace was off, I lied to the desk clerk. My children and I needed asylum for the night. He had a room, and I grabbed up pajamas and school clothes for the next day and slipped out.

Mary had overheard my telephone call and she was giggling.

"You told that man our house was too cold," she said, "but it's really too hot, isn't it, mama?"

I lay awake for a long time in that snug, warm, safe hotel room, listening to the steam in the pipes and wondering what to do. Muv's old expression for having to redo any task that was incompletely or incompetently done the first time was "You've got to lick your calf over." It was plain I had to lick my calf over with Jim, throw him out again—but where? He had no job. There wasn't a dime to spare in the family coffers. I could put his suitcase on the porch and lock the doors except that we had never locked the doors. We didn't even own a key. He could return at will unless I got another peace warrant and I could never do that again.

The next day he was shaky and repentant. He remembered nothing about the knife-brandishing episode and was inclined to think it was a product of Bessie's highly cultivated taste for drama. Knife wielding was such a tacky, poor-white-trash thing to do—how could I believe he had taken it up? I believed it, but when he was sober and the children came to pick me up after work he had them all singing, "Ain't She Sweet?" and I let decision making slide.

Fortunately, a job came up for Jim on the Columbus *Ledger-Enquirer* and he was gone again. He stayed in a hotel. (Rarely could he bring himself to rent something cheaper in any town where he got a job.) So he wasn't able to contribute money at home, but the peace was worth a great deal. He often brought presents when he came home for the weekend, once a glamorous blue nightgown for me, and he had delightful stories to tell of his colleagues on the Columbus paper and their adventures at a barbecue place called The Goat. They ran a tab with The Goat and they kept him off balance by pretending to be people they weren't. Jim's favorite gambit was that he was Roy Chapman Andrews and he just got in from the Gobi Desert. The Goat may not have believed but he gave credit, which was the whole point of the charade.

The Atlanta *Constitution* had merged with the *Journal,* and we all feared the worst. Newspaper mergers usually resulted in wholesale firings. I had never felt vulnerable in that department. I worked very hard and I knew I was low-paid. While Josh Skinner, who sent me the warming "Yes! Yes! Yes!" telegram when I appealed for a job from the Florida fish camp, was managing editor, he had hired as a part-time reporter a beautiful, talented woman, a few years older than I was, at a salary nearly twice as much as mine.

"Why?" I asked. "Why does she make more than I do?"

"She demanded it," he said simply.

"I demand it!" I cried.

He gave me a little raise but I don't think he loved me anymore, certainly not after a bunch of us got interested in the formation of a chapter of the CIO Newspaper Guild. We had not been particularly interested in the Guild but had gone to the apartment of Jim Furniss, then our labor reporter, to have coffee and sweet rolls on Sunday morning and to hear a man from the union talk.

What the Guild had to offer didn't really stir us. We went back to work without committing ourselves to anything. Nor did the Guild representative ask us to. But within a few days the managing editor asked the same group to meet with him. He and our publisher were clearly alarmed at our dalliance with the union, and he began by promising us raises all around. The more he talked the more we wondered if the Guild wasn't a very good thing indeed, and within a few weeks we had launched a lively push to organize. An old gentleman named Wellington Wright, a bona-fide eccentric who had two shirts to his name, a tatty old suit, and a battered, sweat-stained hat, but who had graduated from Harvard, studied at the Sorbonne, worked for the old New York *World,* and served the New York *Herald Tribune* as its Paris correspondent, started a counter campaign. He was for a company union, which would be called the Constitution Editorial Associates.

Despite his seedy appearance, Wellington had class. He began nearly every conversation by mentioning his distinguished alma mater, the New York *World.* "I recall at the *World,"* he would begin. Somehow it had a cosmic ring.

His younger brother, Dupont (a former *Times* man in London), was an elegant-looking gentleman, who wore pince-nez on a black ribbon and covered the courthouse for us. (I subbed for him on occasion and really adored him and his wife, Edith.) He was notable to the staff because he left for a time during the war to work for the Miami *Herald.* And when, like me, he wired for his job back at the *Constitution* he added that Miami was "decadent, rococo and enervating." With a vocabulary like that, we marveled, the Wright brothers were not to be taken lightly.

So in time the National Labor Relations Board held an election and the Wrights' company union won by two votes. Those of us on the Guild side who were not fired joined up. Five people of the original eight found employment elsewhere, Jim Furniss at the Citizens and Southern Bank, where he advanced rapidly to the post of vice-president. But I knew I was not pleasing in Skinner's sight, and at the suggestion of the city editor, Lee Rogers, I made myself scarce around the office. Whatever stories I was covering I could write at the courthouse or the capitol or the police pressrooms, and Lee

165

would dispatch a boy to pick up my copy.

"Just stay out of sight awhile," Lee counseled.

Skinner himself left us for the Miami paper and Lee advanced to managing editor, so I was able to reappear in the office. I wasn't paid any better but my chances of moonlighting had improved. Almost every court or police story I covered was of interest to *True Confessions* magazine. I ghosted grubby first-person adventures of dope addicts, strippers, would-be suicides, and one notable little mountain girl who had sold her unborn baby for $300. Unfortunately, when I tried for the slicks, my freelance piece attracted the attention of the brass and I was called on the carpet.

It was called "Confessions of a Spendthrift" and it ran in the *American Magazine,* the second-to-last issue of that publication before it expired. My effort was to be breezy and amusing about my poverty but it did not amuse my superiors.

"You're putting up a po' mouth," Jack Tarver told me. "People think we are not paying you."

They weren't paying me enough but who was I to argue with three hungry children at home? I promised to be less public with my poverty and went on writing confession stories.

Then the merger came. If we survived, we speculated, we might make more money. *Journal* staffers were said to be far better paid than we were. One young woman with whom I covered the Anjette Lyles arsenic-poisoning trials in Macon made so much in overtime she was wearing a new coat the next time I saw her. I had put in an equal amount of overtime but had not been paid for it. I had a tacit understanding at the *Constitution* that I would work whenever needed, day or night, but if I had a sick child I would take off. It wasn't a profitable arrangement for me because my children's illnesses in no way came out even with the long hours I spent in courtrooms and covering floods and tornadoes, drownings and fires.

But the new regime had help for me. George Biggers, a former *Journal* advertising man, who had become publisher of both papers, called me in to discuss my column. He had not known that I did it with one hand while covering news stories with the other, and that I was paid nothing extra for it. He was willing to pay me well but it involved even more work. The motion-picture business was in the first stages of strangulation by television, and there was hope that it could be revived by advertising. To lend credibility to a new movie advertising campaign I was to go to Hollywood and write about the new pictures that were being made.

My pieces would run in the Sunday magazine and I would be paid $100 for each one!

It was a fabulous assignment and I couldn't believe that I would make so much money. I loved trips to Hollywood and the people I met there. When one of the big studios offered me a job in its publicity department I was tempted—for a little while.

It was more money than I knew existed and although I couldn't imagine a life's work devoted to writing pretty pieces about the movie stars, I certainly would have been privileged to work with many of the publicists. Edward Lawrence at MGM and his wife, Helen, took me under their wing when they heard that I was from Atlanta and that I had even had a brief acquaintance with a colorful old *Journal* sportswriter named O. B. Keeler. O. B. and Eddie met when Eddie was a sportswriter too and they were both covering the exploits of the famous Atlanta golf grandslammer, Bobby Jones. Eddie knew then that he had tuberculosis but he couldn't afford a session in a sanitarium, and he kept working and hoping it would go away—until he met O. B. Somehow he confided in O. B.—a lot of people did—and the old gentleman spoke to Bobby Jones. The next thing Eddie knew, the world's most famous golfer was playing a benefit golf match—the beneficiary, Eddie! He was able to check into a desert sanitarium, where he recovered and met Helen, another patient, and fell in love and was married.

The Lawrences were not only good friends to me but later, when they learned that my daughter Mary had followed her trumpet-playing husband to Hollywood and was living on peanut butter and bread in a sleazy motel, they became her friends, getting her and her husband jobs and a decent place to stay, lending Mary clothes and seeing them through several emergencies.

I loved the Lawrences and their opposite numbers at other studios, including Disney's Joe Reddy, who brought his wife to Atlanta to see us when they were en route to her old home in Virginia on vacation trips. I developed a crush on John Campbell at 20th Century–Fox—an ex-Marine hero, the son of the famous old Los Angeles *Herald-Examiner* editor Jack Campbell, and himself a reporter of distinction until he took up with the movies.

But I couldn't take the publicity job even at the to-me-staggering salary.

"I love California," I said in declining the job, "but I couldn't move out here. It's *so far* from everything!"

The friendly folks at the studios already thought I was quaint. Some of them called me Slow-Talk Sibley. And they laughed and laughed at the notion that California was remote from all the world that counted. But it was to me. I yearned after the *New York Times,* but when a friend at the *Times* came to see me one night with a job prospect I couldn't bring myself to investigate it. I held the *Times* in reverence, as most newspaper reporters do, and I spent my teenage planning to live in Greenwich Village and lunch at the Algonquin, as the literati of that day were believed to do. But when the chance came I looked at the branches of my sweetgum tree against the window panes, listened to the ebb and flow of traffic on Peachtree and West Peachtree streets and thought about how my children would howl at again being uprooted after those years of following Jim from job to job. So I stayed put.

Pap was ill, very ill. He had long had difficulty breathing, which we attributed to cigarettes and now know was emphysema. He had insisted on staying on at the mill in Creola, ostensibly to keep an eye on the Hatter property, after his Uncle Lyles's death, but it made sense for him to be there to look after his own interests. Uncle Lyles, as he had promised when he came back from service in World War II, had left Pap the bulk of an estate valued at a little less than a million dollars. Of course, sisters of the dead man, who had been left out of their father's will in Lyles's favor, and their children and grandchildren came forward to challenge the will. And, while the contest was pending, Pap stayed on in makeshift quarters he had set up in the nearest house to the old commissary and mill. The commissary was gone, the mill was silent but there was still a lot of property, including hundreds of acres of pineland. Pap hired a caretaker to look after the property but remained there himself except for weekend visits he made by bus to Alford to spend time with Muv.

He had a car, but he was terribly weak and liked the bus because he could sleep all the way on the daylong trip. Once he arrived in Alford, he began sleeping in earnest, and Muv, bursting with energy herself, was torn between thinking he was lazy and worrying that he was sick.

168

One Christmas he was not up to the trip to Alford, so I borrowed $65 from Rita and took the children to see him a few days after Christmas. Although he was only a little over fifty years old, he seemed much older and somehow smaller. His handsome face had shrunk because he had had some gum problem necessitating having all his beautiful white teeth pulled. He lacked the energy to get new ones. He sat in the cluttered half-office, half-house, by the heater, while the children and I prowled around the pond and went up to our old house, occupied by a black family after Muv left but now standing vacant. The big dictionary they had bought to help me at school and to help themselves with their slogans and titles was on the floor in a closet, and a primitive oil painting of a three-masted schooner, given to Pap by a German sea captain, still hung over the mantel in the living room.

Muv had never liked the picture or the artist, who had been married to a friend of hers and had deserted her just before America entered World War II. We saw a man who closely resembled him in a newsreel account of a submarine crew arrested in New Orleans, but we were never sure the pictured man was the handsome, blue-eyed, white-haired man we knew who painted ship pictures and, even worse, many stags at bay in mountain streams.

Nevertheless, I liked the picture and asked Pap if I could take it and the dictionary back to Atlanta with me. He was glad to have them find a home and pleased that the children liked them. There was an old rowboat tied to the bank, where I used to tie mine, and the children shoved off in it and paddled out into the pond. There were goats grazing along the creek banks and they begged corn to feed them.

Pap worried that the children might fall overboard or get butted by the biggest billy goat, but I felt absolutely carefree for the first time in years. I sat and rocked and talked to him and assured him that no harm could befall children in that place. It was magic.

"You loved it, didn't you?" he asked, pleased. But mostly I loved him for giving it to me.

Not long after that Muv and her cousin Sister, Aunt Babe's older daughter, came to Atlanta for one of their visits. They always enlivened things at our house, and we were prepared for all kinds of jolly charades by the ladies. But they were surprisingly quiet on arriving, and afterward until the children had had their supper and had settled down for the evening. Then Muv motioned me to follow her to the backyard.

"You'll never believe this," she said. "I'm up here to get a divorce."

"From Pap?" I cried, aghast. "You can't do that!"

"He wants me to," she said. "He sent me to get you to help me."

"Muv . . . he can't!" I said. "He loves us. He doesn't believe in divorce."

It was the old assurance she had given me years before when I worried that he would throw us out if he knew about Henry Colley.

"Well, what he says is . . ." Muv began, and she told me. His sister, Lillian, had found out that Muv had never been properly divorced from Henry Colley, and she planned to use the fact to keep us from inheriting anything from the Hatter estate. If Pap lived until it was settled—and he had turned down his relatives' offer to withdraw his claim in exchange for $10,000—we would be all right. But he did not think he was going to live, and he wanted to be sure Muv had a legal right to his share. His plan, naïve, we learned later, was for Muv to get a divorce from Henry Colley as quickly as possible, and she and Pap would have another marriage ceremony—a legal one.

The next day I met her and Sister during my lunch hour to talk to a lawyer friend, the one who was prepared to represent me in the divorce I didn't get. I told him the situation and he assured me that after all the years they had been together as husband and wife they had a common-law marriage, which was as legal as anything, although it had a vaguely illicit, thoroughly distasteful sound to Muv. She didn't need to press for a divorce, he assured her, but she wasn't sure and wanted to think about it overnight.

That night Pap's brother Clarence called from Mobile. Pap was back in the hospital and not expected to live. We had better come right away.

For once in lives enured to bus travel we tried for airplane reservations and then for accommodations on a train. Planes weren't flying because of heavy fog. The train schedule wouldn't get us to Mobile as fast as the bus. We left the children with Sister and Bessie and boarded a Greyhound for an all-night trip.

The bus was slower in those days and made many stops, and once at some little town in Alabama we got off and walked up and down in front of a closed country store, waiting for the driver to pick up or deliver freight. The cold air felt good after the close, smoky climate

170

inside the bus, but Muv seemed quiet and preoccupied.

"If he should die before we get there," I asked her, "do you think you would know it?"

"I think I would," Muv said.

"Can you bear it?"

She sighed. "Yes, I can bear it. There's only one thing you can't get over and that's the death of a child. Death is natural for a grown person who has had a life and is bad sick. But for a baby . . ."

I knew what she was thinking. All those years she had remembered and grieved for the little baby she lost on East Bay. She had not become reconciled to that unlived life.

When we reached Mobile I called Pap's mother from the bus station. He had died. I turned to Muv and she nodded. She was calm and quiet as we walked up Government Street toward the funeral home, and then we met Coot, our old black friend from the quarters. She and her husband, Po' Jack, Pap's lifelong friend, had been waiting at the hospital and had gotten the word.

She opened her arms to us, and Muv and I crumpled against that warm, loving, substantial body. For the first time we cried.

Jim arrived by the next bus from Columbus, and he and I stayed with Mamie. Muv went home with her friend the German sea captain's deserted wife. The funeral, already arranged for by Mother Dear, was traumatic for me, first a wake, then a service at the funeral home, then a service at the ugly little concrete-block church that had been built beside the Creola cemetery since I had been there last.

Pap had been proud to be a Mason and had worn his little pin whenever he put on his Sunday suit. But I had never known him to go to a meeting, and the members of the lodge Mother Dear had requisitioned to officiate at his funeral were all strangers. I watched and grieved that it couldn't be simpler—a graveside service with Coot and Po' Jack and his close and well-loved friends from the quarters singing a spiritual. When I said something about it Muv shook her head. "Let her have it the way she wants it," she said, looking at Mother Dear. Ervin, Jim's brother, drove us to the funeral and then back to Mamie's house for the night. He had long been the member of Mamie's family who arranged for funerals and comforted the bereaved, and it was a solace to me to have him standing by. But I worried that Jim wanted to go out to a night spot we had frequented before we were married and drink beer and I also worried that Muv

171

was so poised and steady, so gracious to people who spoke to us, dry-eyed and smiling.

Ervin from his experience in funerals—and all Mamie's friends made him promise to take charge of theirs—told me the visit to the beer joint was natural and all right. After-the-funeral tension is released in many ways. Jim and I could have a beer and listen to music; Muv would do it another way.

The next day on the bus to Atlanta we understood what he meant. Muv started talking and laughing, remembering times past, dredging up the details of old funerals in the country when she was a child. Jim accompanied us as far as Columbus, and he and I looked at one another in confusion and distress. She was babbling. She would not shut up. Hysteria was foreign to Muv's nature.

When we got to Atlanta she broke down and cried in anguish so painful and unremitting I finally called a doctor friend, who came and gave her a sedative and put her to bed.

The fight over Uncle Lyles's estate must have picked up tempo after Pap's death, for he had been the principal beneficiary. We never knew how it came out because Muv wasn't interested. Jim talked to her long and patiently about making a claim for her widow's share, but she was so embarrassed by the common-law status she didn't want to enter the fray. We finally were persuaded by Jim to consult his family's lifelong friend and lawyer, a conservative, old-fashioned expert in maritime law, Mr. Palmer Pillians. He seemed to understand her reluctance to be a part of the contest.

"But you," he said to me, "you have a right, I think. His daughter."

Muv and I shook our heads. I was his daughter, all right, but not legally. He would have adopted me but Henry Colley wouldn't agree to it. He relinquished custody. He agreed to having my name changed. But he wouldn't consent to the formality that would have made me Pap's heir.

Muv was philosophical about it.

"We don't have any right to that Hatter money," she said. "We didn't earn it. Besides, it has poisoned everybody who has touched it. Look how that family fought and hated each other all these years. We don't want their money."

Not long after the merger of the two Atlanta papers, the managing editor of the *Journal*, W. S. Kirkpatrick, called to ask me if Jim would be interested in coming to work there on the copy desk. It was possible, Mr. Kirkpatrick said, because the two papers were no longer such fierce competitors. (He didn't mention nepotism, which is used as an excuse for not hiring two members of the same family nowadays, when an excuse is wanted.) Jim couldn't wait to pack his suitcase, give up his hotel room, and move back to Thirteenth Street. As usual, we were glad to see him—for a time.

For one thing, we thought we had found a remedy for his alcoholism. I had been writing some stories about one of Mr. McGill's pet organizations, Alcoholics Anonymous, and I thought it had the cure to Jim's illness. Jim's brother Ervin, who later fulfilled a lifelong desire and became an Episcopal clergyman, was working in construction in Kingsport, Tennessee, at the time and he had learned about A.A.

He began regular weekend trips to Atlanta to escort Jim personally to A.A. meetings. I had had no luck at getting him to go, but with Ervin there in the *Journal* newsroom waiting for him to get off at night, Jim didn't know how to refuse.

He knew how to evade commitment, however. He later explained it to me. Along about 4 P.M. when he was able to take a break from work, he would hurry down to the liquor store, buy a bottle of Century Club, and tuck it in the pocket of an old coat he kept in the locker. When Ervin arrived a little later he was glad to see him and even glad to begin an evening of A.A. activity, listening to the talks of recovering alcoholics, sharing sandwiches and coffee and experiences with them. He really enjoyed the sociability, he said, and was surprised that most of the A.A.s were smart, literate, amusing people.

When the meeting was over and they came to the house, Ervin, weary from his day's labor and the long drive down from Tennessee, would seek his bed. Jim would seek his coat pocket.

He could stand Ervin's brotherly ministrations and the interminable A.A. evening as long as he was secure in the knowledge that he had a bottle waiting for him, he explained.

I fully understood—or said I did—but the truth was that I found I could no longer stomach having a drunk around the house, even if he pulled himself together and managed to get to work the next day. Finally, in a reasonable, non-angry talk I convinced him that he should move to other quarters. He settled, of course, on a downtown hotel a few blocks from the paper.

When it became too expensive for him—and it was one of the

second- or third-class hostelries in town—he picked a cheaper, fourth- or fifth-class hotel with a grand name across the street. He reported to me with pleasant irony that he had packed his bags up and called a bellboy and said grandly, "Boy, take my bags to the Ritz!"

The Ritz was a tired, dejected little place, which catered to tired, down-on-their-luck people. The children visited Jim there once or twice and Jimmy reported to me that daddy had worked out a window-sill arrangement in the unair-conditioned room. He could buy food (he was partial to deviled crabs) and leave it on the sill with the window open enough to keep it cool.

"Isn't daddy handy?" Jimmy asked admiringly.

I warned the children against eating anything stored on the windowsill, particularly deviled crabs.

"They can kill you," I warned.

Something else killed Jim.

One night I was finishing up late in the capitol press room and the office called me. Jim had collapsed on the street, not far from the Ritz. Grady Hospital had sent its ambulance but it was assumed that he had a private physician who should be called.

I called our family physician, Dr. Bill Crowe, and he went and moved Jim to a private hospital, where it was determined that he had a brain tumor.

A couple of weeks later, after the inevitable tests, they scheduled a brain operation. Ervin came and we talked to his mother and sister but there was no chance they could make the trip to Atlanta. Mamie was old and ill, and Everitt, who lived with her and looked after her, could not leave her side.

As it happened, one of my twice-a-year trips to Hollywood was set for the same time. I appealed to Ervin. Should I go or should I stand by during Jim's operation? He said he would stay in Atlanta and sit out the operation and I was to do what I felt I should. I talked to my boss at the paper, Bill Fields, who had succeeded Lee Rogers as managing editor.

"You do what you think best," he said. "How have you arranged things in California?"

I had airline and hotel reservations and interviews and studio visits set up for every day for the coming two weeks, but they could, of course, be postponed.

"Sibley, if you want to postpone the trip, you can," Fields said.

"But I think you ought to remember, you've had to work and take care of your children all their lives. And you still have to. You may want to go on with the job."

In the end I did. The children and I went by the hospital and took Jim toilet articles and pajamas, and Mary made me stop outside and buy him some flowers.

"Mama, he hasn't got a flower in his room," she said in some distress.

I arrived in Hollywood on Sunday night and Jim's operation was set for Tuesday morning. I spent Monday calling and rescheduling appointments and Tuesday sitting by the telephone waiting for word on the operation.

By mid-afternoon it was over and a success, everybody told me. Ervin called, Fields called, our doctor, Bill, called and he put the surgeon, Dr. Mabon, on the phone to give me the details. I went to bed, exhausted and relieved, and cried myself to sleep.

Some time ago the love I had had for Jim had turned to pity. I had sat in a coffeeshop across the street from the paper and watched him come out of the building and walk toward the Ritz, and the love that used to well up in me when I saw his tall frame, his beautiful dark head, his green eyes, wasn't there. He simply looked lonely and shabby and enormously pitiful to me.

Now he was helpless and I was three thousand miles away, but if I had been there I couldn't have done anything for him. I wasn't sure that those who had, had accomplished much. For, when he was out of the hospital and then a nursing home and finally able to show up at the paper, they didn't want him.

He had suffered brain damage, they told me. I didn't believe it and took him to a psychiatrist, who said he had suffered some damage but was making a comeback as he grew in strength and would be able to take on the mental tasks he had once done so well.

Jack Tarver at the paper said he would help him get a job running an elevator.

I was hurt and outraged and did not tell Jim. Instead, I suggested that we look for an interim job in the north Georgia mountains, helping out with cabin and boat rentals at a fishing camp. It would be wholesome outdoor work, not particularly demanding, and Jim would have a chance to spend some time fishing, which he enjoyed more than anything else.

He agreed to it, and to prove that he was capable he came to the house one day and tried to cut the grass. But the effort was too much for him. He went to visit Ervin and Lil for a couple of weeks, and then he went and spent a few days with his mother and sister, and finally he came back and checked in at the YMCA.

The night manager called me as I was leaving the office one evening. Jim was having hallucinations, he said. He had pushed all the furniture up against the door to his room and he was talking wildly and incoherently about somebody being "after" him.

I jumped in a taxi and went to the Y, and with the help of the manager I persuaded Jim to come out and go home with me. Then he was as docile as a child and clung to my hand as I led him out to the taxi.

The little girls were in Alford with Muv, and Jimmy, then fourteen years old, was keeping house by himself. (No Bessie.) He took over the care of his father, fixing lunch for him and helping him to the bathroom and once walking him two blocks down the street to the barbershop, where they had both got their haircuts for years.

That night I noticed that Jim had not got a haircut, and I asked Jimmy why not.

His freckled face went taut with pain and bewilderment. He had held his father's hand and guided him into the barbershop, where Jim went into a frenzy of fear and anxiety. The barbers, Jim insisted, were out to get him. They would kill him.

That night I sat by Jim's bed and tried to puzzle out the strange mental state that had him in its grip. The doctors had not told me to expect anything like that. He spoke calmly for a while and seemed on the edge of sleep, when he heard our next-door neighbor clipping the hedge between our yards.

He sat up in bed, his eyes wild with fear. "They" were after him, he cried. They were saying terrible things about him. They wanted to kill him.

I didn't know what he was going through, if he was insane, or if he was in the throes of some temporary trauma that would abate as time passed. I worried most of all about Jimmy's safety. My friend Margaret Bridges, to whom I confided my worries, arrived the next morning to spend the day with Jim.

She got a book and got on the twin bed opposite the one he was occupying in the girl's room and settled down to talk to him if and when he was ready. He was ready. He talked the whole day through, Margaret said. He would doze a bit and awaken to pour out to her some story of his own wrongdoing, his guilt. He went back into his childhood and spoke of mistreating his sister. He told of every misdeed, every iniquity in his entire life. He couldn't seem to stop talking, and Margaret said at the end of the day that it was like seeing a soul go down into hell.

He was asleep when I got home, and since the next day was Sunday I could stay with him and observe his condition. He was remarkably peaceful and quiet. He seemed somehow purged, purified. During the afternoon Ervin called to say he and Everitt had talked it over and they thought a nursing home in Mobile might be the place for Jim. The beautiful old Government Street mansion of one of his childhood friends had been turned into such a place, and it was in walking distance of his mother and sister's apartment. It might be a better place than our house until he had safely recovered.

Jim was in my bed and I lay down beside him and told him about the nursing home. Would he go?

"Do you want me to?" he asked.

Only if he wanted to, I said. I would go with him and we'd both look it over, and if he didn't like it he could come back home.

"Because I've got my life savings in this house," he said, making an unexpected joke. We both laughed and clasped hands and lay quietly a long time.

Finally he said, "I'll go—but can I come home for Christmas?"

Any time he wanted to, I said. It was his home; we would be his family forever.

Looking back, I don't know how I had arrived at that decision. But it was true. I felt love and pity and responsibility. I would never push him out again.

The next day a temporary maid I had hired for day work after we had to give up Bessie called me at the office. Mr. Little had spent a long time soaking in the bath, she said, and when he got out he was very red and very quiet. He had not spoken since. But he was not asleep. She wondered, she thought he might be unconscious.

Once again I ran out into the street and flagged a taxi. A summer rainstorm was raging, and I was drenched but didn't notice it for hours afterward. Bill Crowe got to the house minutes after I did and called an ambulance.

177

Jim had had a stroke.

I followed him into the ambulance and walked along beside the stretcher, holding his hand as they carried him into the hospital. As the big doors swung shut after us he squeezed my hand. That was the last communication I had from him.

Ervin came and we sat together in Jim's hospital room night and day for more than a week.

He died without regaining consciousness. He was forty-five years old.

As was family custom, Ervin planned the funeral. He and Lil, their children, and Jimmy and I would drive down to Mobile. I called Muv and asked her to keep the little girls. That was Ervin's idea and Muv's too. They saw no reason to let children go to a funeral.

Since that day I've known that we were wrong. They should have been there. For one thing they could not quite believe he was dead, and Muv would permit no grieving. When they would have cried, she stopped them short.

"For goodness' sake," she said impatiently, "he's better off dead and so are you all."

Mamie was unable to leave her bed to go to the funeral. I sat beside her a long time, thinking to talk to her, but she spoke only once.

"My boy's gone," she said, and that was all.

Later Miss Donnie, "the newcomer" in Mamie's "crowd," made a point of seeing me at the funeral home and telling me that Mamie was terribly disappointed in me and hurt that I would go off to Hollywood to have a good time when Jim was undergoing such a serious operation.

The little girls came home from Alford, not certain what had happened and still denied their right to mourn. The youngest, Mary, nine years old and thrilled with a secondhand bicycle Jim had sent to Alford for her birthday, was the most disturbed. She interrupted a tantrum she was having about something else one day to blurt out her fury and her frustration to me.

"You killed my daddy!" she screamed.

She's grown now with children and a grandchild of her own, and she has apologized many times for that childish outburst. But I don't know. Who knows who kills whom in this life?

Chapter Seven

Shortly after Jim's death Margaret Long, the Macon newspaper-woman and novelist (*Louisville Saturday* and *Affair of the Heart*) came up to Atlanta to job hunt. We became friends, she got a job on the staff of our Sunday magazine, and for a time she and her daughters, Margaret, called Sissy, and Catherine, called Bunny, stayed with us.

They found an apartment in the neighborhood and thereafter we were family-close, in and out of one another's houses almost daily, sharing troubles and such triumphs as came our way. Maggie's father had been editor of the Macon *Telegraph,* and she had grown up in the newspaper business, marrying at an early age a fellow reporter named Howard Leonard.

By the time I knew them they were divorced but had remained friendly. Howard's mother was often a welcome guest in the apartment of Maggie and the girls. I had met Howard before I met his ex-wife and daughters. Our paper had hired a man said to be so brilliant, so accomplished, he would take the staff in hand and guide our stumbling steps to journalistic stardom. We heard so much about this paragon before he came that Joe Davis, our incorrigible copy-desk chief, started calling him, sight unseen, "White Hope."

He arrived one week and was gone the next. He had called in sick and, with a heart full of goodwill and compassion, our bosses had gone out to see him, finding him, as they said, falling-down, knee-walking drunk. "White Hope" did not return.

When Maggie heard about it, she nodded sadly. That was why, she murmured, that she was a divorcee.

179

We used to sit over coffee in my kitchen and wonder if there were any men in the world who didn't value strong drink above wives and children, above house payments and school clothes. Our children wondered, too. When a man friend stopped in for a visit or invited one of us out to dinner our broods would look him over carefully, appraisingly, calculatingly.

"Can we marry him, mama?" my Mary asked of one attractive but by no means romantically inclined gentleman.

"Ah, no," I said. "We have our house and he has his house and he wouldn't want to live with us."

"Well," she said reasonably, "he could just drop by and leave off a check."

One day, probably mostly in fun but with an undercurrent of seriousness, our four daughters really took Maggie and me to task for our failure to bestir ourselves and get them new fathers. Other girls had fathers, they pointed out. What was wrong with the two of us, still in our thirties, that we couldn't make it in the marriage mart?

We laughed but we were a trifle dismayed. Maggie, I think, would have liked to be married again. So recently freed by Jim's death from a great deal of agony, I wasn't interested in matrimony. I liked men. I had worked with them all my life. I had a father, step, who embodied all the virtues of gentleness, patience, kindness, and generosity. I liked the way men looked and sounded. I admired their minds, delighted in their humor. But I would see them on the street or coming into our office, their hair damply combed, their shoes hopefully buffed—Willy Loman's shoeshine-and-a-smile armor against an unfriendly world—and my heart would go out to them. They had "back-home" and all that entails on their resolutely squared shoulders. Of course I did, too, but to me men seemed more vulnerable than women, maybe not as tough and mean, certainly lacking that "vein of iron" Ellen Glasgow said resides in the southern woman's heart and spirit. I *liked* them but I didn't want one for keeps. I wanted, I confided to Maggie, not realizing how it sounded, "just a nice gentleman to play with."

Maggie, having a more ribald sense of humor than I had, whooped delightedly and never let me forget it. Later, when we attempted to collaborate on a novel about our adventures, never finished, never published, she insisted on that as the curtain line: "I just want a nice gentleman to play with."

180

Meanwhile, Mary, the youngest of our children, brooded on the get-a-father harangue they had visited on us and put the situation back in the only frame of reference she knew.

"Mama," she said in her gruff, little-girl voice. "It's all right if you don't get us a new father." And then, deprecatingly, "It would just be another mouth to feed!"

We had enough mouths to feed, it was true.

For several years John Cook, a young man in our business office, was often on duty when, in a desperate rush to interview some celebrity, I would rush by and ask for a salary advance of $2 to buy a pair of stockings, get lunch money to my children, or pick up a prescription at the drugstore. A lot of us were in such straits, so it wasn't particularly embarrassing to me, but John worried about me. He was an accountant by training, financially comfortable, and it bothered him a bit to see a hardworking mother of children living so precariously.

"Oh, I make enough to live on, I guess," I said lightly. "I just don't seem to know how to manage."

It could be learned, John told me, and supposing that he could show me the intricacies of this mysterious matter in a few minutes I pleaded with him to come out to the house, look over my income and outgo, and reveal to me the strange and wonderful technique for being solvent. He came one Sunday afternoon during one of the periods when Jim was at home and drinking and we were trying to housebreak a new puppy. The house was in an uproar, but John was game. He sat down at the dining-room table with the whole sorry mess of bills, paid and unpaid, past due and threatening.

When he looked up and put his pen back in his pocket I knew he had not hit upon any magic solution. It was going to take time and discipline and some skinny living.

"Show me how!" I pleaded. "Take over, please! I'll pay you whatever you ask!"

John smiled. "You can't afford to pay me," he said. "I'll do it because it's such a challenge."

There followed several years of rigorous budgeting. The first thing John did was to take my checkbook away from me and put me on a $25-a-week allowance, which, with the exception of Bessie's salary, had to cover all household and personal expenses, children's school

181

needs, even church and charitable contributions. I put my salary check in the bank and the bills in an old tin deed box on a chest of drawers in the living room. Once a month John picked them up and somehow made what was in the bank cover what was in the tin box. Gone were the days when the cut-off men from the electric and gas companies hovered over our threshold. He even paid so promptly that we got the discount for early payment—unheard of in our household.

It wasn't always easy. Often I ran out of carfare and lunch money between paydays and had to walk to and from the office, but it was only a three-mile hike and rather enjoyable in good weather. I found those heavy thirty-five cent lunches I had been enjoying with some of my co-workers were not at all essential. An apple or an orange from home served me well.

A bachelor, just then contemplating marriage, Mr. Cook wasn't always realistic about children's needs. When I asked for something extra to outfit them for school, he magnanimously told me to keep an additional $30 out of my paycheck. I laughed hollowly, barely squeezing out a pair of shoes all around, but I didn't protest. I was too afraid he would quit us and that was unthinkable. I had grown used to not hurting with anxiety. We didn't give up an occasional splurge, and when the need was imperative I found Mr. Cook always came through. Braces for Susan's teeth threatened to be a horrendous expense, but John Cook insisted that I go and talk frankly with the orthodontist and see if I couldn't pay $10 a month. I did and it worked.

He was sympathetic to cultural needs. The way he was reared, youngsters received music and dancing lessons, and he wanted mine to have them, but only if I could arrange moderate monthly payments. Surprisingly, I could. The girls went to Girl Scout camp and Jimmy, given a scholarship to Fork Union, the Virginia military school, received $200 worth of catchup dental care, required before admission, and was outfitted with the splendid, expensive gray uniforms needed. Even the railroad fare to Richmond would have been an insurmountable obstacle to me before John Cook.

Astonishingly—and I know it would have pleased him immeasurably—Jim's death brought us unexpected windfalls. Each child received a small monthly Social Security check, and there was about $3,000 left from the newspaper's insurance policy on him after his hospital and funeral expenses were paid. At the time the hospital bills were due I was able to borrow money from Jim's sister, Everitt, and I signed my rights to his insurance over to her. When she had deducted for his bill and funeral expenses she sent me the remainder, with a suggestion that I "salt it away" for the children's education.

Even John Cook laughed at that.

The children's education, as well as their daily bread, had always been my concern and mine alone. I was indignant that she would think I needed to be told to look after them. My friends, who of course heard all about it, promptly started planning a joyful caper in which I would borrow a friend's Rolls-Royce, press him into service as a chauffeur, deck myself out à la Auntie Mame, and turn up at my sister-in-law's door and say, "See, this is what I did with your brother's insurance money!"

I thought it was a delicious idea, but, of course, it died a-borning. Everitt wouldn't have thought it funny. In fact, she probably would have been hurt, and she had certainly been good to rally when we needed her.

The way John was able to spread that sum of money, not a stupendous inheritance by some standards but the most we had ever seen, was little short of miraculous. He invested most of it in AT&T stock for the children's education, and out of the rest managed to eke out a new car and a new stove, the first of either we had ever had. Our stove was still the one we had bought for $10 and it still required a broom handle to prop the oven door closed. Our old car Miss Guided, which always smelled like rotten eggs when it warmed up, had long since fallen by the wayside.

Looking back, I marvel at how much trouble John went to in his effort to get me the best bargain in a car. We traveled to a little town thirty or forty miles east of Atlanta, where a dealer was trying to get rid of his last-year stock to make way for the new models, and John spent hours dickering with him, checking out tires and under-the-hood appurtenances, squatting by the side of the car, chewing on a straw, and saying nothing for long moments. Not knowing the finer points of car bargaining I sought the warmth of the waiting room and yawned and waited.

The car, when John was finally persuaded that it was a satisfactory deal, was a stripped-down model but so unaccustomedly fresh and shiny-new, so reliable about running, the children and I were dizzy with excitement. John even opened a charge account for us with our

183

neighboring mechanic friend, Skinny Roach, mainly to be sure our chariot got essential maintenance, but allowing a little leeway for gas and oil. The danger of running out of gas and having to walk home had been ever-present with us and it was downright luxury to be able to drive into Mr. Roach's station and say grandly, "A dollar's worth of regular, please." (For all his new lenience John was not about to authorize so profligate a gesture as "Fill 'er up, please.")

One of the first trips we took in our new car was to the mountains to see a rough deer-hunter's, trout-fisherman's cabin on a beautiful little stream called Holly Creek.

Herbert Tabor, an Ellijay insurance man, who was born in the mountains and had traveled over them all his life, taking the first Model-T Ford some mountaineers had seen into the remote coves and hollows, was the *Constitution*'s correspondent in the area and a fast friend to all reporters and photographers. He had an infallible eye for a story, and when he called or scrawled a tip on one of his memo pads, our state-news editor dispatched a reporter-and-photographer team to the scene immediately. Sometimes it would be a spot news story, more often a Sunday feature. Many of us took a turn at prowling the mountains with Mr. Tabor and fortifying ourselves for the trip with hot rolls and country ham in the kitchen of the tall white Victorian house where he and his wife, Frances, lived.

When my turn came, I fell in love with the mountains and with the Tabors. Coastal-reared, I had no acquaintance with the crisp, cool mountain climate, with summer evenings when the fragrance of sourwood and ripening apples filled the air instead of the ineffable scent of mosquito-repelling oil of citronella, when a sweater would feel good and so would a blaze in the fireplace. The stories Mr. Tabor knew or learned about delighted me. Many of the old-time country fêtes continued in the mountains long after they had vanished in the metropolitan areas. I attended cane grindings and hog killings, cemetery workings, quilting bees, fiddling contests. With Mr. Tabor I visited herb gatherers and herb doctors, drank sweet wild-fox-grape wine with one family, got lessons in growing ginseng from another. I watched one woman make soap, another sitting at an old handmade loom guiding a shuttle threaded with home-grown and -dyed wool through the warp of a coverlet of Elizabethan design. I was totally charmed by the mountains, the beauty of the rhododendron- and

184

hemlock-clad slopes and peaks, the flashing streams, the people and the climate.

"If you ever hear of a house up here that I can afford, let me know," I begged the Tabors.

A few days later Mr. Tabor said he had two houses for me to consider. One of them was a five-room house on five acres of land with a stream, for $2,500. The other was a two-room shack on a creek with not quite an acre of land to go with it. Price $500.

"Let me look at the five-hundred-dollar one!" I said without hesitation.

The following weekend Muv and the children and I packed a picnic lunch, piled in our new car, and headed for the hill country. It was November and the mountains were still awash in brilliant autumnal color. From a paved main road, which crossed the top of the state, we followed a winding gravel road back into the woods through caves of dark green spruces and pines, and blazing hardwoods arching overhead, beside a rushing stream, singing as it splashed over boulders and down rocky passes. I had seen much beauty in the mountains, but it seemed to me when I saw the two-room shack, backed up to a wooded mountain, facing that little creek, I had never seen anything that overwhelmed my senses and latched onto my heart with such beauty.

Muv was less than enthusiastic. "What do you want to be back here in this old spooky place for?" she kept saying.

The children were already loping up little woodland paths, hopping from rock to rock in the creek, and I was very busy building a fire in the old wood range Mr. Tabor's hunting, fishing friends would throw in with the sale of the cabin. There were also a trash-burner heater in the other room, a double bed, a big rough deal table, a shelf of rat-marked, spider-webbed dishes, a few pots and skillets, and a teakettle.

It was the teakettle that engrossed me. I took it down to the creek and scrubbed it with some sand and left-behind soap and walked across the road to a spot to fill it where a spring rushed out of the ferny cleft of a rock. In a little while it was singing on the old black stove, and Muv had spread our picnic cloth on the six-foot-square open platform that served as an entrance to the cabin. The Tabors arrived with a sumptuous contribution to our picnic, and we all sat on

185

the edge of the deck or squatted on the ground, drinking in the color that engulfed us, shivering delightedly in the mountain coolness, pronouncing the tea made from spring water the best we had ever tasted.

Muv still was unconvinced, but I wasn't.

"Tell the owners I want it," I told Mr. Tabor. "Tell them I haven't got $500 but I'll get it. Don't let them sell this place to anybody else."

A week later I went to south Georgia to make a Rotary Club Ladies' Night speech, and the hosts paid me an unprecedented $75. I dispatched it to Mr. Tabor immediately. He persuaded the owners to accept it as a down payment and to let me send $25 a month until I'd paid it all. I didn't have an extra $25 a month and I wasn't disposed to tell John Cook that I was buying what is called a "second home." He would have been flabbergasted at my folly. But I knew that somehow, some way, we had to have Holly Creek cabin.

There followed years of happy "pioneering." We somehow managed the $25 a month and, looking back, I don't quite remember how. The girls had baby-sitting jobs, Jimmy signed on as an usher at the neighboring Peachtree Arts movie house—the one, sad to relate, to which Margaret Mitchell and her husband were headed the night she was struck and fatally injured by an automobile. Skipping lunch and walking to and from the office became a privilege when I could accumulate as much as $5 a week to send to Mr. Tabor.

Long before it was paid for, of course, we had established residence in the little shack, chasing out field mice and squirrels and spiders and at least one snake. With Mr. Tabor's help and that of friends he brought to see us, such as County Commissioner Cicero Logan, we made what we considered vast improvements. We added a screened porch across the front, not more than two steps from the banks of the creek, built a fireplace in the front room, and rearranged what we lovingly thought of as the layout of the house by making the bigger room a kitchen and living room combined and turning the former kitchen into a bedroom.

Two dollars' worth of wallpaper covered the hunters' grease spots on the sheet-rock walls, and Mr. Tabor himself installed a window at the kitchen end of the main room and hooked up a secondhand sink beneath it. Not that we had running water in the cabin, of course, but having a sink with drain running out to a spot beneath a rock in the backyard turned out to be a surprising convenience. You didn't have to walk outside to pour out half a cup of cold coffee, for instance, or to empty your washpan after what passed for a bath at the cabin.

We spent every weekend at the cabin, summer and winter. The children learned many valuable lessons—how to clean and fill kerosene lamps, how to chop wood for the cookstove and the fireplace, how to keep the water buckets filled at the spring, and how to sweep and lime the privy, which they approached singing and beating on tin pans to frighten away snakes.

They nearly always brought a friend each, and as they grew older and had pressing engagements in town, I would go up to the cabin with some friend of my own, most often Margaret Long, who liked walking and swimming and reading by the fire as much as I did. I have a special recollection of Maggie bundling up in pea jacket, knitted cap, and mittens for a winter's trip to the privy. She had her cigarettes and lighter in one hand and a copy of *War and Peace* in the other. She paused at the window of the cabin as she went by and held up the book.

"I won't finish it this time," she said.

I sometimes think of another Margaret—Margaret Bridges—squatting on a rock in the creek scrubbing a pot. Wild asters were blooming, the creek sang as it rushed past her, and she lifted her face to the wheat-colored sunshine with an expression of near reverence.

"This is the way you should wash dishes," she said. "And clothes. Machinery has taken all the soul out of housework. It's something you should do sitting on a rock in a creek."

As it turned out I did many things in that idyllic, if peculiar, position.

On one of my trips to Hollywood I had started a book. It was really busywork, done because I had a roomette on the Super Chief and found it lonely being shut off from the day-coach crowd. On all previous trips to the West Coast I had flown, but it began to seem a waste to me—all the country I was passing over and not seeing. So on one fall trip I took a train to Chicago, spent a wonderful day sightseeing there at the direction of a woman I had picked up on the train, went to a matinee of *Guys and Dolls,* and boarded the Super Chief for Los Angeles in the late afternoon. It was a novel experience and seemed totally glamorous to me for a day and a night. Then it began to pall. Reared a day-coach traveler, I missed people—holding wet babies, sharing shoebox lunches, the whole sociable business of journeying poor folks. On the Super Chief every passenger was hermetically sealed from every other passenger, some of them in roomettes, some of them in drawing rooms, and all of them, I reflected bleakly, isolated and cut off from the human race.

It happened that I was taking a small snake to Actress Jean Peters, the gift of our movie editor, Paul Jones, who had learned of her affection for snakes while she was in Georgia making the Okefenokee swamp movie, *Lure of the Wilderness.* This reptile was small and innocuous, I suppose, but I was terrified of him just the same. Not wanting to admit it, I stuck the glass jar with ventilating holes in the lid down in a narrow, covered basket to be sure I would not have to look at the snake. So he was no company, except for the fact that dining-car waiters learned about him and came in two or three times a day with flies they had caught in the kitchen for him to eat.

Lacking anything else to do, I started a murder mystery. I opened up my portable typewriter and between looks at the wonderful, fearful scenery of the desert and bare-bouldered West, I plugged along on a story about death in an Atlanta newspaper office. It wasn't *Gone With the Wind,* but it kept me happily occupied until I arrived at the Los Angeles train station, where I was met by a publicist from 20th Century–Fox, Miss Peters, and the studio's herpetologist.

One look at the gift snake and the studio publicist decided he was too puny and unimpressive to warrant any attention from the Los Angeles newspapers. Right away somebody was dispatched to rent a *real* snake, and presently the herpetologist, Miss Peters, and I were posing for newspaper pictures with a boa constrictor draped over the herpetologist's shoulders. After some debate the experts agreed that Miss Peters's fans might be offended if she got *too* cozy with the snake, so she merely patted his head. I, the supposed donor, was caught fearfully backing into the woodwork.

Sometimes I wonder what happened to that scrawny, fly-fed little snake who, probably against his wishes, was hauled from Georgia clear across the continent on a glamorous movie-star railroad train and then, like many another film hopeful, found inadequate.

The murder mystery I started probably had a happier fate. I took it one night to read to a group of writing friends, who met occasionally to read their deathless works, exchange great dollops of praise, and encourage one another to newer and loftier endeavor. The group had started out at our Sunday magazine, under the maternal eye of a prodigious writer named Wylly Folk St. John. Wylly was always looking for story ideas, and she found a small item in the newspaper one day that appealed to her as a plot germ. She persuaded five of us, co-workers, to take the bare bones of the story and try our hands at writing something around it. We turned out a variety of prose, including a short story, a novelette, a dog story, a magazine interview, and a television play. After work one afternoon we adjourned to Wylly's old-fashioned, tree-shaded front porch in Kirkwood with beer and sandwiches and read aloud.

It was so much fun, so really stimulating, we made a regular thing of such meetings, and our group expanded to include some already-successful published writers. Among these was a delightful woman named Nedra Tyre, whose first novel, *Red Wine First,* had been critically acclaimed before she turned to writing murder mysteries.

Nedra was present when I read the eight opening pages of my Super Chief opus.

"Go on with it, Celestine," she said. "Finish it."

"Oh, I don't have time," I said. "You know I don't have time."

Nedra leaned over and touched me on the shoulder.

"Just fifteen minutes a day, Celestine," she whispered. "Just fifteen minutes a day."

It was the best writing advice I ever received. Nedra knew what I was to learn, and that is if you force yourself to sit down and write for fifteen minutes every day you might find that you stick to it for an hour or two.

Even with a shortage of writing time I got about thirty pages written and saw it off to Doubleday, whose $1,000 advance I had never repaid. David Creviston, that publisher's Georgia representative, was a friend of mine and he volunteered to take my manuscript to New York and give it to Isabelle Taylor, who presided over the company's output of murder mysteries, called the Crime Club.

To my amazement and delight Mrs. Taylor wrote me right away that she liked the story, except for a flaw I didn't perceive—it was smart-alecky in spots. If I could remedy that, she would offer me a contract and a nice cash advance. For days to come I couldn't be separated from that dog-eared manuscript. I read it on the bus, when I went to bed at night, when I awakened in the morning. I couldn't see how it was smart-alecky, but I was determined to find out.

Wylly came to the rescue. We had lunch one day and she went over my opening chapters carefully, pencil in hand. When she finished we had agreed to eliminate eight words.

Nervously, without much hope, I sent it back to Mrs. Taylor. Lo and behold, killing those eight words had been enough. She liked the start, wanted the rest of the book as soon as possible, and enclosed a check for $1,000, less the $1,000 I owed Doubleday.

The cabin at Holly Creek seemed the natural place to go for the necessary uninterrupted peace and quiet in which to work. It was summer and the girls were visiting Muv, so I took some vacation, and Jimmy and I loaded the car and headed north. The temptation to clean up the place, make improvements, and move in ferns and other wildlings to the yard was great, of course. But I managed to stick to the typewriter, which we set up on the screened porch. When the sun reached the porch and it was too hot to continue there I would take the portable and sit on a rock in the creek with my feet cooling in the icy stream.

Jimmy was in charge of the commissary department and fed us regularly, if monotonously. If I reached a pause in my writing and thought about it, I got tired of peanut butter and jelly sandwiches and sardines and crackers, but I mostly jogged along with what he provided, grateful for his help and the fact that the few dishes involved in Jimmy's cuisine could be set in the creek and presently the motion of the water and the swirling sand would scour them clean.

A welcome break in our fare came on those days when we looked out and saw the Tabors crossing the creek on the foot log. Frances invariably had a foil-covered dish containing freshly cooked vegetables from their garden, cornbread or homemade rolls, an apple pie or a chocolate cake.

With such friends, such a peerless retreat for working, I should have turned out a monumental work of the caliber of Maggie's *War and Peace* or, at the very least, a latter-day *Gone With the Wind.*

Instead, it was a pleasant, I think, but fairly slight murder mystery of Doubleday's "Damsel in Distress" persuasion.

In the spring of 1958 not everybody in the world had a new book out, as they seem to have at almost every season nowadays, so my first got a lot of generous attention. From everybody but the *New York Times,* that is. The *Times's* reviewer gave it two or three paragraphs, pointing out that I knew a lot more about newspapers than I did about opera. (I used opening night in Atlanta to get some of my murders off the ground.) Anthony Boucher, the review king, was absolutely right, of course, but my feelings as a new author were young and tender, and since I admired him and his works so much I was wounded as many another author has been, to find him picky about my prose.

Other reviewers were uniformly kind, however. Our editor, Ralph McGill himself, did the *Constitution*'s review, saying, "a great many thousands ... already know how well Celestine can write" and urging the book on them as authentic newspaper and good mystery. He explained the title, *The Malignant Heart*, which I took from the Georgia code's definition of murder: "The act of an abandoned and malignant heart." I was grateful because a lot of people thought it might be a medical tome about cardiac problems. There were parties and autographings and Isabelle Taylor came down from New York to see me through the first ones. The possibility that a store will buy up a lot of your books, throw a party to which no one comes, and there the store and you are stuck with all those unread, unwanted volumes haunts every writer, I suppose. I have had that experience but not with the first book, thank goodness. It would have thrown my fiction writing into permanent, traumatic arrest.

The kickoff for any book by a Georgia author used to be at Rich's and I knew the system. If the clamor of the reading public for a book was so faint as to be unheard, the book buyer would put hats on the clerks and walk them by the author. Not many authors knew that but I did, and I started out looking with suspicion at everybody who came toward me with a book to be autographed. Are you from hosiery or housewares? I wanted to ask. Fortunately, I was saved by friends, who rallied round spectacularly.

When you have had the mayor and the governor and half the legislature as well as all your neighbors and newspaper friends at the first party, then you start worrying about the second one. You are going to be, you reflect bleakly, *all alone with all those books.* Davison's department store, now called Macy's, gave me a gala celebration on its book mezzanine, but even as they set out the cookies and punch I worried that nobody would come.

Just as I reached the point of doing what I used to do at high school dances, retreating to the bathroom, I heard a commotion on the up escalator. Half the Atlanta police department, pals all, led by Chief Herbert Jenkins, was arriving. Before they had bought their books and moved away, the Salvation Army, trumpets, trombones, and tambourines, arrived. I couldn't see to autograph for the tears in my eyes.

Now I really have used up my friends, I thought humbly. There's nobody else left in the world to care that I've written this little book and to want a copy. But the escalator was bringing me a new and surprising wave of the faithful.

The summer before I had spent a week or ten days in the little south Georgia town Vienna, waiting out the death of the state's senior U.S. Senator, Walter F. George (the one, you recall, President Roosevelt tried unsuccessfully to purge because of his opposition to packing the Supreme Court). A *Journal* reporter, the late John Pennington, was also there, and we spent the long, hot days with Madge Methvin, editor of the local weekly, or visiting with her friends at the drugstore or the town's morning-coffee gathering spot. In that space of time I grew fond of the town and the people I met, especially Madge, who was the George family's spokesman and our contact with Mrs. George and the Senator's doctor. Because she worked so hard to help us, allowing us to use her newspaper office as our headquarters and taking us home to hot midday dinners, put on her table by a peerless black cook named Beulah, we volunteered to help Madge put out her paper as press time approached. It was my first experience with working on a weekly and I enjoyed it and Madge Methvin tremendously.

Now I looked out toward the escalator leading to Davison's book department, and there came Madge and a whole congregation of friends from Vienna.

I got up from the autograph table and tottered to meet them, gasping, "What on earth . . . ?"

"Oh, we just decided to have a motorcade to Atlanta to get this book!" said Madge blithely.

There must have been fifteen or twenty of them, beautiful and unforgettable.

There were other parties and kind attentions from many quarters—I even got Sigma Delta Chi and Theta Sigma Phi awards, and me not a member of either group!—and it was a good thing because there's nothing like your first book. After that there may be a pleasant bustle here and there. You may get to go to New York to be on the *Today Show* or to book-and-author dinners around the country. (The one in Richmond, which the *Atlantic*'s Edward Weeks used to emcee,

192

is a don't-miss if you're ever invited.) But there will be lulls, dry spells, times that the author Harnett Kane described as occasions of such isolation that you are grateful when somebody stops by and asks you the way to the ladies' room. I once had such an experience in his beloved New Orleans, selling but two books and I bought one of them.

So everybody who writes for a living probably does what I have just done and relives, fatuously, the triumph of that first book.

A year after *The Malignant Heart* was published the women's journalism sorority Theta Sigma Phi gave me an award at the height of a banquet. I was leaving, clutching my Brenda, a chocolate-colored nude figure in plaster, when I saw Jack Strong, a newcomer to our reportorial staff.

"You're not covering this, are you?" I said, surprised.

He shook his head.

"Came as a fan," he said. "Paid my own way."

I laughed, not really believing him. That handsome young man, who came to us from Lockheed, where he had written textbooks, drawing on his experience as a Navy fighter pilot for background, could not possibly be interested enough to buy a ticket and spend an evening listening to speeches. It was the kind of thing reporters avoided if they could and never, never did on their own time.

But I found that Jack Strong did many pleasant and unexpected things on his own time. If I wrote something he liked he called me to talk about it. If I got a new dress he noticed and complimented it. He read a lot, and if he found a book he thought I would enjoy he dropped by my office and left it off with a note. Harold Martin, who was a contributing editor to the *Saturday Evening Post* and wrote a column two or three days a week for us, shared an office with me; he noticed the attention I was getting from our young colleague and teased me about it.

"Aw, he's just a kid," I said, embarrassed.

Then I wrote a column about Jimmy's old car, a $25 number I had bought him for Christmas just before he wearied of high school in his senior year and elected to get in the obligatory six months in the service, the Coast Guard his choice. The car was a dog but his own, his first. We had bought it from our friend novelist Maggie Davis, who claimed that its only flaw was a leak in the gas tank, which she mended with a wad of chewing gum. It wasn't really effective but she only bought a gallon of gas at a time and managed. Jimmy thought he could manage, too, and went off to the Coast Guard, admonishing me to exercise and feed his steed enough to keep it in health until his return.

Naturally I did not. But he was on his way home and I hurried to make amends. The old car was dead, dead. What to do? I wrote of my dilemma in a column and Jack Strong called and said he would be glad to take a look at my son's machine. He was reared in his stepfather's automobile-repair shop down in Biloxi and had some little mechanical skill. He came by the house one morning, crisp and neat in clothes I considered totally inappropriate and at risk in our dirty old garage. He waved aside my demurrals, raised the hood, and poked around for a few minutes, hit something with a wrench and told me to try the starter.

Miraculously, the engine coughed to life. In a follow-up column I mentioned that it took a lad in his twenties or younger to cope with an old car. Jack called me, amused and irritated.

"I'm twenty-nine years old, soon to be thirty," he said. "I'm as old as you are."

He wasn't by about twelve years, but I found myself unaccountably pleased that the difference in our ages wasn't greater, and out of gratitude for his help I asked him to Sunday dinner. He came and was full of praise for my pot roast and the rice, which he said he had not found so light and fluffy since he left the Gulf Coast. Susan and Mary, who were going to Brenau Academy, a small boarding school for girls forty miles north of Atlanta in the town of Gainesville, were home for the weekend with a classmate who was a music major and a marvelous pianist. Our old upright, bought from a friend for $50 when the girls started taking music lessons, had never sounded so fine as when Leila's young fingers took charge of its keyboard. To everybody's delight the young man from the office was a singer! He knew all the music Leila played, had been a choir boy in the Catholic church of his childhood, had sung in the glee club in college, and had had a brief stint with an opera company in New Orleans.

Our old house reverberated with the wondrous sounds of piano and a winsome tenor voice, sometimes lifted in a solo but most often leading the young people to sing harmoniously the hymns, show tunes, and Kingston Trio numbers they all knew. I listened and thought wistfully that it was a shame Jack Strong was too old for my

194

daughters and too young for me. He was such fun!

Amazingly, Jack didn't seem to know his age was out of synch with any of ours. He cut up with the children and their friends, inviting them over to his room in a nice old house half a dozen blocks away to listen to his jazz records. He went to Holly Creek with us all, called almost daily, invited me out to dinner once or twice a week, and on at least one occasion took me to a glossy nightclub to dine and dance. I was having a good time and the children knew it and applauded.

He was in the naval reserve and was able to arrange with his flying buddies to give Jimmy and his sailor friends rides back to their Coast Guard base when they came home on leave. He himself flew them to Norfolk once when they were threatened with getting back disastrously late. Muv delighted in him and he in her. One weekend when he was getting in his monthly stint with his reserve squadron we were all up at Holly Creek. Muv was with us when a Navy plane came over the mountain, followed the creek a little way, and buzzed the cabin.

Determined that the pilot would see us, Muv grabbed a pillow case off one of the beds and rushed out to a clearing to flap it in the wind. Jack didn't see the pillow-case signal or any of us but he had made an impression on Muv.

"Somebody in this family ought to marry that man," she said. "If you or one of the girls don't grab him I will."

Sometimes the subject came up. We were spending a lot of time together. I had been down to Biloxi and to New Orleans to spend weekends with his mother and stepfather and several dearly beloved aunts and uncles. Jack's own father had died when he was three years old and he had been raised in the midst of a loving family, all of whom were very close to him. They came to Atlanta to visit him, and although he had moved into an apartment he didn't have room for all of his relatives, who came in batches of six, and we naturally caught the overflow. We delighted when they all came to dinner and we got to hear the stories of his Uncle Frank Guttierez, a raconteur so gifted he could have made a fortune as a standup comic if he hadn't devoted his life to shrimping and running a boatyard.

We liked them and knew that they liked us. Muv was especially fond of Jack's parents, seeing in them a close and comfortable resemblance to our own family. Once when they were all visiting, Muv and

Jack's mother and aunts shared a bottle of wine, which loosened Muv's tongue alarmingly.

"I'd like to know," she said to Jack, "when you're going to make an honest woman of my daughter?"

Horrified, I cried, "Hush, Muv! I *am* an honest woman!"

A silence fell on the group and then somebody tactfully changed the subject. Jack brought it up later, asking me if our association was making me uncomfortable. Did I want marriage?

I knew that I cared about him, probably more than I wanted to admit, probably more than I had ever or would ever care for any other man, but that twelve-year difference in our ages bothered me.

"You don't have to 'make an honest woman' out of me," I gibed. "I'm already honest enough to see that I wouldn't want to spend the rest of my life wishing I were twenty years old!"

We dropped the subject—for about twenty-five years.

Inevitably, I suppose, there would be other women to interest Jack through the years, and even when they were affairs of shallow depth and brief duration I suffered. Once Muv heard about one of these romances—not from me, I hasten to say—and she said to Jack's mother, Julia, loudly and disloyally, "I don't blame him." The inference was that he could do better, much better, than to tie himself down to a plain older woman with a houseful of children who would be trouble of one kind or another for years to come.

Seeing the logic in that didn't ease my pain. I grieved that I wasn't young and beautiful and found little to comfort me until Jack returned and set me straight on a few of my fantasies. A woman I had imagined was everything he wanted—French and musical and probably endowed with a wonderful classical education, turned out to dye her hair, pick up men on airplanes, and douse herself with strong perfume. I should be jealous of her! I gloated.

One I was able to dismiss when I lucked into a letter from her on Jack's desk and discovered to my delight that she was banal, ungrammatical, a bad speller, and already married. A third wasn't so easy to brush off—a divorcee with two or three children, living in a house she couldn't afford, and eager to find someone to support her. I couldn't find any redeeming faults in her and could only wail desperately to my daughter Susan, "I bet she can't even cover a murder trial!"

Susan would have liked to comfort me, but she confessed years later that she felt at the time the things I found wrong with these women—dyed hair, bad spelling, ignorance of the finer points of covering a murder trial—might not be deterrents to love and marriage for Jack.

Something was, because he came back each time and we somehow managed—without bitterness and with a minimum of recriminations—to resume our deeply caring involvement in one another's lives, families, friends, jobs, pleasures, griefs, and pains.

The success of any book is really a foot in the door for an author. *The Malignant Heart* was doing very well. It had been taken by the Detective Book Club, sold in England and in France, and one day I got a telegram from Isabelle Taylor telling me that it had sold to an Italian publisher for 40,000 lire.

She didn't tell me how much real money that was and I assumed that it was a fortune—until I called the bank. It was something like $40! But still they had wanted it, and Mrs. Taylor felt that it was time for me to come through with a second book. I had an idea, which she liked, but literally no time at that point in my life. I was covering the Georgia legislature by day, doing my column five days a week, and staying late to work on Sunday stories.

But Mrs. Taylor herself had an idea that I found irresistible and, remembering Nedra Tyre's fifteen-minutes-a-day formula, I decided to give it a whirl. At that time several publishers were bringing out books about America's cities. I had read and loved Cleveland Amory's *Proper Bostonians,* and when Mrs. Taylor suggested a book about Atlanta I visualized myself as writing something comparable, not Chamber of Commercey, not history nor yet geography, but a smart, literate, funny book, which incorporated all three with something extra, an irreverent look at the mores, the quality of life in our town. I was glad to sign a contract. And there followed three years of drudgery.

It wasn't enough to set down the funny and wise observations I had picked up from such people as Margaret Mitchell and a marvelous old street character named Ina Mae Smith. Anecdotes and character sketches, which I reveled in, weren't going to replace facts—and digging those out was wearying and time-consuming. I remember complaining to Mrs. Taylor that I was pregnant with the Battle of Atlanta one entire summer.

Peachtree Street USA—An Affectionate Portrait of Atlanta came out in 1964, again with fanfare from bookstores and the loyal, supportive acclaim of friends.

If the timing was right for another book, Jack asked, why didn't I offer them the Christmas stories I had done for a number of years to run serially in our newspaper?

"Aw, they don't want them," I said. "I sent them to the juvenile editor and had them rejected a long time ago."

Jack suggested that we have a talk with Clif Devereaux, who was Doubleday's new man in the region, having succeeded Dave Creviston and Don Parker. I didn't have copies of the stories, of course, being very bad about keeping such things, but at Jack's insistence I tackled the microfilm machine in our reference department, a slow, eye-straining operation in those days, and got five of the stories together. We took them out to the Devereauxes' house, and while we sat at their kitchen table drinking coffee poured for us by Judy, Clif's wife, they reread the stories. Clif said immediately that they would make a salable book, a small one but a good Christmas item. He would take them to New York himself.

This time, with the murder mystery already a good seller, Doubleday was interested. *Christmas in Georgia* came out in time for Yuletide shoppers that very year, 1964. Clif, who had had a hand in its birthing, determined that it would be a bestseller. With him zealously beating the bushes throughout Georgia, stacking copies of it on shelves some storekeepers didn't even know they had, *Christmas in Georgia* became that year the third from the top on Doubleday's list of sales, and Clif Devereaux was invited to write a paper for salesmen on how to turn a little regional sleeper into a bestseller. He ultimately moved to New York as Doubleday's sales manager.

Meanwhile, my boss, Bill Fields, viewed the hullabaloo sheepishly.

"Sibley, for God's sake don't tell anybody I only paid you twenty-five dollars apiece for those stories," he said.

Naturally I told everybody—delightedly. It was one more proof that the newspaper did not properly appreciate me and would pay me as little as possible whenever it could. But at the time I did the stories I was grateful to Willie for letting me do a little extra work to make Christmas money for my children. He could have gotten them for less if he had but known. He was my friend, and his death in 1987 a loss that will be with me always, but he was handicapped in any generous payment of the staff by his feeling that it was his job as managing editor and later executive editor to save money for the paper. He lost many outstanding staffers that way, among them Jack Strong.

Jack got a job working for his cousin Billy Waters in the oil industry in Louisiana. He didn't particularly want to go, but he was restless in his job as our courthouse reporter and the salary struck him as insulting. He had left Lockheed at a financial sacrifice because he wanted to return to newspapering, at which he had worked in college and in Mississippi before he went in the Navy. But, when it appeared that he was never to get beyond the courthouse and a starting reporter's pittance, he began looking around.

Fields called me in. "I hate to lose Jack," he said. "Why is he going?"

"Money," I said. "His cousin has offered him twelve thousand dollars a year."

Willie let out a long whistle. "I'd go for that myself," he said.

Jack left one autumn morning. I took him to the railroad station and would have cried to see him go except that his mother, Julia, was with him. Before the train pulled out *she* cried—at the sad, dejected figure I presented standing there in the station, I think. All I could do to comfort myself was to reflect waspishly on how this departing fellow had churned up my life, turned it around, changing it completely before he took off.

By the day after Christmas Jack was back—to stay. But it was perfectly true that my life had undergone changes, a lot of changes, some he wrought, some fate visited on me, and some, I suppose, were self-inflicted.

The children had grown up. Susan had graduated from Brenau Academy. (John Cook got married, changed jobs, and quit as our business manager or he might have vetoed a private school, which I had grabbed as a last resort when Susan quit public school six months before graduation. She liked it so well and flourished there, so I persuaded them to admit Mary, too.) She had enrolled in the University of Georgia journalism school, and I had sold the AT&T stock John Cook bought us and opened bank accounts for her and Jimmy, who was going to Georgia State, then a branch of the university in Atlanta, now an independent university in its own right.

Neither stuck.

Susan announced that she was in love with Edward Bazemore, a lanky Georgia Tech senior, who was a friend of Jimmy's and had been

199

a regular at our house, playing records with Jimmy and his friends, working on old cars in the driveway, and apparently courting Susan in a quiet, unobtrusive way. In order to be ready to marry Edward the next spring, when he would have graduated from Tech and put in the ROTC's requisite number of months training with the U.S. Army engineers in Virginia, she felt it imperative to come home, get a job, begin accumulating a trousseau, and planning their wedding.

It wasn't what I would have chosen for her. She is bright and energetic and would have done well at school and in any field she chose, I knew. When she had a summer job working with a public-relations firm she had excelled. I knew she could write. But no amount of talking changed her mind, and I was so worried about Mary I had little time or energy to expend on Susan.

Jimmy had quit Georgia State and taken a job in the advertising department at Davison's, a menial job that taxed his considerable talents very little and paid less. But he considered himself grownup enough to move out of the house and to an apartment with friends. Mary at seventeen was not old enough, but she insisted on following suit. She and a girlfriend from Brenau moved into a building half a block away, handy for running home to use the washing machine and eat a meal. I knew, as friends suggested, that I was just fostering her rebellion and enabling her to stay away in an environment that was worrisomely loose and maybe even dangerous. But I couldn't tell her not to come home for a meal—or for any reason. I wanted her back home at any cost.

Susan's wedding brought them all home. It was to be in April and we went by our church, North Avenue Presbyterian, to make plans. One look at the main sanctuary and Susan screwed up her freckled face in distress.

"We couldn't fill this place if we gave away a set of dishes to everybody who came," she wailed.

So we checked out the chapel, a pretty mini-sanctuary that would seat only a hundred people. It seemed perfect.

Money was a problem, of course, and we started planning how we could "do a wedding" on a shoestring. I would make Susan's dress and my own, thereby saving a wad. Mary and Edward's sister, Zu-lette, who would be bridesmaids, lucked into a sale, miraculously finding suitable, fitting dresses for themselves at a manageable price. Muv shelled out for an ashes-of-roses lace with dyed-to-match slippers for her role as grandmother of the bride.

There had to be flowers. I called my friend Helen Ayre, who ran a very chic florist shop.

"Are you going to do flowers for Susan's wedding *cheap,*" I asked, "or will I have to steal them from West View Cemetery?"

"Honey, I'm gonna do those flowers so cheap you'll *think* you stole them," said Helen.

Engraved invitations were out of the question and they struck me as pretentious anyhow for so small a wedding, so I insisted that Susan write personal notes to our friends. Bill Fields was amused that she wrote him: "You have seen us through so much, please come and see us through this."

Music was no problem—at least not much of a problem. Our doctor, Bill Crowe, was a pianist of no small stature, having served as the Emory University Glee Club accompanist in its heyday when it toured all the capitals of Europe, performing before kings and queens. Music remained his hobby, and we spent many pleasant evenings at his and Sara's house singing around the piano or just listening.

"I'm going to play for Susan's wedding," he announced immediately.

"But, Bill, the chapel just has an organ," I said. "Do you also play the organ?"

"Not yet," said our doctor, "but I'm about to learn."

Susan wanted Jack to sing, and she chose "Ave Maria." That would have created no problem except that the organist and the singer met at the chapel at lunchtime to practice, and some militantly Protestant ladies heard them and called me in alarm. Did I know, they asked, that Bill Crowe, a lifelong member of the church, was planning to play "Ave Maria" at Susan's wedding? I saw no objection, but I called the minister, Dr. Vernon Broyles. He saw no objection either. "Ave Maria," he said, is a prayer to Mary, and although Protestants don't pray to Mary, it is a beautiful, reverent classic and he saw no reason not to go ahead with it.

Jim's brother, Ervin, had by that time fulfilled his lifelong desire to become an Episcopal clergyman, giving up his job in construction and going to the seminary. He was a full fledged Episcopal priest, and in his priestly garb was a stylish addition to the wedding when he arrived to give the bride away. He made another contribution, which Susan and Muv especially valued. He had a nice, black, shiny clerical-looking automobile to transport the bride and her grandmother to the church, and we were down to a secondhand wooden station wagon at that point. It had mushrooms growing out of the back and the hood had blown off and been lost forever on the expressway, when Jimmy was driving it one day.

Muv looked at the engine naked and exposed to the world and vowed that she would not ride to the church in such a vehicle. Susan felt the same way.

"At least you could have made a slipcover for it," said Muv.

Ervin's nice car saved me that.

Jack's mother and Aunt Secessia arrived from Biloxi and New Orleans. Jim's sister, Everitt, arrived from Mobile. The Crowes gave an elegant after-rehearsal dinner, with champagne that Jack bought at bargain rates at the Navy commissary. Dr. Broyles had persuaded me that a reception, however small, could better be held in the church parlors, where they were already equipped with china and silver and splendid antique accessories, which wealthy members had in time bequeathed to the church. He called in the woman in charge of food at the church, and she said blithely that she could provide punch and coffee and party sandwiches—"not churchy fare but cocktail-party goodies, shrimp and all"—for one hundred people for $35. We had only to bring the cake.

Helen Ayre had an inspiration about flowers for the reception, which she assured me was not uncommon for shoestring weddings. Have one of Susan's friends assigned to grab the bouquet off the altar as soon as the chapel emptied and rush it upstairs to the reception table. She would make sure the flower arrangement was suitable for both.

We were managing fine, I kept telling myself. It was going to be a simple wedding but lovely and memorable for Susan and Edward and all of us. We were even having pictures taken. My friend Hugh Stovall, a newspaper photographer with whom I had worked for years, had announced ahead of time that he and his wife, Mary, would be at Susan's wedding and he would have his camera in hand.

The only trouble was that I kept being terribly tired. If I stopped moving I fell asleep. If I had a moment alone, I cried. The reason was that just before the wedding when I tried the bridesmaid dress on Mary it was tighter than it had been when we bought it. I couldn't imagine why, and as I knelt there on the floor with a mouthful of pins, she told me.

She was pregnant.

Seventeen years old and she was pregnant!

She had, pretty valiantly, I realized, not wanted to say anything that would detract from our pleasure and excitement in Susan's wedding, but she and Richard Fleming, another seventeen-year-old and high school dropout, who played a mean trumpet, were secretly married. Richard, called Cricket, was one of the teenagers who had hung around our house with Jimmy, playing records and, of course, his trumpet. He was a handsome, well-mannered boy—but a boy, not a husband and prospective father. I thought I would die, and, of course, it was no time to tell anybody, least of all Muv and not even Jack, who had opposed the apartment for Mary for some time, feeling that something like this might happen. My reaction was bone tiredness, utter exhaustion.

On top of that, the $35 check I gave the church for the reception bounced!

In the end Jack was the one who rallied. He treated the newly-weds—*those* newlyweds, Mary and Cricket—to a weekend honey-moon at the Biltmore Hotel, Atlanta's finest at the time, and had a small dinner party–reception for them at his apartment. All I could do was sag tiredly and wonder where we all were going.

As it happened, I was going to the country.

For some time Jack had wanted to buy a piece of land in the country. I had gone with him to look at advertised property in all the rural counties surrounding Atlanta. He had finally arrived at liking the area north of the city best, the farmlands and pine-clad hills and little creeks that were the beginning of the mountains, which on a clear day you could see rising in blue peaks against the sky. I went with him a lot to look at land, and occasionally we would stop by a country store and collect sardines and crackers and cold drinks for a picnic before some dilapidated, long-abandoned old farmhouse.

One such house, standing on a little hill in the midst of eroded, weedy, long-neglected fields, appealed to us both for a time. We even went so far as to take our decorator friend and Jack's neighbor Edmund Bocock out to look at it.

Edmund was an effete city type given to designer clothes and elegant furnishings. Plainly horrified at the aspect of both the land and the house, he narrowed his eyes and tilted his head in a parodied inspection.

"Versailles *revisited!*" he finally intoned, lyrical in his sarcasm.

A week or so after that some friend of Jack's at the courthouse told him about a physical therapist a few blocks away who had bought and fixed up an old house in north Fulton County, thirty miles from town, and who dabbled a bit in real estate. His name was Winston H. Smellie, called Doc, and he knew and loved the area. Jack made an appointment with him to look at a couple of pieces of land and we drove out one Saturday afternoon.

On the way to look at twenty acres he thought might suit Jack, Doc drove by to show me what he felt was an interesting old log cabin, said to have been built in 1842, used for a time as a schoolhouse but vacated by human inhabitants back in the 1930s and now choked by undergrowth, weeds, briars, and honeysuckle, its rusty, lopsided tin roof barely visible from the road.

I loved it. And Jack loved the twenty wooded acres a quarter of a mile away, with a beautiful little creek winding through an old field and a stand of assorted hardwoods, a lake site, and a hill idyllically suited for a house designed to make the most of a view of the future lake and the sweet indigo silhouette of Sweat Mountain ten miles away. Jack didn't commit himself immediately, but we were only halfway back to town when he pulled in at a pay station and phoned Doc that he would buy the land.

It took me a few months to buy the cabin. We all worked on Jack's land, the children and all their friends and I spending weekends helping him firm up the old wagon road that led into the place, picnicking on the hill, and putting in our first garden on the creek bank. At some point during almost every working day some of us would slip away and visit the old log cabin, picking wild strawberries, daisies, and the rampant Seven Sisters roses in the yard, and when fall came, gathering the fragrant purple muscadine grapes, which hung in swags and loops from the tall trees in the hollow.

It made no sense but I loved that little cabin and I wanted it. Finally, I persuaded Doc to make the owners an offer. They took it—$1,000 for the cabin and an acre of land.

It seemed an exorbitant price. After all, land in the area was selling for less than $300 an acre at the time, but where would you find a cabin of such wonderful vintage so close to Atlanta? It even had a name: Sweet Apple for some decrepit sweet apple trees, which were gasping their last in a pine thicket next to the house.

Paying for it was no breeze. I had to find extra writing chores, for my regular pay couldn't encompass such a wild expenditure. I was so busy worrying about the vast debt I didn't think what I was going to do with the cabin when I got it until the day after Susan's wedding in April 1962.

Susan and Edward had departed on their honeymoon, Ervin and Everitt had gone their separate ways, and the only out-of-town guests remaining were Muv and Jack's mother, Julia, and Aunt Secessia. We had made no plans for entertaining them, but when in doubt, I always say, have a picnic. The wedding viands were long since gone, but we rustled up some hot dogs and a bottle of champagne and headed for Sweet Apple.

Muv surveyed the sad little cabin, which stood on its rock pillars looking like a picked chicken since we had been clearing away its swaddling of vines and brush.

"You've got as much use for this place as a hog has for a saddle," she snorted.

But, when we moved the tattered, mildewed deckchairs I had bought at the Salvation Army for fifty cents apiece into the shade of a crooked, wormy, but gently flowering old peach tree, a mellow mood descended on us all, Muv included.

The ladies discovered they had been reared on some of the same country songs, and, sipping the champagne, they sang together a gem that begins: "Oh my little darlin', I'm sorry for you. . . . Told you that I love you but I don't believe I do!"

Our closest neighbor, Clarence Johnson, who lived just out of sight up on the paved road, walked down to see us and to offer to plow us a garden. Jack and I walked over the spot Clarence recommended, and I inwardly planned. Clearly I was going to be out of children, with both girls married and gone. What need had I of a big-city house when I could sell it and put windows and doors and a new roof on this dear cabin and spend my declining years here?

The decision, I think, was made that day, but it was a full year before I could carry it out.

Selling the house on Thirteenth Street didn't take long, but it was

205

more of a wrench emotionally than I could ever have foreseen. Susan came up from Fort Benning, where Edward was stationed and where she was experiencing the first pleasures and pangs of pregnancy, to help me move. Mary, who lived in an apartment not too far away, was present to oppose Susan's firm—we thought ruthless—decisions about what to give away, what to throw away, and what to return whence most of it came, the Salvation Army and Goodwill.

Mary grieved over the loss of all her favorite dolls and one or two dresses she had cherished. I walked over the house mournfully, trying to relinquish memories—the seventeen growing-up years of my children, all spent there.

An old house lends itself to nostalgia anyway and that one had the imprint of most of our lives all over it—the spot on the dining-room wall where a red Christmas candle had splattered wax, the dusty outline where the piano stood, the view from most windows of our precious sweetgum tree, standing tall against the sky, the penciled notations of the children's growth on a kitchen-door facing, the telephone numbers scrawled on the wallpaper over the telephone shelf in the hall, the secret cache of Social Security numbers kept in the hall closet against the day when a job-hunting child would call up crying, "Mama, I can't remember my Social Security number!"

The big window in the dining room framed a chunk of our lives. It faced a little hill that climbed steeply up toward Tenth Street, and through it I had watched, gnawing my knuckles, as each of the three had soloed in an automobile. When they started dating I waited there, agonizing over the sounds of screeching brakes or speeding motors on Peachtree and West Peachtree. When I was frightened or sad I stood at that window staring outward, but searching inwardly for solutions.

There was the day when I had come home from covering a lurid murder trial in Cedartown, Georgia. North Georgia had been blanketed by a history-making snow and ice storm, the worst in recollection. I could not get home even when the trial ended and the jury's verdict was in. Electric power and telephone service were out. Roads were impassable. Trains and buses were not running. Cedartown citizens crowded into the town's only hotel, where I was staying, because it had gas stoves and they could get food and some warmth. The jury deliberated by candles stuck in Coca-Cola bottles, and when it brought in a verdict of guilty with a life sentence for the murderer, the other reporters covering the trial and I were stymied over how to communicate it to our offices.

A friend tipped me off to the name of a ham radio operator, who lived within walking distance of the courthouse. A state trooper kindly accompanied me and introduced me to the radio hobbyist. Within minutes the verdict was radioed to the *Constitution* and I had scooped all opposition.

It was a triumph of sorts, but I had another problem—how to get home and how to be sure my children were all right. They were teenagers and competent but I worried nonetheless. I should have known that Jack would walk over and check on them.

He did better than that. He arrived bearing ham hocks and dried red beans and cooked for them that coastal specialty for washdays, blue Mondays, and times of stress. The house smelled fragrantly of garlic and red beans and rice when I finally hooked a slippery, skiddy ride home with one of the reporters I had scooped, one who happened to have a big, heavy-haunched car, more suited to icy roads than the U-Drive-It I jettisoned in Cedartown.

Standing before the big dining-room window, I remembered that snowy afternoon. People were instructed not to travel, warned that the streets were hazardous and they should hold to their houses if possible. A number of daredevils insisted on braving that hill, and Jack and my children stood at the dining-room window shouting out encouragement, cheering them on, booing when they skidded and lurched into sidewalks and lawns, and rushing out to help them when they caromed to a stop at the bottom of the hill and couldn't move. It wasn't exactly benign sport, but it was so merry I couldn't help being relieved and cheered that Jack was there and I had made it home to them all.

Now the window—and the rest of the house—were going. The buyer was planning to tear it down and erect a small apartment building. While work progressed slowly on Sweet Apple cabin, I had rented interim quarters in an apartment complex a few blocks away. It would not begin to hold the furniture we had kept, so we put some in storage, stuck some under plastic under the trees at Sweet Apple, and deployed what we could wedge in around the three-room apartment.

We had to wedge in more than furniture.

Mary's baby was born—a beautiful little boy named Richard. Susan

207

and I had taken her to the hospital, and Cricket, who had given up high school completely and was trying to make a living playing his trumpet at night spots around town, joined us in the waiting room when his gig ended. I took him home with me to the apartment and made up the sofa for him to sleep on.

In a week I took the sofa and gave him and Mary and the new baby my bed. It was crowded and I felt sad at the young couple's shouldering even such a dear and priceless responsibility as a baby. Little more than children themselves, they seemed caught in problems beyond solution. Besides that, they could not even be alone.

Some nights, to offer them a little privacy, I would walk around the neighborhood. One night I walked up to our old house, which the wrecking crew had not yet tackled, and sat down on the front steps. The street light, shining through the red-oak leaves, still touched the white clapboard walls with a radiance made to dance by the wind in the tree branches. I let my fingers trace in the granite block by the steps the weathered name carved there by that old man who had built the house in 1914 and loved it so much he kept it for himself, when all the others he built were sold.

Suddenly everything was too much for me. I lay down on the cool red tiles of the porch and cried. I should have kept the house. I should be within its spacious walls now with all my beset children.

A couple of weeks later I learned that one of my beset children had never departed from the old house.

Jimmy's job had run out. His apartment mates had moved and he had no place to go. He told nobody but went back home and was camping out on the old sleeping porch, where we had left an unneeded mattress. Gas and lights were off, but the water still functioned, so he had that to drink and could take cold baths. But he had nothing else.

The day I found him there was just before Easter, and I was on my way to Holy Week services at the church. On impulse I made one last, farewell stop by the house. Jimmy was asleep on the floor in almost exactly the same spot where I had lain, caught up in exaltation over owning a house and a tree that first night seventeen years before when his father and I had moved into the house.

"Jimmy!" I cried in shock and distress.

He opened his eyes and grinned at me.

"Just call me 'Onie,'" he said lightly.

Only Jimmy, only Jimmy, thin, hungry and a little drunk, would draw a literary comparison at such a moment. He saw himself as the strange, half-crazy little man who refused to leave when the new owners and bulldozers moved onto the land in *The Grapes of Wrath* but lurked like a shadow in deserted old houses or in the woods.

Hiding from the neighbors, starving himself, now dirty and alone, he was almost exactly like a John Steinbeck character. And typically he thought it was funny.

Naturally I did not, particularly when I learned that he had been selling his blood for drink at one of those seedy laboratories that used to cater to winos. Between anger and tears I hauled him off the mattress and back to my apartment for a bath and some food, and then made him go to church with me on the chance that some miracle would happen there, that within those sacred old walls, where he had spent so many hours of his childhood, he would somehow be turned around and gain strength and hope.

The one-bedroom apartment was getting crowded, and Mary and Cricket and enchanting baby Richard needed the first escape. We found it in a small but charming apartment in the basement of a pretty, nicely kept Morningside house. Its back doors opened into a pleasant shady yard with a sunny spot on a small terrace for the baby to sleep in his carriage. It was more than they could afford, since Cricket was able to work only sporadically, and to keep us all afloat I had to dip heavily into the house-sale money, which amounted to only a few thousand dollars after the mortgage was paid, and which I needed more than I had expected for all the expenses of repairing and making habitable the little log cabin.

A team of carpenters from a neighboring small town had moved into the cabin, tacked plastic over the lopsided rectangles that had served previous owners as windows. Glass window sashes were unknown to those first settlers, and they had equipped the crooked holes with shutters, which had long since disappeared. Our workmen had the fireplace for warmth and cooking and we had brought the refrigerator from Thirteenth Street. An electrician came and ran lines to the new pump in the old well, a drop cord in the ceiling for light, and an outlet for the refrigerator. Jimmy and occasionally Cricket worked with them some, camping out on cots in the one room.

Jack and I headed for the cabin nearly every Saturday morning. Except for building an equipment shed to house his tractor, newly acquired, work on his twenty acres had come to a standstill. We were concentrating on adding what the old-timers called "a shedroom" to the log room at Sweet Apple, and that involved finding the right old timbers and material to make the new walls match what was there. We were fortunate to meet a hardware merchant in the little town of Alpharetta five or six miles away, who was razing an old frame hotel to build something else. He said we could have all the material out of the hotel that we could tear out. We labored mightily to wrest old hand-planed paneling from its moorings, delighted to find that it had not been planed on the backside, which, facing out, would be rough, red brown, and marvelously suitable for Sweet Apple's shedroom walls.

The carpenters usually went home on the weekends, and we and our friends took over, doing what work we felt qualified to do or could, by trial and error, learn to do. Jack went down in the old well twenty-five feet below the surface, slimy, weedy, with a small snake in the first bucket of fetid water he sent up. He persevered until he had deepened the big hole, opening up new streams of water, which ran sweet and clean and served us for more than twenty years.

It was his idea to buy at ten cent apiece the cobblestones that surfaced Atlanta streets in the old neighborhoods and that were being torn up to make way for expressways. Everybody who came to help brought as many of these beautiful old granite paving blocks as the trunks of their cars would hold, and Jack, though unschooled in stone masonry, fetched a book from the library and built a coping around the well. I knew nothing about mixing the cement needed to hold the blocks together, but I figured it was no harder than any other kind of batter and, using my biscuit-making technique, I stirred and troweled.

Jack designed and with the help of the boys constructed an old-fashioned well house to shelter the well from the rain—all of this while the cabin itself was still a shambles of rotten logs pulled out and still not replaced with the few sounder ones we had been able to locate. The roof had been divested of its rusty tin, exposing the ancient curling shakes, which had not stood up too well to 120 years of life. Holes in the floor were covered with flattened Prince Albert tobacco cans, and holes in the wall let in the wind and the rain.

But we were having a good time with all the projects involved, and we went happily to the woods every time we could. When Thanksgiving came, Jack and I conceived the idea of spending it at Sweet Apple and cooking our festive dinner in the fireplace. Roast duck would do splendidly, we decided, and I checked to see if the children would join us or if they had plans of their own.

Mary and Cricket had half plans. His parents, still unreconciled to the marriage, had invited Cricket to come to them for dinner, bringing the baby. Mary was not asked.

I urged them all to share our roast duck at Sweet Apple. Cricket accepted his parents' invitation but did not take Richard. Instead, Mary brought the baby to the country with us, and in the midst of lumber piles and sawdust and shavings, with no furniture but the old deck chairs and a wobbly table, we prepared our feast. We stuck candles in the holes between the logs and chilled our wine in a plastic bucket of cold water from the well.

We improvised a crib for Richard's nap, using the carpenter's bedding, and when he awakened, rosy and smiling, Jack took a picture of him on a quilt in the firelight.

It was the only picture we ever got of him. Two weeks later Richard was dead.

He had been a beautiful healthy baby—my first grandchild—and I saw him often. Sometimes I kept him while Mary went to some night spot to hear Cricket play, and I grew accustomed to the way his little body felt in my arms, the texture of his soft baby hair when his head was tucked under my chin. I couldn't remember such pure sensual pleasure in a baby presence.

That night in December 1962 I drove by Mary and Cricket's apartment just for a glimpse of Richard on my way home. He had had his bath and his bottle and he was ready for bed. I rocked him and played with him a little while, marveling at so charming a smile in one but three months old. He already knew me, I bragged to his mother.

Around midnight the telephone awakened me. Mary was on the line, sobbing.

"Richard is dead!" she cried. "Richard is dead! I think I killed him. Oh, mama, please come!"

I couldn't make any sense out of it, but I got directions. They were at a hospital in Cobb County twenty-five miles north of town. I called Jack and threw on some clothes and he came to get me.

We found Mary walking the floor, sobbing. Cricket, white-faced and silent, stood just outside the emergency-room door. Richard couldn't

211

be dead, he just couldn't be, I kept telling myself. It was some cruel joke. But they let us in to see him and I knew, the still little body, the perfect little face, waxen and colorless.

I went to Mary. Jack was wiping her face—a teenager's face, smeary with makeup she had put on for a big evening at some roadside night spot where Cricket was playing, now crumpled and old with grief. She and Cricket and another couple had gone there together. Cricket went in to play and Mary and the two friends took turns sitting in the car with Richard, who was asleep in his basket on the back seat.

Mary went in to hear Cricket's solo and returned to the car to relieve her friends and check on the baby. He was cold to the touch. She snatched him up and ran for help. By the time they reached the hospital a few miles away she had decided that he either smothered or froze to death and it was her fault for bringing him out.

Neither was true.

The interns in the emergency room knew that much. They weren't sure of the cause of death. Our pediatrician, a long-time friend with relatives who were neighbors to Muv, had taken care of Richard since his birth, and we called him immediately. From his examination he knew it was the terrible unannounced killer called sudden infant death syndrome, which tackles babies anywhere for no apparent reason. To be absolutely certain, he asked for an autopsy.

Many times through the years I have felt called upon to find fault with Cricket, but that night in the emergency room, when he signed consent for his baby's autopsy, putting his name down as Richard Sr., and his age, eighteen the next day, my heart went out to him in grief and pain.

The next day our doctor explained to me about the so-called "crib death," which has taken babies for generations but was not recognized or defined until fairly recent years. He took pains to make it clear to Mary and Cricket that Richard's death was not caused by anything they did, that it would have happened in his bed at home or even if he had been in the sterile constant-care atmosphere of a hospital.

To be freed from the intolerable burden of blame helped, but there wasn't much comfort for our loss. I went alone to pick out the little casket and went back to stand beside it and ache for the baby who would no longer smile or latch onto my finger or curve his warm little body against my breast.

Mary told me that Cricket's parents wanted to pay for the baby's funeral, and knowing how much keeping the little family had cost me, she thought I'd be relieved. I was furious. They had not wanted to pay for his birth, or even to be there. They had not known and loved him as I had, had not been a part of his short life as I had. Not knowing him, how could they love him? I wouldn't let them buy him a hole to be buried in or a box for his little body, I cried hotly.

That being said, I burst into angry tears and Mary tried to comfort me. She had only thought, she said, that it would please Cricket to have them help, and Cricket needed his parents.

When his parents took Cricket *and* Mary home with them I regretted my angry words, my senseless animosity. They were the losers; they had not known Richard. They were slow getting to know Richard's mother.

The little funeral service, performed by our dear Ervin, was private, graveside only, and I don't remember if I spoke to Richard's other grandparents, who arrived early and sat in the front row. I was too moved by our mountain friend Herbert Tabor, who also arrived early for the funeral and said with wonderful, blunt sympathy: "Frances said I shouldn't come; this is a *private* funeral. I told her, 'I'm a private friend,' and here I am."

I clung to him and cried brokenly.

Jack invited the funeral party back to his apartment for lunch. Jimmy was there and I looked out at the front walk and saw Susan, very pregnant, lumbering toward us.

So many times through the years I had worried that my children fought. I had rejoiced that they were close in age and, from my point of view as an only child, there were so many of them. They would always have one another, I thought. But they fought constantly and I was bleakly convinced that they would never be friends.

But Susan coming up the front walk saw Mary on the steps and held out her arms. Mary rushed into them and they held to each other and cried together. They do love one another, I thought; they'll always have one another.

We learned that day that not only Susan but Mary, as well, was pregnant. Susan's baby, a big boy with swirls of red curls like his mama's, was born at the Fort Benning Army hospital in February.

Hovering grandmothers were not allowed to attend births in that military installation, so mother and baby were at home in the barracks-like apartment just off the post when Jack and I flew down for our first look at him. Jack had acquired half interest in a small plane with another reporter, and one of our first trips was to Columbus.

To my consternation, Susan, just out of the hospital, drove to the airport to meet us. The Cuban missile crisis was on, and Edward and all other officers and men were restricted to the post in a state known as readiness. Susan was in blooming health, perfectly capable of ferrying her relatives about, and very proud of the little boy asleep in his bassinet. His name: John Edward, for his father and grandfather.

The birth of Mary's second child was more complicated. With Jack pushing him, Cricket had been accepted in the Army music school and, after basic training in Fort Jackson, had been assigned to Anacostia. Mary had been working in the office of our friend Margaret Bridges's husband, Dr. Glenn Bridges, and sharing an apartment with another girl, but as time for the baby's birth approached she wanted to be near Cricket and Walter Reed Hospital, where military personnel could claim free maternity care.

One day we went shopping for maternity dresses, and a few days later I saw her off on the train for Washington. She found a room in an old house not far from the music school and wrote letters so cheerful I did not know for a long time that she was terribly lonely, often hungry, and frightened that all was not well with the little life inside her body.

Muv was on her way to Atlanta for a visit the day Mary called to say that she was in the hospital. Something had gone wrong; the baby was threatening to be born two months early.

Jimmy and I met Muv at the bus station and took off for Washington, driving my Volkswagen bug.

Charles, named for his late uncle, arrived early, blue and weighing only four pounds. He had to stay in an incubator in the hospital, but Mary was allowed to go home and was waiting for us on the front steps of the old house in Anacostia when we drove up around midnight. She was almost pathetically glad to see us.

She had engaged a room for Jimmy and me to share, and Muv was to share her bed, since Cricket was often restricted to the base.

The Mobile Press-Register *used this picture to announce my marriage to Jim.*

In a borrowed brown lace dress, photographed just before marriage.

Jim (James W. Little) before marriage.

*Jim in front of the
P.K. Yonge home in
Pensacola—the first place
we lived after we were
married.*

*Susan and Jimmy
about 1942.*

Dazzled by Walter Pidgeon in Hollywood, about 1952.

Clark Gable had stopped giving interviews by this time but when they told him I was from Atlanta and knew Margaret Mitchell, he talked to me—freely. On the set of Across the Wide Missouri.

Interviewing Lana Turner on the set of The Merry Widow *at MGM.*

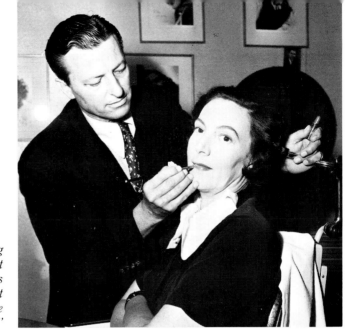

Wally Westmore, making me up at Paramount, hurt my feelings by telling his secretary not to interrupt him: "I'm doing Bebe Daniels!"

Went to Hollywood as a guest of Walt Disney to preview Song of the South. *Here with its juvenile stars, Bobby Driscoll and Luana Patten.*

A nice man, a pleasant interview: Van Heflin on the set in Hollywood.

Wearing Esther Williams's dress for Quo Vadis *premiere. Ida Jean Kain (left), exercise newspaper columnist, is telling me about exercises to correct flat-chestedness—a problem with Esther's dress.*

I couldn't go to Hollywood to accept the Christophers' national award for my column about Mary asking the blessing in a coffee shop. Father Keller ran Loretta Young in my place.

*Woman of the Year banquet at the Piedmont Driving Club. Congratulatory kiss from Jimmy while Mary (*left*) and Susan (*right*) hold prize antique silver entree dishes (Photo by Ken Patterson).*

Editor Isabelle Taylor on hand for debut of my first book, The Malignant Heart.

Photo Ken Patterson took for jacket of Peachtree Street U.S.A.

Miss Mayhayley Lancaster, star witness of the John Wallace murder trial, telling my fortune—almost.

Sweet Apple cabin with Jimmy scattering grass seed after we had cleared the yard of underbrush but before beginning to rebuild.

At a 1967 signing for A Place Called Sweet Apple *with the legendary Ann Poland Berg of Rich's public relations department, Faith Brunson of Rich's book department (supplying rabbit ears), and the hoping-to-become-legendary Larry Ashmead of Doubleday's editorial department.*

On our way to cover the Beatles' visit to Atlanta a photographer made me wear a Beatles wig.

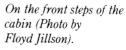

On the front steps of the cabin (Photo by Floyd Jillson).

Jack Strong and me in the kitchen at Sweet Apple.

"Are you hungry?" she asked. "I have plenty of peanut butter and jelly!"

To Muv, who had never eaten peanut butter and jelly in her life, except perhaps on an ill-planned picnic, that symbolized almost heart-breaking poverty.

"Poor child, poor child," she kept saying. "She's got 'plenty of peanut butter and jelly'—and nothing else."

She did have a little son in precarious health, and except for an old friend and former neighbor of Jack's, an octogenarian named Miss Kate McBride, called Bridey, who had moved from Atlanta to the Eastern Star retirement home in Washington, she had nobody to accompany her to Walter Reed Hospital once a day to stand outside a window and watch her baby breathe. Cricket often couldn't leave the music school, and when he did he didn't want to spend an hour in the apparently futile business of simply looking at the little mite in the incubator.

Valiant old Bridey caught a bus and met Mary at the hospital every evening, and they went and stood together at the plate-glass window that isolated the nursery, willing little Charles to keep breathing, to live.

I choked up over the poignant picture they made, the old lady and the young girl, neither of them strong, clinging to one another and standing for the full hour the hospital allowed, their eyes riveted prayerfully on the tiny body in the incubator. Muv and I stood with them (Jimmy went out to a neighboring pub to drink beer with Cricket) until the baby was said to be out of danger. Then we went shopping for a bassinet and a month's supply of diapers, bottles, and milk before we left for Atlanta.

In a month we were meeting Mary and the baby, now called Bird, at the Atlanta airport. The baby, still pitifully scrawny, had measles—and Mary was pregnant again.

"Isn't he beautiful, mama?" Mary kept saying. "He's so beautiful."

He wasn't to a grandmother and a great-grandmother accustomed to plump, rosy, picture-book babies, but Muv and I came swiftly to Mary's conclusion. We kept Bird a month so his mother could go to Newburgh, New York, and find a place to live. Cricket had graduated with honors from the music school and was being assigned to West Point, where he played for such returning heroes as General Douglas

215

MacArthur and for football games, and daily he played the despised—by him—"Reveille" and "Taps."

Muv took the daily duty with Bird, and when I came home from work I became night nurse, terrified, as Mary had been, that his evening bout with colic might cause him to quit breathing, as Richard had done. But he flourished. He gained weight and took on color in his cheeks. By the time Mary had found a place to live—a trailer not far from the Point—and our friend, Charlie Hooper, who was flying to New York on business, offered to deliver Bird to his mother, we thought he was as handsome and healthy a child as we had ever seen.

In May 1963, two months before Bird was born, the cabin at Sweet Apple was pronounced habitable, if not totally restored. The yard had been skinned of underbrush and planted to rye grass, the log walls were as straight and true as their nature permitted, glass-paned sashes gleamed in the sunshine in the two newly-squared windows in the main room, and there was a fairly roomy shedroom kitchen just waiting for its appliances. Our carpenter had replaced the ladder leading to the loft bedroom with stair steps and installed a bathroom.

The new roof covered with old shingles filled me with proprietary delight. I had had a hand in putting it there.

One of our best-loved neighbors, an old gentleman named Mr. Lum Crow, knew I wanted authentic white-oak shakes for that roof, the kind that the builder had put there 120 years before. A mountain man with a keen blue-eyed gaze and silver hair, he was, at seventy-nine years, as lean and erect as an old Indian and as tireless. He came almost every weekend to see if he could help us, delighting me with his knowledge of the old days in the area, when he had gone to school in the Sweet Apple cabin, sitting on puncheon benches and having to pull the boards off the cracks between the logs to get enough light to see by. At that, Mr. Crow did not learn to read—at least the printed word—but he unerringly read the seasons and the earth. His sharp old eyes never missed a bird's flight, a shift in the wind, a ripening muscadine, a young fox's track, or the passage of a rabbit.

Our old neighbor took seriously my need of hand-rived white-oak shakes for the cabin roof, and he introduced me to craftsmen who could still do the work, but as one of them, Mr. Jim Taylor, plaintively explained to me, "City people moving in has messed up all the good

216

timber." He simply could not find white-oak trees of the right size to make my shingles.

One day a timber cruiser in north Georgia called me and said he thought he had found a cache of shingles in an old buggy house near the little town of Jasper. The man who had rived them forty years before had carefully stacked them out of the weather with a rock to weight them down, but he had died, his widow had moved to town, and the timber cruiser thought she would be willing to sell the shakes reasonably. I couldn't embark on such an enterprise without expert guidance, and I called on Mr. Crow for help.

On a frosty January Saturday he and I embarked, followed by another neighbor with a truck that we had hired for the day. We found the buggy house without any trouble, and I waited for Mr. Crow to inspect the shakes. He took his time, lifting the rocks, picking up one roughly-rived, tapered shingle after another and sighting down it as he would the barrel of his squirrel rifle.

Finally he turned to me and delivered his accolade. "Them's good boards," he said.

He and Clint Goodman, who had the truck, and I loaded the shakes for an hour. The sun came out and melted the frost, and we shucked our jackets and caps and hefted shingles from buggy house to truck bed. It was good work, and I was eager to get back to the cabin and display my find to Jack and the carpenters.

But there was a little delay. Mr. Crow had a cousin who lived in the small town of Canton, twelve miles north of Sweet Apple, and he asked if I would mind stopping by her house on the way home. Willing, of course, I urged him to go see his cousin and I would wait in the car. It was a short visit, and Mr. Crow appeared cast down when he came out of the house.

"How was your cousin?" I asked.

He shook his head gloomily. "Not good," he said. "She used to be a fine-looking woman. Weighed over two hundred pounds. Now she's as pore as a snake."

Our chief carpenter, Judson Carter, was as pleased with the shingles as we were and immediately started preparing the roof for them, marking out courses with a chalky plumb line to make sure they marched along in straight rows. So jubilant were Mr. Crow and I to have come through with the proper "boards" that we climbed the

217

ladder to the roof, donned nail aprons, and hammered along with the carpenters. If there had been traffic on the road in those days we might have drawn a crowd of spectators, two real carpenters, a middle-aged woman, and a seventy-nine-year-old man perched precariously on a rooftop nailing away at forty-year-old slices of silver-and-rose oak wood.

When our day's work was done and the sun had gone from the new rooftop, Mr. Crow went to his ancient pickup truck and brought back a sackful of sweet, fragrant little lady apples, which he passed around to us his co-workers.

It seemed to me that day—and it still does—that an old house you helped to restore to usefulness and happy living has a spiritual pull on you that no other structure can match.

For we were happy at Sweet Apple, despite the problems of a rapidly expanding family. Jimmy had moved into Sweet Apple with me, and Jack had given up his apartment in town and fixed up quarters in the rough building he had intended for an equipment barn on his land. We all worked on Jack's apartment, when we had time, the boys nailing down flooring from a torn-down dancehall in town and staining the outside walls barn red, I hauling up wild plants from the woods and making a sort of garden by the front walls, Doc supervising the construction of a deck to expand the little house. We had all helped Jack build a lake, a clear, fern-fringed body of water fed by the pretty little creek we had first admired. To reward ourselves we swam in it often, and one day, sitting on the little strip of sandy beach we had hauled in, I looked in amazement at the family gathered there.

First there were none and now there were eight adults—Jack and me and my three children and the people they had married—and *their* five children!

Jimmy had gone to work in Rich's book department, where he met and married a pretty girl named Marie Eubanks. They had a little boy named James for his father and five fathers before him. (We called him Jamie.) Mary and Cricket had come home for Cricket to finish out his military stint at Fort McPherson in Atlanta and Mary to give birth to their first daughter, a dark-eyed charmer named Celestine Sibley for me and, at my insistence, called Sibley, Tib, or Sissy. (Not Celestine, please!) She was so close to Bird's age, with a difference of only eleven months between them, that they seemed almost like twins in their affection for one another but not in appearance. He was fair-haired and blue-eyed; she had tawny gold and brown gypsy coloring.

Susan and Edward had two little boys, John and Ted, both red-headed.

"Ah, the strength of those genes!" Edward said in mock despair, looking at his wife and sons with their fiery, coppery heads together.

I didn't tell him then—maybe I shouldn't tell him—that they owe that shining titian coloring to a restless, wandering woman also named Susan, who roamed the earth many years before, faithful to nobody and no place. Sue, headstrong and impetuous—how would she have liked being grandmother, great-grandmother, great-great-grand-mother in that gathering by the lake on the sunny afternoon? If Muv had been there she would have pondered once more the only clue she had to her mother's whereabouts and death. She believed her mother had been on welfare in Jacksonville and Muv had sent regular, if small, contributions to a caseworker who hadn't known either if the old lady she watched over was her correspondent's mother or just a similar person in need. Muv needed to believe her Cousin Albert's theory. He sent her a newspaper clipping about an old woman who had lost her life in the path of a speeding automobile while pushing a baby in a carriage to safety. He believed that irresponsible, turned-funny Sue had died a heroine.

None of us ever knew for sure—but we do have Sue's red hair, in abundance.

Since I had three books out and doing pretty well, Mrs. Taylor wanted me to keep them coming, and I *needed* to. Long ago I had read that the great English author Samuel Johnson had turned out a full-scale novel to pay his mother's funeral expenses while her body waited in the next room for burial. I didn't think old Sam had a patch on me when it came to urgent places to put money. Thankful though I was that we were all in life and reasonably healthy, I could but reflect that a funeral isn't necessarily the most pushing need for money. Muv was having trouble with her ears and her eyes, the bright brown eyes that always saw so much and reflected so much humor and malice and compassion and cunning. We got her equipped with a hearing aid, which she tried to wear for a while and finally deposited in a dresser drawer and forgot. Then I took her to an eye specialist and found that she had cataracts on both eyes, needing operations, if she was to have any sight at all. Her insurance would pay some but not all of the bill, and I was very glad that Mrs. Taylor would keep the advances coming as long as I was able to keep the books going her way. I never made a lot on a book, but then I never made a lot as a reporter-columnist. In those days it was assumed that women either didn't need as much as their men colleagues or were not worth as much, although Fields, while refusing to hire women reporters when I would see a good one and urge her on him, sometimes told me that in spite of my evil disposition and other deplorable traits I was the best reporter he had.

His appreciation, acid though it often was, meant a lot to me, and I never pressed for more money, fearing, as women have for generations, that I might lose my job and the little I was making. I pieced out by doing magazine articles when I could get them, confession stories, trade-journal pieces on the opening of drugstores and new laundries. And now books.

Clif Devereaux had talked to the people in Doubleday's New York offices about the possibility of a book on Atlanta's famous old department store, Rich's. There had been highly successful books about Macy's by Margaret Case Harriman, the *New Yorker* writer, and Marshall Fields in Chicago by Emily Kimbrough, the humorist and Cornelia Otis Skinner's pal and collaborator (*Our Hearts Were Young and Gay*).

Clif and his superiors in New York felt that Rich's had the personality and character for good reading, and Rich's and I agreed. Dick Rich, grandson of the founder, was alive then and intensely interested in presenting the famous and in many ways totally unique old store in the most readable fashion possible. I had, like everybody else in Atlanta, an abiding relationship with the store and close friends who worked there. Funny and heart-warming and amazing anecdotes were all there for the picking, I believed.

We signed a contract. Rich's was to pay the advance, but I would be entitled to the usual royalties from the sale of the book. Mr. Dick, as everybody called him, assigned me an office with a phone and a desk in one of the big mirrored fitting rooms, where Atlanta women went to try on their designer clothes. I knew it was too grand for me. I had learned that years before when I was nominated Atlanta's Woman of the Year and was compelled to show up at a banquet at the elegant Piedmont Driving Club. A friend of mine, who was a clerk in the specialty shop, called me very mysteriously one day and asked me over.

220

When I went slopping in, wearing muddy loafers and a beatup raincoat, I thought I saw bewilderment and perhaps a bit of chill on the faces of the other saleswomen in the department. But my loyal friend Mary Dunlap looked at her co-workers and said persuasively, "It's all right. We're going to fix her up."

The mystery was that someone—Mary wouldn't say who—wanted to buy my outfit for the big evening—dress, shoes, gloves, bag, the works. I pressed for the name of my benefactor. Mary wouldn't tell me. I insisted. She balked.

Finally, I said I couldn't take such an expensive gift from somebody whose name I didn't know, and slogged on out through the ankle-deep carpet.

The next day Mary called me back. The donor of my finery was our publisher's wife, a perfectly lovely woman I didn't know well but admired a great deal, Mrs. Clark Howell.

"I'll take it," I said. "And thank you."

So my friends in the rich and splendid precincts of the specialty shop knew I could be made worthy to work among them. But I was back in raincoat and loafers.

"My dear," said one of the artfully corseted, opulent-bosomed ladies in black which shrieked of gold, "while you're in here wouldn't you like us to help you to something . . . a bit . . . well, you know suitable."

"Suitable? I'm just working," I said. "What I have on, does it matter?" I yanked at a rumpled blouse, which kept working its way out of my skirtband and stuck a loafered foot under my chair, hoping she wouldn't see the run in my stocking.

They let the subject drop, and I got busy on the phone, making appointments, setting up interviews.

In spite of my sartorial unsuitability, the ladies in the specialty shop and I became great friends, and they were the source of many rich anecdotes about the store and its customers, including one about the lady who paid $2,000 for a dress and had to borrow money to get out of the parking lot.

The store really was legendary, sustaining a quixotic credit, return, and exchange, customer-is-right-right-right policy, which students of department-store techniques came from all over the world to study. Customers held the store in more than high esteem, rather in love and respect accorded a generous old uncle. As one competitor remarked derisively, to people in the South's Bible Belt Rich's was "the true church." It had a history going back to 1867, the days of scorched earth and bitter Reconstruction, of pitching in and helping individuals and the city in time of crisis.

So I had a good time working on that book, going to the store after I had finished my stint at the *Constitution* every afternoon and often laboring there after closing time. I developed a real affection for Dick Rich, who gave me my head, turning over to me bales of records and correspondence, including sentimental poems that customers sometimes wrote to the store, and directing employees to talk freely to me.

One day I decided I needed to see the grave of the founder, Morris Rich, Mr. Dick's grandfather, and Faith Brunson, the book buyer, and Anne Berg, the public-relations director, both long-time friends, decided to make a picnic of it. Anne collected a lunch from Rich's tearoom, and we set out for old Oakland Cemetery, where most of the city's founding fathers and such luminaries as Margaret Mitchell are buried. We found the grave in the Jewish section and spread our lunch there.

"I wonder what he looked like," mused Anne as we read the headstone and munched our sandwiches.

"Slender, dark-eyed, five feet eight," I said promptly.

Faith whooped. "She's ready to write the book," she said. "She's got it."

Writing it was not all that easy since weekends and nights were the only times I had to devote to it. Once when I sat by the window in the cabin struggling, I saw a black snake headed my way on a trellis outside. He was chasing a little green frog, which found refuge through a hole in the logs and dropped on my typewriter. I feared the snake would do the same.

At that moment the phone rang. Anne wanted to know how I was doing with the book.

"Can't talk, Anne!" I cried. "There's a frog and a snake after me. I got to run 'em off!"

"You'll do anything to keep from writing," said Anne and hung up.

The book came out in 1967, named *Dear Store* from one of the fan letters in Mr. Dick's file. We were all delighted with the reception it got from an awed and gratified public, not just employees and customers, although customers seemed to regard it as a personal family story. Years later there was a movement afoot for me to update the book, but by that time Dick Rich had died, the store had become a part of the big Federated conglomerate, and had changed. I did not want, as my mother often put it, to lick my calf over.

Meanwhile, I was acquiring a new editor at Doubleday. Mrs. Taylor was grooming her young assistant, Lawrence Ashmead, to succeed her. This was a development the publisher's Atlanta authors viewed with alarm. He came down from New York for *Dear Store*'s debut and several writers left their typewriters to try to curry favor with a welcoming party. Faith and Anne invited him and me to lunch at Rich's, an occasion that bordered on a disaster when Larry remarked innocently that he had just had his thirtieth birthday.

"Thirty!" we cried, looking at one another in trepidation.

The gentle, perceptive Mrs. Taylor, southern born, in fact the daughter-in-law of a former Alabama congressman, was turning us over to this stripling, this wet-behind-the-ears youngster, who probably thought Miami was the South. We were in for shoaly waters, we feared, and there was but one way to handle it.

"Don't ever mention your age again!" one of us said harshly.

And Larry Ashmead, my editor for twenty years now and the editor of several other Georgia writers, has not so far as I know ever said another word on the subject. This is remarkable in view of the fact that I have attended several of his Fourth of July birthday parties in New York and on Long Island, where he and a friend shared a beach house.

The last book I did at Mrs. Taylor's suggestion was edited jointly by her and Larry. It was *A Place Called Sweet Apple,* an account of acquiring and restoring the old cabin. Both Larry and Mrs. Taylor came to town for the pub-day festivities, staying in the country with us, Mrs. Taylor at Sweet Apple with me and Larry in Jack's former tractor shed with him.

Loyal friends at Rich's rallied and had a tea featuring the old country recipes I had included in the book. I had collected them from my mother and from old-time neighbors, who had them handed down from ancestors in Appalachia, on the theory that if I didn't make haste to save them they might be lost. Just before the party got underway Anne Berg murmured to me that Mr. Dick would like to see me in his office. He had the usual congratulatory words to offer and something else: a Steuben glass apple, still one of my most cherished keepsakes, reminding me of a special day and of the gentle, imaginative man who was my friend and all the South's.

Larry, knowing of my enthusiasm for tilling the soil, suggested that I try my hand at a gardening book. As usual, I was enthusiastic. I always seem to be when somebody suggests a story or magazine piece or a book. My impulse is to say, "Sure! When you want it?"

Delivery is tougher, and it was very tough for that one because it was the summer that the well-known author Jesse Hill Ford (*The Liberation of Lord Byron Jones*) was being tried for murder in Humboldt, Tennessee. I was sent to cover the trial.

I had picked up a few misgivings about my ability to write a gardening book, recognizing that my personal experience was pretty limited and my knowledge and skill inadequate. The only thing that reassured me was that as a reporter I often wrote about subjects not within my personal ken. I interviewed experts. I could do that on the subject of gardening, and I set about talking to those who had demonstrated that they were, if not landscapers and horticulturists, at least gardeners of proven ability.

The trial came up during my research. The book was past due, and I had called Larry to apologize and explain. His assistant said he would deliver the message, but he knew Larry would be embarrassed to explain my delinquency to his editorial board. I went off to Humboldt, vowing I would deliver that manuscript somehow, someway as soon as I could get back.

Jesse Hill Ford was acquitted. He had shot a man he thought was an intruder in his driveway, but the man was black, and racial tensions being what they were at the time, the author was indicted and tried. It was a tough time for Ford and his family, but those of us assigned to cover the trial enjoyed a certain fraternal sociability. After work we shopped for food at the nearest market and assembled in one or another's motel room for sandwiches, beer, and good newspaper talk.

When I got back I fell to and finished the gardening book. Larry was content that while I celebrated the joy of being a striving neophyte I depended on others for my solid how-to information, but he made a joke, which serves him to this good day.

He came to Atlanta for the publication of *Sweet Apple Gardening Book,* and we assembled a few friends for a brunch in his honor at the cabin. It was March and my patch was still in the throes of winter deshabille. Musing on its dilapidation before the party I remarked that I hoped no guest would feel impelled to look it over.

Edited by my editor, that story comes out that I made a frantic plea for somebody to take up a post in the backyard and turn back all prospective lookers. For years I have wailed, "But, Larry, it was March! Nobody's yard looks good in March! Besides, the book plainly says that I *enjoy* gardening, not that I'm good at it."

Larry is now a gardener himself, spectacularly successful in a small plot at his weekend and vacation home up the Hudson River. But he knows about the uncertainties and the near-misses, and someday he'll give up that story about me and the gardening pretensions I never had. Or I'll give up and enjoy it.

Chapter Eight

Children, at least *my* children, are bad about turning your most impressive pronouncements, your fondest recollections, against you. When we have traveled through rural counties and small towns of Georgia, I have often launched what I considered to be fascinating conversational gambits with "I covered a murder trial here."

Instead of pressing me for the absorbing details of the life-and-death drama, they hooted derisively, and at the next crossroads somebody in the back seat would yell, "Slow down! Mama covered a murder trial here!"

Sometimes a trial took me out of the state. The trial of Arthur Bremer, the strange young fellow who shot Alabama Governor George Wallace while he was campaigning for President, crippling him for life, was such a one. That went on for a week in August 1972 in Prince Georges County courthouse in Upper Marlboro, Maryland, ending with the twenty-one-year-old defendant being held sane and sentenced to sixty-three years for assault with intent to murder Wallace, a Secret Service agent, an Alabama state trooper, and a woman supporter, who stood near the governor as he spoke to a crowd at a Laurel, Maryland, rally.

The Bremer trial was peculiarly troubling to me. For one thing, I was lonely. It had brought out a lot of newspapermen and women, but none were old friends, members of that sizable national coterie of one-time Atlanta reporters. Many of them lived in the Washington and Baltimore areas and went home at night and, hating to eat alone, I usually went back to my motel room, ate cheese crackers, made a cup of instant coffee with my little submersible heating coil, went to bed

226

early, and lay awake puzzling over the life of the bespectacled young defendant, who attended the trial with the bright expectant expression of a child on a picnic. Obviously aware of the artists in the courtroom, who were sketching him in the absence of photographers, who were barred, he obliged them by turning around in his chair and directing sunny, almost serene, smiles at them. In his diary, which was read to the jury, he proclaimed his desire to be another Sirhan Sirhan, who killed Robert Kennedy. He wanted to kill *somebody*—anybody—whose assassination would get him worldwide attention. He had considered killing J. Edgar Hoover. He had stalked President Richard Nixon for months, losing his chance to shoot him once because of his own fanatical cleanliness. (Before pulling the trigger he went back to the motel to take a bath and brush his teeth.) He had thought of killing Hubert Humphrey and George McGovern, temporarily shelving the idea of Alabama's governor for the reason, as he wrote in his diary, that the newspaper headlines would read: WALLACE DEAD. WHO CARES?

The shootings he failed to pull off caused him to reflect sadly, "I am a failure. I hope my death makes more sense than my life."

What happened to him? I wondered as I couldn't sleep. One psychiatrist testified that genes have a lot to do with the way a child turns out, that some of us are "programmed to fail" from birth. But that did not keep Bremer's attorneys from dwelling on his unhappy childhood and his inadequate parents. He had not had a "stable relationship" with anybody in his entire life, they said.

A woman in the courtroom spoke to me at a recess. "I thought for a minute there they were trying Bremer's mother," she said.

I smiled and nodded, accepting the fact that mothers are practically always suspect. But then Bremer's father came to court, took the witness stand for only two or three minutes, and then did not look at his son or mention his name. Asked if his wife, a woman their son had called "aggravated and aggravating," had accompanied him, the elder Bremer said in a loud voice, "She did not."

"Did you ask her to come?" the defense attorney asked.

"I did," Bremer replied. "She said she couldn't make it."

Mulling over the tragedy of Arthur Bremer and the senseless shooting of two officers and a woman bystander, who happened to be in his line of fire, as well as what was to be lifelong pain and near helplessness for Governor Wallace, I had trouble getting to sleep.

As always when I was out of town on assignment, I had to call my children before I slept. A stable relationship we might not have—I wasn't even sure what that was—but love, ah, I loved and missed them.

The John Wallace murder trial, later to be delineated in a book (*Murder in Coweta County*) by Margaret Ann Barnes and a pretty inept television play, starring Johnny Cash, June Carter, and Andy Griffith, took me to a little town but thirty miles southwest of Atlanta. I suppose I could have commuted to the trial each day, but there were night sessions of court and you never know what apparently extraneous ingredient in a trial will lead to a good story.

Miss Mayhayley Lancaster was such a find.

A tall, gaunt woman with one eye that had a stubborn fix on the ceiling and one that ran rheumily constantly, Miss Mayhayley wore a little hat with a long-stemmed flower bobbing crazily from its brim. To my mind she was the most fascinating witness either side presented during that ten-day trial. I took out after her at recess and then followed her to her home.

A man variously called William and Wilson Turner (he was a deserter from the Army and sometimes used his brother's name and 4-F draft card) disappeared after being run down, severely beaten, and hauled from a Coweta County motel dining room by three big men, while witnesses looked on.

A widespread search ensued, involving a lot of people—one group sympathetic because he left behind a wife and little son, another group because one of the men who pursued and hauled away Turner was the area's most prominent landowner, John Wallace, known to be a harsh dealer with people who crossed him. The sheriff in Wallace's county, Meriwether, a long-time Wallace friend, was old and ill and didn't bestir himself in Turner's behalf, knowing him as a bootlegger and accused cattle thief and probably dismissing his disappearance as good riddance.

A young and diligent sheriff named Lamar Potts in the adjoining county of Coweta did take an interest. The Sunset Motel, where Turner was snatched up, beaten, and taken away by Wallace and two of his friends, happened to be just over the line in Coweta County, thus empowering Potts to enter the case.

I didn't get into the search at first. Our police reporter, Keeler

McCartney, trudged through thickets and swamps with the officers for days, and I was finally sent in search of Turner's wife, who had fled the county, supposedly in fear of Wallace. Photographer Floyd Jillson and I found her in a lonely, remote old house in Heard County, hiding out with relatives. I never forgot that interview. We found the house and knocked on the door, and after a long time a ragged shade stirred at one of the front windows and I found a pair of crossed eyes watching me.

It was Julia Turner. She apparently considered Floyd and me harmless because she let us in and talked freely while her little boy tore up a seed catalog, chewed the paper, and pushed it through the big cracks in the floor.

Meanwhile, the two principals in the case, Wallace and Sheriff Potts, sought out the area's self-styled "seer and oracle," Miss Mayhayley Lancaster, for information and what amounted to direction.

"I told them both the same," Miss Mayhayley testified, "that Turner's body was in a well with blue flies around it and that it was soon to take a trip on horseback."

The location of the body was of course known to Wallace, but he accepted Miss Mayhayley's words as omniscient, and that night Turner's body, beaten and bloody and bullet-riddled, was hauled out of the abandoned well, put on horseback, and transported to a funeral pyre in a swamp. There it was reduced to ashes and an almost negligible assortment of bones—so few that the state's famed crime doctor and toxicologist, Dr. Herman Jones, brought only a matchbox full to court to establish corpus delicti. Sheriff Potts took Miss Mayhayley's words to heart, and the next day he found the well and by following the tracks of the horse, trampled grass, and signs of blood, was able to trace Turner's body to the swamp and the ash pile where it had been cremated.

Wallace was convicted after a long, rambling account of his troubles with Turner, who had been a tenant on his place and, he said, a trouble-making moonshiner and cattle thief. He contended that he was merely trying to teach Turner a lesson when he had him on the coping of the old well, but his attention was diverted by a passing train and the gun in his hand went off.

"I'm just as innocent of this man's death as you are," he told the jury.

229

But the jurors didn't believe him, and he was sentenced to die in the electric chair.

I went to see the fifty-eight-year-old prisoner a few months before he was electrocuted and found him affably directing the activities of the prisoners in his bull pen and optimistically predicting that he would not be executed. He had got religion in jail, he said, and found scripture promising that he would be spared by prayer. Besides, he had Miss Mayhayley's word that he would live to be eighty-eight years old.

"If there was ever a time when I hoped she was telling the truth, this is it!" he told me.

Miss Mayhayley and I became friends—for a very pragmatic reason on her part. My stories about her stepped up the fortunetelling business astronomically. Famous for hanging around the courthouse square in Carroll County telling fortunes for "a dollar and a dime" apiece she raised her fee to $2.75. She was suddenly a wealthy woman, building herself a ten-room house in the town of Franklin, which had been, so she told me, "one mile measured" from her rude cabin in the country.

I never saw the fine painted town house. The last time I visited Miss Mayhayley she and her sister, Miss Sally, were still ensconced in the log cabin. I did see some signs of lively commerce, in that the weed-choked area next to the house had been cleared and turned into a parking lot for customers, and one of Miss Mayhayley's cousins had erected a stand to sell soft drinks and sardines and crackers to those who had to wait in line.

Miss Sally was alone in the cabin when photographer Ryan Sanders and I arrived and eager to tell of her recent illness, during which she "couldn't keep a thing on my stomach but parched corn and whiskey." Miss Mayhayley, coming up from the cow pen, gave no evidence of the new affluence. She was wearing her World War I visored Army cap and a long khaki, government-issue coat, which brushed her high-topped shoes. It was late afternoon and very dark in the cabin. Dogs and chickens swirled around Miss Mayhayley's feet indoors and out, and when I asked her to tell my fortune she had to light a pine torch to see by.

I had heard stories of those rare customers whose fortunes she emphatically refused to tell, foreseeing that they were going to die on the way home. There was no such impetus when she examined my future. She took one look at the cards, glanced at my palm—and went to sleep!

"Some boring future you got!" my buddy Sanders said, packing up his camera to leave.

He was wrong, of course. Boredom has never been one of my problems. One reason is those murder trials.

Half a dozen years after John Wallace was put to death, I was deep in the case of Anjette Lyles, a plump, sweet-faced thirty-three-year-old restaurant operator in the mid-Georgia city of Macon. Platinum-haired and charming, she had been a favorite of lawyers and judges who ate at her establishment across from the courthouse. She was highly regarded by her minister, who shepherded one of the biggest and most-stylish congregations in town, and, as we say in the South, she was "connected with some very nice people."

She was charged with having fed a clear, colorless ant bane to two husbands, a mother-in-law, and the eldest of her two daughters, nine-year-old Marcia. They all died horrible, excruciatingly painful deaths. According to the testimony of nurses at the hospital and some of the workers in her restaurant, she solicitously took buttermilk and lemonade to her loved ones and insisted on preparing their meals with her own hands. Some of the food she carried to them was kept in the hospital refrigerator, a potential peril to other patients.

As Miss Mayhayley figured in the John Wallace case, so did root doctors, spiritual advisers, and soothsayers in the Lyles case. Bill Wilson, a photographer, and I arrived a couple of days early for the trial of Mrs. Lyles and spent some time researching old Macon murders (this one was the worst in fifty years, I was told) and checking on the alleged devil worshipers who held her in thrall. In a neighboring small town we found a very respectable-looking middle-class housewife who said she had indeed instructed Anjette in the use of candles and mystical rites.

On the witness stand, making an unsworn statement, which was required by law in Georgia at the time, the cameo-faced but heavy-bodied defendant smilingly admitted to the attraction of voodoo artifacts.

"I have been burning candles a long time," Anjette told the jury. "I believe in them. I went to root doctors. I went to fortunetellers. I went to spiritual advisers. I talked to one every day. I believed in it and liked it."

She said she burned a long green candle for luck and money, a red one for love, a white one for peace, an orange one "to keep down talk," and a black one to break up her most recent lover, an airline pilot named Bob Franks, with his other girl friend. She said she sprinkled salt in four corners of her restaurant to make business good and in her house to bring luck and love to it. She put green garlic under her rugs in the confident belief that it would "bring back anybody who walked on it," and she put Frank's picture in a sock under her bed and in a stocking in the north corner of her dresser drawer, also calculated to guarantee his return.

There are "certain roots," she said, "if you put them in your mouth when you talk to people you can get them to do what you want them to do," and one root named for Adam and Eve, which, if rubbed on your forehead three times before the morning sun would "get you what you want."

Obviously Mrs. Lyles was not equipped with roots the day she told her story to the jury. It did not believe her protestations that she loved her slain relatives and wouldn't hurt them for the world. They seemed to think her interest in $40,000 insurance money and her purchase of an expensive car immediately after her second husband's death did not indicate heartbreak.

She was found guilty and sentenced to die in the electric chair by a jury that deliberated only an hour and a half before reaching its verdict.

Her sentence was later commuted to life in the state hospital for the insane, and for some reason Anjette wanted me to have the scoop on that development. She had the jailer call me and Bill Wilson and I rushed down to Macon to interview her.

Always carefully groomed, she was especially well dressed that day and was holding court in a room at the jail. Grateful to her for giving me the break on the commutation story, I said ingenuously, "Anjette, I know you have always worked. There's a sewing room at the hospital. You might try to get in there."

She laughed her low, throaty laugh. "Celestine," she said, "I couldn't sew a seam if my life depended on it. The only thing I'm good at is food. I hope they put me in the kitchen."

Wilson and I left Macon, gloomily predicting that Anjette's contribution to food preparation in our big mental hospital might wipe out our mental-health problems in Georgia or, at least, end overcrowding in our mental institution.

It happened that Anjette was assigned to food preparation. She died at Milledgeville Hospital fifteen years later. I never learned of a single arsenic death at the hospital during her tenure in the kitchen, but then, after they exhumed those four bodies in Macon, they outlawed ant bane in Georgia.

Many stories of national and even international import have happened during my years with the *Constitution*. I covered all or parts of most of them, including some aspects of the funny, shocking "Double Governor" hiatus, when the state was caught without a governor in 1947 following the death of Eugene Talmadge before he could assume office. His son Herman, elected by the state legislature on the strength of a wad of absentee ballots, some of which were cast in his home county by citizens long dead, took over the chief executive's office in a late-night foray which the outgoing governor Ellis Arnall compared to the acts of a "pretender in a Banana Republic."

I also knew Jimmy Carter when he served in the State Senate and later in the governor's office, and I went to New York to see the Democratic National Convention nominate him for President of the United States. I had always wanted to cover a national political convention, but until this one—and the Republican convention of the same year—it was an assignment editors reserved for themselves. Half a dozen of us got to go to the Carter convention, of course, traveling up to New York in the private plane of the paper's owner, Anne Cox Chambers.

Madison Square Garden, which I had never seen, dazzled me with its color and its crowds, but it wasn't easy for even an accredited reporter to get close to the action. The best seats went to the wire services, television reporters, and such papers as the *New York Times* and the Washington *Post.* By sheer happenstance I was able to beat that. The second day of the convention was gray, with a drizzling rain. I went back to my hotel room to get my raincoat out of the cleaner's bag I had brought it in and found a tag on the lapel that read: "This garment has received our VIP treatment but we could not remove some of the stains."

The VIP stood out in clear black letters, the disclaimer in small print. I decided to wear the coat with the tag attached.

It was magical. First I went up to the suite of that celebrated elder statesman the late Averell Harriman. His secretary started to tell me that he was very busy with a schedule jammed with appointments, and then her eye fell on my cleaning tag.

"But I know he will want to see *you!*" she said hastily and admitted me.

Mr. Harriman was a charming man, maybe the most politically savvy at the convention, and a good interview. I left him to go up to the Plaza in search of Candidate Carter's mother, Miss Lillian, who was being honored by the cast of her favorite soap opera, *All My Children.* People spoke to me on the subway, asking how the convention was going. In the restaurant where I stopped for lunch, the proprietor came out and asked me who was going to be nominated for Vice President.

I was very authoritative. I told everybody that Texas Congresswoman Barbara Jordan, whose keynote speech I had heard the night before and found very impressive, had the job. They nodded sagaciously and spread the word. A bona-fide VIP had told them.

By keeping on my raincoat, I got a good seat in the Garden and was able to trip down to the convention floor and stand with the Georgia delegation when our governor, George Busbee, moved to make Carter's nomination unanimous.

Unfortunately, Barbara Jordan didn't see my cleaning tag and I was not able to get an interview with her. It served her right that Walter Mondale got the vice-presidency.

A snowstorm hit Washington the next January about the time the Peanut Brigade from Georgia hit it for the inauguration. Our fashion editor, Raymond Alexander, went up to cover the parties and the clothes and was, of course, fashionably equipped for the assignment. She wore a raincoat lined with sable. Whatever I wore—the same old raincoat, I think, but without the VIP tag—was not enough. Our photographer, Billy Downs, saw my shivering dilemma and brought me one of the two suits of long underwear he had packed for himself for the trip. Another photographer, Bill Mahan, went out on Pennsylvania Avenue and found a street-corner vendor selling knit watch caps for $1 each. He brought one back to me.

Our fashion editor assured me I wouldn't make *Vogue,* but I was almost comfortable in the cold winter wind that attended the swearing-in ceremony and was able to walk along parallel to the Carters when they made the now-historic hike from the Capitol to the White House. Earlier I had weathered the dawn service at the Lincoln Memorial emceed by Martin Luther (Daddy) King, Sr., by far the most moving of the many events attending the inauguration. The famed Atlanta Boy Choir, which has sung for royalty all over the world, sang that morning, and I don't think a soul but me, hearing their lovely young voices raised in the cold air, noticed they were wearing Baggies over their shoes.

Martin Luther King, Jr., was a story I mostly missed. The paper wasn't really assiduous in its coverage of the civil rights battle. Our editor, McGill, who had spent years paving the way for integration, and our political editors, Bill Shipp and Reg Murphy (he who was later to be kidnaped—and I did cover some of that story), made occasional sorties to the battlefront, but we didn't give it our all-out best.

I didn't particularly covet the assignment. I was too provoked with Mary. She was fifteen and spending every minute she could hanging around the edges of the black college students' rallies and marching with them to demand equal accommodations at Rich's department store. I was embarrassed because I owed Rich's for the very clothes on her back and annoyed because she was about to fail history.

She did fail history and was sentenced to make it up at summer school.

Shortly after the summer session opened Jack's parents and his aunt and uncle came up from the coast and we took them for a couple of days' visit to the cabin on Holly Creek. We had been there but one night when our friend Herbert Tabor arrived with an urgent message for me. Jimmy and Susan had called. Mary was missing from school and hadn't come home the night before. They checked with Margaret Long and learned that she had gone with Maggie's daughter Sissy to join the King crusade in Montgomery, even then prepared to march on Selma.

That was the end of the Holly Creek house party. I hurried home and got on the telephone to Martin Luther King, Jr.

"My child should be *passing* history, instead of *making* it!" I wailed. "She's not even sixteen years old yet!"

He laughed quietly and reassured me. He would find her and send her home, he said. And he did—on a plane that afternoon with a patient, kind black lawyer accompanying her.

Years later, when Mary was married and living with Cricket and

235

Bird and Sibley in Shreveport, I was on my way with John, then five years old, to spend a weekend with them. It was a dark night, raining heavily, and John was asleep on the back seat when music on the radio was interrupted by a fierce crackling of news. I pulled over into a truck stop parking lot to wait for better visibility and to try to hear the news bulletin.

It came out of the stormy night strong and clear: Martin Luther King, Jr., had been assassinated!

My impulse was to call the office, to head for Memphis, but I was miles away with a sleeping child behind me. For long moments I sat there, listening to the terrible news and crying.

That good man, concerned with my fears for my little white child, while children of his own race were being beaten and put to death . . . I couldn't even remember if I had thanked him.

Members of the staff were always welcome in Mr. McGill's office. In fact, *everybody* was welcome there, business and civic leaders perhaps less so than colorful politicians, a black waitress seeking a job for her son, the retired farmer who sold flowers down at the corner. The ubiquitous "meeting," which is as essential to today's newspaper operation as computers, was then as unheard of, and since Mr. McGill liked to cite the *Constitution*'s ancient policy, going back to the days of Henry Grady, as "hiring writers and letting them write," there was little direction from the top.

More often reporters went to his office to borrow rent money, to get him to co-sign notes at the bank, to tell him their troubles, or just prop their feet up on his desk and talk.

In the late afternoon, while he killed time before some night meeting or speaking engagement or waited for Mary Elizabeth, his first wife, to pick him up (he did not drive a car and almost always rode the bus to work), he liked to open a book of poetry and read aloud. He tried his hand at writing a little verse and became shy and diffident as a schoolboy if anybody sought to discuss it. Once I had the effrontery to tell him I thought the phrase "silver hoofbeats of the rain" from one of his columns was banal. He considered this criticism carefully and then with consummate good humor said that I was right.

Oddly enough, he never picked apart anything I wrote until the day after Atlanta high schools were integrated and I wrote a column different from his in its interpretation of attempted interference by some kids from outside the city. We both had been present at the

236

arrest and arraignment in police court. I regarded the boys as misguided. Mr. McGill called them "young punks." I wouldn't have worried that we had different versions. Hadn't he said the *Constitution* hired writers and let them write?

He changed his tune that day. He burned my hide with a memo so scorching I went to the bathroom and cried and then went back and started clearing out my desk to quit.

Eugene Patterson, then executive editor, later to go on to the Washington *Post* and the St. Petersburg *Times*, was far closer to McGill than I was. He came in and put his arm around me and soothed me into reconsidering.

"You know Pappy," he said. "He just can't stand to have somebody more compassionate than he is."

Actually he had the edge on everybody in compassion. When I took up collections to help some family burned out in a fire I had covered or to send our pregnant-out-of-wedlock church editor to a maternity hospital, Mr. McGill was the biggest contributor. He was a regular employment agency for the displaced and desperate. At the office he was prompt with presents and flowers when there was a new baby. He liked to give babies their first books of poetry, and sometimes when there was a death in the family he would also send poetry. Once when I grieved over the death of a friend, he wrote me a note in longhand and put it between the pages of Stephen Vincent Benét's "John Brown's Body."

He traveled the world covering national and international stories, going back to the times when he happened to be in Cuba when the revolution broke out and in Europe on a Rosenwald fellowship when Hitler, "the evil evangelist," launched his takeover in Germany.

Inevitably he had return visits from foreign dignitaries and foreign newspaper people. (He steadfastly refused to call a member of the working press a "journalist," insisting that the term applied to "one who carries a cane and borrows money from newspapermen.")

One afternoon a member of the British Parliament talked late in McGill's office and he called Mary Elizabeth to say he would like to bring the visitor home with him to supper.

Mary Elizabeth, as warm and friendly as her husband, was delighted. She was waiting for McGill and the British statesman in front of the building when Icky, a seedy, unwashed fellow who would be called a "street person" today but was sometimes a *Constitution* newspaper street salesman then, walked up with a ragged, dirty woman, who was either his wife or the other "newsie" he courted by barking at her like a dog across Marietta Street. Mary Elizabeth wasn't sure which it was but Icky said they needed a ride to get a package they were carrying home.

"Get in," she said, hospitably opening the door to the Ickys and, simultaneously, to the British visitor. The package they carried, wrapped in soggy newspapers, turned out to be what Mary Elizabeth later described as "the biggest, the deadest, the stinkingest fish I ever smelled, right out of a Broad Street garbage can."

She said McGill fidgeted and urged her to drive faster and faster to the slum where the Ickys lived. There was no report on the Britisher's reaction, except that he did open the window nearest him and thrust his head into the night air.

Born on a hardscrabble farm in East Tennessee, thirty miles north of Chattanooga, a spot now covered by a TVA lake, McGill responded deeply to the pull of the land, but, as Harold Martin wrote in his fine biography of our editor, "He was like Dante in that 'to him all the world is native country, just as the sea is to fish.'" He loved it all, but he agreed with "Marse" Henry Watterson, the famed Louisville editor, who contended in a bit of poesy:

> *Things have come to a hell of a pass*
> *When a man can't flog his own jackass.*

McGill flayed the South and the nation about the inequities of segregation, about the Ku Klux Klan and the demagogic politicians represented by Eugene Talmadge. Talmadge didn't take McGill's assaults on his brand of politics lying down. He incited his followers to near riots at political rallies throughout the state when he lit into McGill.

"Tell 'em about Rastus McGill, Gene!" the group called "the tree-climbing Haggards" would shout. And ol' Gene would reply, as if on cue, "I'm a-comin' to that!"

It introduced a litany that enlivened barbecues and campaign stops, but back at the shop we worried about our boss. He and his family had been bomb-threatened and marched against by robed and masked Klansmen. He was the target for nasty phone calls. Sometimes at the office we were able to field them for him, particularly if he was away.

238

He handled those that came to his house with typical imagination. He had a little dog he named Rastus and trained to bark into the telephone. So when in the middle of the night he was jangled awake by the phone and a voice said, "Is that you, Rastus?" he would say calmly, "You want to speak to Rastus? Just a minute."

He would hold the receiver out to the dog, who would leap into action, barking vociferously until the caller, ear drums aching, hung up.

Being older and perhaps mellower than most of us, McGill could take defeats and disappointments with better grace. After a hot summer's campaign during which the paper supported a Marietta attorney named James V. Carmichael for governor, some of us came to regard Eugene Talmadge, his opponent, as evil incarnate. I did a series on Carmichael and his family and fell in love with his parents, a couple who had a big old-fashioned house on the old Atlanta-Marietta streetcar line, with a big general store down by the tracks and his grandmother's old farmhouse across the way. On election night I was sent to sit up with the elder Carmichaels until the results were in. It didn't take long. Jimmy, their son, swept the state with the biggest popular vote ever won by a candidate for governor, but through the archaic county-unit system of vote counting, since abolished, Talmadge was the winner. I went back to the office ready to cry—and I did at the sight of our crusading editor shaking hands with Gene Talmadge and escorting him to the newspaper's radio microphone to make a victory statement.

McGill did it pleasantly, graciously, and some of us thought traitorously. It might have been necessary but did he have to be *nice* about it?

He was also to oppose Gene's son, Herman Talmadge. While Herman was governor, later to become United States Senator, I got caught up in a campaign to buy an elephant for the city zoo. The climax of the big push was a carefully orchestrated welcome in front of the *Constitution*'s almost brand-new building, catercornered across the street from the old Victorian pile where the paper had operated since 1884. McGill had agreed to emcee the show and, although the governor declined our invitation to welcome the elephant, the first lady, Betty Talmadge, agreed to let their little boys appear and be photographed giving the elephant his first taste of Georgia peanuts. Instead of performing for crowds and cameras, the little boys, Gene and Bobby, took one look at the elephant and broke away howling.

McGill snatched up the elder, Gene, and whacked him across the seat, setting him back to do his duty. He later apologized to Mrs. Talmadge and explained that it was just reflex action, the old recurring urge to hit a Talmadge.

McGill became a friend of both John and Robert Kennedy, bringing them through the newsroom for the staff to meet when they visited Atlanta, and accepting an invitation for himself and his family to dine with them at their Palm Beach house. He was boyishly pleased that the *Constitution* was one of the papers President Kennedy read each day and offered to pay for it himself when Jack Tarver as publisher pointed out that getting our paper on the White House breakfast table every morning was horrendously expensive.

McGill had been with Richard Nixon in his "kitchen cabinet" meeting in Russia and seemed to like him, but as Harold Martin wrote, "The only way McGill could have supported Nixon was for him to have been running against Count Dracula." He did not live to see Watergate.

As the years passed and pressures of his celebrity grew, Mr. McGill became less close to the staff. He regretted this, liking, I think, the image of himself as mentor, father figure, to us all. Sometimes he took a few of us to lunch at a health-food place he patronized when he was on a diet, which was often. And sometimes after work he would invite us to sit around a scrubbed kitchen table in the basement storeroom of Max Muldawer's restaurant-delicatessen a block away on Broad Street. There among the boxes and bags of groceries we sipped red wine, ate cheese and cold meats, and read poetry.

These favorite places were razed out of existence and McGill's leisure was nearly so. This bothered him. He wanted to know the younger members of the staff and, remembering his first days as a sportswriter in Atlanta, when he slept on a cot in the apartment of his friend Ed Danforth, the sports editor, he was concerned that they might be homesick and lonely.

One day when Mary Elizabeth was out of town he asked me to assemble the young away-from-home ones and he would cook dinner for us all. It was a marvelous meal—he was an expert cook—but the talk around the fire afterward was even better. Our boss talked of old political campaigns and old shenanigans on the paper—and then, after

240

we all went home, he washed the dishes and pots and pans himself because he didn't want to burden their long-time cook-maid the next morning.

After the *Constitution* was merged with the *Journal* we were all commanded to appear at the annual banquet of the 4-H Clubs of Georgia, an event the *Journal* had promoted for years. McGill liked young people, particularly those who were involved in farm life, as he had been at their age, but he dreaded the long evenings of speeches and awards at the banquet. So he took members of his staff, who had to go, to the Capital City club and bought us pre-banquet drinks.

"We have to be fortified against all that clean-limbed youth," he remarked wryly.

After one such banquet I confided to the members of our group that I was going out with a Hollywood publicity man I had become friends with on assignments at the movie capital. He was to be in town only that evening and I was looking forward to seeing him. To my everlasting chagrin McGill led a march on my friend's room, towing along six convivial friends, who sang their way through the corridors of the Biltmore Hotel. Even worse, when he met my young man he demanded to know what his intentions toward me were. Unfortunately, the poor man had no intentions—and I haven't seen him since.

Mary Elizabeth McGill died in 1962 after lingering in the hospital for three months. Their son, Ralph, Jr., was seventeen and soon to leave for college, but none of us really suspected how very lonely McGill must be. He was not only a famous man with time-filling engagements all over the world but he was a very popular man, numbering among his many friends women we all thought would like to marry him.

Late one afternoon when I was finishing up a day's stint Mr. McGill paused by my desk to chat a moment. After discussing the day's news a little he changed the subject. "You've been a widow awhile now," he said. "It's lonely, isn't it? Or do you have somebody?"

"Well, sort of," I began. "Friends . . ."

He sighed and turned away and then he turned back.

"The worst of it," he said bleakly, "is coming home from a trip and getting to the airport and having nobody to call. All these years I've called home and said, 'I'm back.' Now there's nobody there to hear . . . or care."

There was no use telling him that we at the paper cared, that we would be glad to hear from him. That wasn't what he needed. A moment later I saw what he needed.

"There's this young woman," he said. "I'm attracted to her. I think I want to marry her . . . she's a lot younger than I am."

His voice dwindled off and he looked uncomfortable. I had to repress a smile. He must know that we wouldn't be newspaper reporters if we hadn't already found out that "the young woman" was Dr. Mary Lynn Morgan, a children's dentist—and we had decided that we liked her fine and would give them our blessing when they were ready for it.

Some months later, in April of 1967, a note on the newsroom bulletin board bid us all to the wedding of Dr. Morgan and McGill—a wonderfully happy event in the life of a lonely man. I was sure of that in November 1968 when were preparing to cover the trial of James Earl Ray for the murder of Dr. Martin Luther King, Jr.

Every newspaper in the world wanted to have a reporter at that trial and of course the Shelby County courthouse in Memphis could accommodate only a comparatively small percentage of them. The *Constitution* was the Atlanta paper, maybe the only one in Georgia, to receive a courtroom pass. We knew it was because of McGill's status. He was not only one of Tennessee's most-distinguished sons, he was perhaps the most-famous newspaperman in the country.

But he didn't see it that way. He considered the job of reporter the important thing, and since I was assigned to cover the trial, the ticket to the press section was mine.

"Except," he said, "when you have to go to the ladies' room. I'll use it then."

We had to go to Memphis in November to be mugged and finger-printed and given a security clearance by the sheriff's office for the trial still months away. Right off I observed my boss in the role new to me—not the august editor but a working reporter.

At the airport he chided me for buying a tourist ticket on the assumption that the paper wanted me to travel that way and ex-changed it for first class to match his. In Memphis he was annoyed that I even thought of checking with the office before ordering a special telephone line to the city desk from the courthouse press-room.

"Don't ever ask!" he barked. "Order the phone and ask later."

242

We were in Memphis a day and a night and McGill was busier than any of the reporters there, leaving no angle to the upcoming trial uncovered. He had been in Memphis hours after the shooting of Martin Luther King, Jr., and he took a group of us to the Lorraine Motel to see the slain leader's room, by then a little museum. He walked us across the parking lot to the shabby rooming house and showed us the murky, unwashed window through which Ray had fired his assassin's bullet.

He told us about the jazzman W. C. Handy, and went with us to a little park dedicated to the black musician's memory. He insisted that all reporters stay at the famous Peabody Hotel, then shabby and rundown, now restored to its former glory. It was our duty, McGill assured us solemnly, to encourage fine old hostelries with interesting histories to stay in business.

After dinner, which we had at the Holiday Inn chain's flagship establishment on the river, I waited in the lobby while McGill called Mary Lynn. Some friends of mine, led by my former tenant's husband, Martin Waldron, of the *New York Times,* came by and invited me to join them in a suite upstairs where a party was forming. I thought McGill, then seventy years old, would be tired and ready to go back to the Peabody. But they said bring him and I mentioned the invitation.

"Let's go!" he said.

A dozen or so wire-service and big-city reporters were in the living room of the suite, some of them from London and France. They greeted Ralph McGill with shouts of pleasure. They all knew him.

Within minutes he was ensconced in a big chair in the middle of the room, and they were deployed around him, on chairs and on the floor, asking questions, reminiscing about other stories in other parts of the world. He had a terrific evening, and before he left he called Mary Lynn once more to report and tell her goodnight.

The assignment had revealed to me that he was two things: a happy husband and a whale of a newspaper reporter.

McGill died of a heart attack the following February, one day before his seventy-first birthday. He was buried from All Saints Episcopal Church, where he and Mary Lynn had been married, with famous people and humble people gathering by the hundreds to mourn him in the church and along the funeral-procession route.

Minutes before the service was to begin, the Reverend Frank Ross,

243

the pastor, received a bomb threat, which none of us gathered in the half of the sanctuary set aside for newspaper people knew about until much later. Police checked the church and decided it was a false alarm.

At West View Cemetery I found myself standing behind former Vice President Hubert Humphrey and his wife and near a troop of black Boy Scouts, who had presented themselves as an honorary honor guard.

In March the James Earl Ray trial was slated to begin, and I heard from the sheriff. He sent me the identification card he had had made for McGill after our November visit. I handed it to Harold Martin, who quoted a column I wrote after McGill's death, which began, "If he should have to be identified at heaven's gate, I think he will be happiest if St. Peter says, 'Lord, this is Ralph McGill, newspaper reporter.' "

Harold noticed what I had not noticed about the card the sheriff had sent. On it the editor, publisher, and Pulitzer-Prize-winning columnist was identified simply as "Ralph McGill, Reporter, the Atlanta *Constitution.*"

I went back to Memphis alone to cover the Ray trial, which ended in a matter of minutes with a plea of guilty. Two years later, when he attempted to withdraw his plea in an appeal in federal court, it took longer—more than a week of testimony—with the same result: Ray's return to prison to resume his life sentence.

A smaller group of reporters was present to cover that, and three or four of us were old friends from many assignments in the past. One day, mindful of all the dinners my friends had insisted on buying for me at Memphis restaurants, I decided to reciprocate in the only way they would let me by assembling a picnic lunch in the park outside the federal building, overlooking the Mississippi River.

It was a long recess and we lingered in the sunshine, watching the slow movement of the river and talking of the man who meant so much to all of us and who certainly would have wanted to be there. In fact, McGill would have insisted on bringing the wine.

244

Chapter Nine

Space was a recurring problem at Sweet Apple. We decided to add a screened porch across the back, even if it didn't match the age and architecture of the cabin. The little boys could sleep out there, but cots and pallets filled the living room when they were all home, and I wearied of stumbling over bodies on the floor in the dark.

One day our neighbor Ralph Dangar called to ask if I would like to buy another cabin of the same size and same age three miles down the road. Jack and Doc, who had been involved in the restoration of the original cabin almost more than their time and strength allowed, set up a shout: *"No! No! No more log cabins!"*

"How much?" I asked Ralph. When he told me $1,200 I had to express regret.

A week or so later, when neither Jack nor Doc was present, Ralph called again. If I wanted that cabin I could have it for $750.

"Oh, I want it!" I cried. "But, Ralph, I haven't got seven hundred fifty dollars."

"How much have you got?" he asked.

"Two hundred dollars," I said.

"I'll take it," said my neighbor.

By the time we were ready to tear down and move the second cabin I had paid off my remaining indebtedness to Ralph and high-heartedly participated in the big move. Our carpenter friend Quinton Johnson and his son Larry carefully pulled apart the old square logs, numbered them, and hauled them to Sweet Apple's yard, where they had to stay for the wintry rainy months, waiting for rebuilding weather and for me to accumulate rebuilding money. When that time arrived, we found the numbers had been washed off the logs. Quinton had put them on in chalk!

Before we could get what the children called The Annex and our friend Edmund Bocock called Fort Apache under construction, tragedy struck our family again.

Jimmy called me at the office one afternoon with the frantic report that little Jamie had been hurt. Jimmy was on his way to meet Marie and the baby at Henrietta Egleston Children's Hospital. Jack and Susan and I followed as fast as we could.

With both his parents working, Jamie had been in the care of a young woman who was the daughter of the Eubanks' long-time friend and servant. She was reliable and truthful, and they could only trust her when she reported that the baby had fallen out of his crib and struck his head on a little red rocker I had given him.

The head injuries were massive, so great, said our doctor, that he couldn't believe they had been suffered in so short a fall. He had seen their like only in automobile crashes where the car was traveling at a speed of eighty miles an hour.

Jamie died within the hour.

For months to come I would grieve and wonder if something else happened to that baby. I took to driving by when I got off work and walking to the yard back of the apartment, where there was a ten- or fifteen-foot drop from the window in the baby's room. Could he have fallen out there? I wondered. Could it be that the young nursemaid was too frightened to tell us? Would even that distance have hurt him so cruelly? I saw no sign of blood, no evidence that the ground had been disturbed, and the neighbors had seen nothing.

We never found anything to believe beyond the nursemaid's story.

Without the baby, Jimmy and Marie eventually found their marriage dissolving. One day Marie walked out of the pretty old-fashioned, close-to-town apartment they had fixed up together and told Jimmy, in effect, it was all his. She wanted none of the silver or the dishes or the pots and pans so painstakingly acquired. He was welcome to the furniture with the bright slipcovers she had made. She went home.

They both married again in time, and I don't think there was ever any anger or resentment between them. Such was not the case with Jimmy's second wife, a pretty, sexy-looking young divorcee, who did not like me one bit. She forbade his having any contact with his family and I could understand her hatred of me. I had been somewhat (somewhat? viciously!) critical of her. But, when Jimmy failed to call or come to see his grandmother on her visits to Sweet Apple, it broke Muv's heart.

That marriage lasted but a year and that wife walked out, too.

Happily, many years later he would marry a warm, loving, indestructibly cheerful widow named Peggy Carter, the mother of six children and a woman with whom he has every appearance of trudging, hand in hand, into his old age and beyond.

When Edward finished his tour of duty with the Army Engineers he and Susan came home and settled down in Atlanta, first in an apartment and then in an almost new suburban house, which Susan promptly hated because it *was* new and suburban. What could you do with such a place? she wondered. Enjoy, said her grandmother, Muv, whose idea of comfort and status was to live "in a nice brick home with hardwood floors."

None of us had ever lived in a new house, but it was Muv's dream and Susan might have been content with it except for two things: (1) Mary's children came to stay with her while their parents job- and house-hunted in California, so it seemed to have drawn in its walls and become a very small house. (2) She got a job with a real-estate man, whose specialty was old houses in the once-fashionable area called Inman Park.

The neighborhood had deteriorated. Old settlers had moved out, leaving their Victorian mansions to be cut up into many light-housekeeping rooms and dingy apartments for the poor and the displaced. But there was a movement to restore and renovate and Susan was very excited about it. She talked Jack and me into pooling our resources and putting small down payments on two big houses, which were going for $15,000 and $18,000 each. The rents from the many apartments in each would make the monthly payments, she promised us.

The system worked for seasoned slumlords. But not for us. Jack named Susan our agent and rent collector, and after a few months decided that she had no head at all for business. She wasn't making many collections and some tenants were seriously in arrears. He undertook to show her how the rental business should be handled.

The nearest example he proposed to deal with was an old lady keeping two or three of her grandchildren. We waited outside while

247

Jack stalked purposefully to the door. He was gone a long time, and when he came back he looked decidedly sheepish.

"Did you get the money?" Susan asked brightly.

"Well," began Jack, hesitating.

"Okay," said Susan. "How much did you give them?"

Jack was defiant. "Only ten dollars," he said. "They need milk!"

It was clear that we weren't intended to be slumlords or landlords of any stripe. I got a call at the office one busy day that police cars and an ambulance were in the hard-beaten, beer-can-littered yard of one of our houses. I hurried to the scene.

There was a dead man in the dismal old room that had once been a stately library or back parlor. He had been dead for a considerable period of time. Only an oppressively evil smell would have impelled anybody in that house to investigate.

The man, old and seedy and a wino, had been shot. Nobody knew by whom or even who the victim himself was. It was so distressing I vowed I couldn't go back to that house. But Susan had resigned as our agent, to be succeeded by a young fellow who, with his wife and several children, occupied the front parlor, cooking in what had been the dining room. We gave him the title of resident manager and reduced his rent.

One day I decided to skip lunch and go down to Inman Park and show our resident manager and his family how we wanted the premises spruced up. I bought a pair of pristine white sheets to curtain the big front window, thinking it would hide the squalor inside and bring a touch of elegance to the front porch, where I had already hung some flowering baskets.

My dream of showing the resident manager how to pick up beer cans and rake the yard went a-glimmering. He was the proud possessor of a broken arm.

"Cain't do a thing," he said happily. "Gon be weeks."

I went out with a plastic bag to make a start on the garbagy yard. I had barely begun when the resident manager, so called, summoned me.

"You better come here!" he cried. "The man in Number One's set the bed afire!"

He had indeed. The mattress was smoldering, the emaciated old fellow on the bed was coughing and heaving. And the resident manager, because of his disability, couldn't do a thing.

I picked up the old man and laid him on the porch and hauled the foul-smelling mattress to the curb.

"Good thing you're stout," said the resident manager admiringly.

But I wasn't stout enough to stick out that restoration project. It was clearly something young people with boundless energy and ambition could do *if* they lived on the premises. I had no intention of deserting Sweet Apple for Inman Park, as much as I admired the neighborhood. Susan and Edward agreed to relieve us of that house (we gladly threw in our equity) and we sold the one next door at a loss.

I noted that when the resident manager and his family decamped they took the new sheets and the hanging baskets with them.

Susan and Edward and almost all the other young couples who so hopefully acquired the dilapidated mansions in Inman Park had to take their time with restoration. First they had to evict tenants right and left, and that was a heartbreaking business. The rent these dejected dwellers paid by the week was by no means cheap but that's the way they got their money and that was the only way most of them could pay. There seemed to be few places for them to go, and while Susan waited out the departure of some of the people in their house she found herself becoming friends with them.

There were a couple of tough, self-reliant little boys in whom she took a special interest. They were older than her children but of an age to enjoy some of the same sports, she felt. When she took her John to Pop Warner football games, where at age eight he was learning to be a tackle, she invited the two neighborhood boys along. Conditioned by back-alley and vacant-lot sports, they apparently found this athletic endeavor pretty puny stuff. The bleachers were filled with proper, well-heeled parents when Susan's guests began loud coaching from the sidelines.

"Grab him by the ass, John!" cried one.

"F—— the bastard!" directed the other. "F—— him, John!"

Susan's only hope was that there were many boys on the teams named John, but her son, John, reported miserably that there was no confusion about whom the instructions were directed to.

Susan admitted that she might not be doing so well in her efforts to be a friend to the boys, and she turned her attention to their sister, a stringy-haired teenager with one pair of blue jeans to her name. She checked with a few friends who had daughters and collected some very nice young-girl clothes. Folding them tenderly in tissue paper so they wouldn't look like past-their-prime hand-me-downs, she put a gift wrap on them and left them, under cover of darkness, at the little girl's door.

The next morning she awakened in time to see the child's mother putting the clothes, box and all, in the garbage can. She glanced toward Susan's bedroom window as she left and said something Susan not so much heard as recognized instinctively. The mother had the same four-letter vocabulary as her sons.

When the house was finally cleared of tenants, it needed a lot of work. Removing bathrooms that had been stuck on the porches, pulling out sink and gas pipes, which reared their ugly heads through the living room's fine old parquet floor, tearing out the makeshift partitions that had converted one gracious big room into three squinchy ones were all a part of it. But the thing that got priority was a room for the new baby who was approaching.

Having allowed eight years to elapse after Ted's birth, Susan and Edward decided they wanted a baby, preferably a girl.

"But I haven't got a decent place to set up a baby bed!" cried Susan. "Edward wants to worry about the foundation and the roof. I just want some paint on the walls and some curtains at the window!"

We waited until Edward was working late one night and I arrived in jeans with ladders and brushes. We swiftly turned a little dressing room, off one of the upstairs bedrooms, into a spiffy clean nursery. Edward would have preferred a more careful job with the removal of old wallpaper and the scraping of woodwork, but he said nothing because in a month red-headed, brown-eyed baby Susy had arrived and was occupying that room.

"Well, howdy, Sue Barber," said Muv when she saw the new baby. "I reckon you're the caboose. We won't be getting any more young-uns till the next generation."

She confessed to me a little chokily that she was glad what was likely to be the last of our babies was a gal youngun with her ill-fated great-great-grandmother's name and red hair.

The little gal youngun's name and dark auburn hair endure, but Muv didn't live to know that she was by no means the last of our babies.

For in the spring of 1976 Muv's indomitable old heart started giving her trouble. She had to check in at the Jackson County hospital thirteen miles from her little house in Alford, and when I got there her dark eyes were snapping with fury. They had put her in a shorty hospital gown, exposing more of her "quivering old flesh than I *ever* let anybody see" and she was held captive by shining tubes and clicking monitors. I stayed a week and then Jimmy took over to let me run home, get my clothes and my typewriter, check in at the office, and get back.

Larry Ashmead had left Doubleday for Simon & Schuster, turning me over to his fellow editor Carolyn Blakemore. At her suggestion I was in the midst of writing what purported to be a sunny, light-hearted dissertation on the joy of living, making grist for your mill out of the gritty substance of misfortune, learning from adversity. It was to be called *Small Blessings,* and while I believed in the book and believed in the title, it wasn't easy to prop my little portable typewriter on my knees and write joyfully while I sat by her bedside and listened to my mother breathe.

In 1969, 1970, and 1975 I had turned out small upbeat books on assignment from Larry, including stories about my favorite old street people, friends I made in jail and the county almshouse. The books were celebrations of Christmas and motherhood and humanity as I knew it, with one of them, *Day by Day,* a sort of distillation of wisdom and philosophy I had picked up from people and books. I had loved doing them, cherished the people I wrote about, and enjoyed the success of each when it hit the bookstores.

But, sitting there in the hospital, frightened that my mother might be right when she announced calmly that she was going to die, I had trouble remembering anything in the world beyond the big pine trees in the hospital yard and the sign that read "AMBULANCE ENTRANCE." I felt as I had so often felt in a courtroom when the jury was out and lawyers and court attendants sat for hours awaiting the verdict. There was no world beyond that room, no people closer to me than the ones who had been involved for days in trial. Except that courtroom talk, particularly between judges and old-time criminal lawyers, is rich and funny, and the talk of illness and death is incomprehensible and terrifying. Readers were good to me. One woman who had recently lost her husband sent me a sitting-up-at-the-hospital Care package, including notepaper and a pen, hand lotion and mints and postcards and stamps and some paperback books she knew I'd enjoy.

But then I took Muv home, and although she was glad to be there and enjoyed moving around her little house, talking on the phone and seeing her neighbors, I again felt trapped. I couldn't leave her and there was very little that I could do for her. I set up a table for my typewriter at one end of the enclosed porch, where she grew those standbys of the elderly gardener, African violets, and tried to remember good things, blessings, if you will.

Muv slept a lot, and when she awakened, never the sweet, saintly silver-haired-mother type, she was often cranky. I could leave her and ride my bicycle to the store and post office when her friends had seen the soap operas they called their "programs" and came calling. She reached a point of not wanting to get out of bed, and I could only persuade her when it was time for Walter Cronkite and the six-o'clock news to put on a dress and walk as far as the living room or her screened porch. (Later when I saw Walter Cronkite, alone among anchormen, get to his feet and stand at attention for the playing of "The Star-Spangled Banner" at the Democratic National Convention, I mentioned it in a story and had a nice note from his mother. I meant to reply—I hope I did—that I was personally indebted to him because he was the only reason I could get my mother on her feet and in motion toward the end of her life.)

Some days when Muv felt rebellious at being ill and annoyed at me for any reason at all, I brooded on the fate of grownup daughters who have to stay home and nurse elderly parents, bestirring themselves over such trivial matters as whether to latch the kitchen screen or lock the door—all of urgent importance to Muv. Is that what I've come to? I wondered.

Then I got a letter from the Columbia University School of Journalism, asking me to serve on the next Pulitzer jury! It was the opening of a door into the world again. Like all newspaper reporters I respected—and coveted—the Pulitzer Prize, and to serve on the jury awarding it was an honor unmatched by all the plaques and certificates and even cash prizes I had won through the years. I sang when I took my bicycle ride that afternoon, even after my vehicle turned over in deep sand, flipping me off and bruising my knees badly.

The next door was opened by Jack's parents. Julia called one evening to ask after Muv and then she said, "Lee and I have been wondering what we could do to help you and Muv. We decided that we would take a week and come down and stay with her so you can go home for a while."

It was inspired generosity. Muv loved and enjoyed Julia and Lee. A visit from them would be a tonic for her, a wonderful change from a daughter who either sat at a typewriter writing about blessings or latched the wrong door. I was ecstatic. I hadn't realized how homesick I had been. I called Jack with the news.

"Good," he said. "I'm glad they're coming, but if I were you, when they get there I'd wait at least fifteen minutes before I left."

They stayed a week and then Susan and Susy stayed a week, and I went back with the intention of getting somebody in the neighborhood to help out. A woman who would shop for Muv, check on her daily, and perhaps even sleep in her house at night was what I had in mind. Muv was indignant. I insisted that the alternative was having me or somebody in the family with her all the time.

That persuaded her. With a malicious light in her eyes she said, "If I got to have some old heifer hanging around in my way all the time I'll pick her myself."

She finally settled on a plump, sweet-faced woman who lived a few doors down the street and was famous for her kindness and loving care of several old people in her family. I went to talk to Bertha and we made a deal. Her presence and, of course, that of neighbors who were close and concerned, would enable me to go back home and to work.

While I was getting things in order, taking Muv's prescriptions to be refilled and buying new sheets for her bed and summery cotton nightgowns for the hot days ahead, my daughter Mary called from New Orleans. She and the children had gone there to join Cricket, who was playing pretty regularly at a Bourbon Street night spot, but they had been unable to find a place to live. She had a little job in a souvenir shop and she hated leaving the children to their own devices during the day. They had been staying with friends, but it wasn't working out too well. Could they come for a visit?

I was delighted and I knew their cousins in Atlanta would be thrilled to have them back. For a few weeks it was a happy summery time at Sweet Apple. Jack was away and we took his pickup truck and rode around the countryside, going to swim in his lake every afternoon with all the Sweet Apple dogs racing us to get there first and get in the water. We took long walks and Bird discovered Euell Gibbons and made us edgy cooking up wild food. We rode bicycles along the country roads, and one day when I was at the office I got a call from

253

our druggist friend in Roswell, Dr. Max Staples, to reassure me that Bird, twelve, and Ted, eleven, were perfectly fine after a seven-mile ride from the cabin; they were just settling down to milkshakes. I hadn't known they were on such an expedition and I was nervous about leaving them alone after that, particularly when Sibley embarked on some kitchen project and sliced Bird's hand so it needed stitches. Our neighbor Doc rushed to the rescue then.

Surprisingly, the *Small Blessings* book seemed to be going along very well. While the four children fished and explored the woods or played in the hammock, I sat on the back porch and worked.

But one June morning I got a call from Muv. "That pain," which had sent her to the hospital, was back.

"Get Bessie to take you to the hospital," I said. "I'll be there as fast as I can."

"No, I'll wait for you," Muv said.

"Muv, it will take me six hours to get there," I said. "Go on to the hospital!"

"I may and I may not," said Muv and hung up.

As fast as I could I hit the road, depositing the four children with Susan and picking up Jimmy to go with me. We stopped for gas in Columbus and I called Muv. No answer. I tried her neighbor, Bessie, who was reassuring. She had just been over to check and Muv was sleeping peacefully.

Two and a half hours later we drove up to Muv's little house to find a police car in the yard and neighbors standing under the trees and on the porch. Stupidly, I didn't realize what had happened, thinking first of some household disaster.

"Your mother died about an hour ago," her neighbor Buck Barnes said gently, walking over to open the car door for me.

It seemed to me that I could not sustain that blow. I knew she was old, eighty-three years old, and very ill. But I had never had a day or a minute of my life when my mother wasn't there, ready to help me, to give me strength or comfort, to make me laugh. If I had only been with her, I thought, I could have done something to save her. I *should* have been with her!

A hearse came to get her body, and the little black poodle she had named Jackie for Jack, who gave it to her, trotted along behind the stretcher and attempted to climb in after it. I picked Jackie up and took her in my arms back into the house. She returned to her post on the rug beside Muv's bed and would not leave it. For two days we could not persuade her to come out for water or food.

Jimmy made the requisite telephone calls to Susan in Atlanta and Mary in New Orleans, to Jack and his parents in Biloxi, to my boss, Bill Fields, at the *Constitution,* to Larry Ashmead in New York, and to the friends listed in Muv's little directory by the telephone. I prowled the house, seeing the things she had done just hours before, for, as always when she expected us, she had "prepared"—this time a fresh pot of turnip greens and one of her special jelly cakes. I prowled the yard, wondering once more how the things she had planted, the sweetheart rose by the back steps, the lilies by the tool shed, had the temerity to survive the hands that put them there.

Susan arrived, having left all five children with Edward. ("I couldn't find that many shoes and clean clothes so fast," she explained.) Bill and Hazel Fields, who would have been celebrating a wedding anniversary, arrived with our mutual friend Fran Brown, widow of Joe David Brown, whose books (*Addie Pray, Stars in My Crown, Kings Go Forth*) Muv had loved. Jack was there within hours, followed the next morning by Julia and Lee, bringing Mary with them. ("I got as far as Biloxi and ran out of gas," Mary explained wryly.) Cricket had not wanted to come, nor had he felt it necessary for Mary to come.

Fran and Joe David Brown had always loved dogs and had half a dozen of their own. The day Fran arrived she walked into Muv's bedroom to see Jackie and knelt down beside her, rubbing her curly ears and speaking to her softly. When Fran stood up to return to the living room, Jackie followed her, going eventually to her food and water bowls.

"Fran, will you take her?" I begged. "You're the only one she has responded to."

Muv had extracted a promise from Jack to have Jackie put to sleep if and when she died because she couldn't visualize my being able to make such a devoted, one-person dog happy, as much time as I spent away from home. Fran welcomed her to her farm called Covey Rise near Sparta, Georgia, where Jackie lived happily for ten more years.

The funeral was in the new, modern-looking Methodist church, which Muv had opposed their building as a replacement for the old steepled, white clapboard building she had known all her life. But I noticed that a little brass plaque at the end of the pew where the family sat said it had been contributed by Muv and by me. And I

255

thought I had sent her that money for repairs to her roof!

Bob Lamb, a fine reporter on our staff, had been assigned by Bill Fields to write Muv's obituary. He mentioned the thousands of letters she had received from readers of my column, who often just addressed her as "Muv, Alford, Fla." Both Bob and an editorial headed simply "Muv" quoted my old office roomie Harold Martin as saying: "She was the eternal matriarch, strong and wise, merry and brave, and at the same time warm and loving—holding things together through times of trouble. The passing of Muv will leave a lonely place not only in the lives of Celestine and her children, but in the lives of all of us who came to know her through Celestine's column."

It took years for me to become reconciled to the fact that I hadn't been there, that Muv had died alone. And then I realized she had done what she wanted to do. Disinclined to go back to the hospital and the sessions with tubes and monitors, she had willed herself to go into her own room and die.

Death, she had once told me, might be "the brightest wagon in the caravan."

Before we left Alford, Bertha came to see me. She had not worked a day for Muv. "She ran me off the day you left," she said, smiling.

Muv's death came on June 17, and a few weeks later Mary and the children settled in in Muv's house to wait out Cricket's summer job playing at a Cape Cod resort. Jimmy Carter's campaign for the presidency was shaping up, and before Bird and Sibley went to join their mother in Alford I had to leave them for a day's trip to Plains, Georgia, to do a story on the Carters.

Jack said he had work for the children to do and I could leave them at Sweet Apple with an easy mind. When I came home from Plains, late and tired, I saw what that work was. As I drove into the yard a light came on back of the garden in the old abandoned plastic greenhouse I had worked in with such pleasure before its heater had gone crazy and spewed soot over everything.

That night it glowed like a gray pearl and I got out of the car running. Jack and the children had spent the day putting new plastic over its black pipe ribs and cleaning up the interior for my fall gardening projects.

It was the finest kind of surprise, and I couldn't settle down to do anything about food but kept walking around, examining the green-house inside and out.

"That's all right," said Bird. "We've had our supper and I've been digging sassafras. I'm gon make us all some tea."

We drank it happily.

It was the last time of accomplishment and good companionship we were to have with Bird and Sibley at Sweet Apple for many years.

A time or two their cousins and I went down to Alford to visit them, and once Jack and I picked them up and took them to the Gulf Coast on a fishing trip with his parents and Louisiana cousins. But a few days after Thanksgiving both children were with their father in New Orleans, presumably to start school there while their mother packed up and moved to join them.

Bird went first, riding the bus from Alford. Sibley followed a few weeks later by plane from Atlanta. We all waited for a call that she had arrived safely. The call came and Mary turned from the phone, white-faced and trembling.

She was not to join them in New Orleans. Cricket was filing suit for divorce. He would get custody of the children. She could see them "after court," not before.

Everybody has troubles. Grief and pain and loss dog the footsteps of even the most fortunate. Looking around me through the years, I knew a great many people had worse troubles than I had. By contrast I felt I had been very lucky.

Our losses through death had been painful—my beloved Pap; Jim, a tragically ill man; Mamie, a dear friend and almost mother; two babies; and, hardest of all to sustain, Muv, the whole family's strength and comforter.

But this was different. It was desertion, for it became clear after many desperate efforts to find them and bring them home that Bird and Sibley *wanted* to stay away. Cricket, we learned, intended to marry a young woman he had met during the summer's engagement at Cape Cod. He and the children were living with her and they planned marriage as soon as his divorce from Mary became final.

After a time of heartbreak and shock Mary became resigned to the loss of Cricket. She even admitted to Susan and me for the first time that they had not been happy most of the time they were married, and the happy face she had presented to us was mostly false. But the

257

loss of her children threatened to kill her. And me.

She spent days tramping the streets of New Orleans looking for them. We both spent all the money we could borrow or beg hiring lawyers and detectives. Mary appealed to their other grandparents, who hung up on her. Jack and I joined her in a search in New Orleans, organized by a detective we hired, involving a day-long "stake-out," coming to nothing.

For almost six years Mary would get a job and work at it long enough to save up enough money for another trip to New Orleans. Susan and I went to see Cricket's parents in Indiana; they were pleasant and hospitable but contended that they did not know where the children were.

It was senseless, I thought. Other people got divorces and made civilized arrangements on child custody with a minimum of trauma to the children and the other parents.

Then I started looking around me, talking to lawyers and court officials and reading stories in our paper. The country, even our town, was full of people searching for children who had been taken from them and whisked across state lines, where court orders could not reach them. My daughter Susan knew a woman who had come home one day to find her house totally emptied by movers and her two children gone. She did not find them for twenty years. Many prominent citizens in New York and other eastern cities hit the news occasionally with their search for missing children—and they had far more money to spend than we had.

It was not simple cruelty, I decided, it was evil, wickedness in the Old Testament sense.

And then one day it struck me that it might be punishment for what Muv and I did to Henry Colley. She had taken me from him—and I had gone along docilely, believing her when she said he was worthless, cooperating in whatever deception she felt needful.

I found his name in the Pensacola phone book and called him.

He showed no particular excitement at hearing from me. "I hear your mother died," he said. "And Mr. Sibley, did he die too?"

"Years ago," I said.

He said he was sorry and then he added, "You know your mama quit me. I never quit her."

I made a half-hearted attempt to bring him up to date on my life, job, children, grandchildren. He wasn't noticeably interested. I asked about his life and if there was anything I could do for him.

He laughed. "What could you do for me?" he asked. "I got everything I need. This little house I live in, I had it built. I got one room eight feet by eight feet and another one a little smaller. Plenty big enough for me. I'm six feet, seven inches. Got a window and the lady next door sets my plate of food on a shelf there every day. She's a mighty good neighbor. The welfare pays her."

He said he was glad I had called and he would call me up some time—but he never did. It was after that I found the paper he signed relinquishing custody of me to Muv and Pap and allowing them to change my name.

I should worry about him, I thought. But I did, and a few years later I learned that he had died virtually blind. William Wells, the East Bay teacher and historian, took him to a doctor and he belatedly had a cataract operation.

"The little house he had," said Bill, "belonged to a judge. One time your father said he planned to will it to you but he said you told him you didn't want it. It wasn't much of a house. He had ropes strung out to guide him through it. When he died the judge took it back."

"Was he sick long before he died?" I asked.

"Well, you know he had sores on his legs all his life," Bill said. "He had two dogs and put a sign on the front of his house which read, 'My dogs licked me well.' For a while it looked like his legs had healed, then sores broke out again on his ankle and he got blood poisoning and he lost that leg. We were away when he died. But he died in Pensacola Hospital and is buried in a cemetery there. I don't know which one."

The last time I talked to him, I have often thought, was not for affection or concern. A guilty conscience impelled me to make that call. I was trying to expiate guilt for all the years of absence and alienation. Somehow I thought if I atoned for that, if I claimed him for my father and made some kind of return, we would get Bird and Sibley back.

It hadn't worked that way.

Bird and Sibley didn't come back. We didn't know where they were. And the worst of it, both Mary and I worried about how their father would care for them. My fears went back to the basic ones of my childhood. Were they hungry? Did they have a roof over their heads? Suppose they got sick?

No matter what we did, part of every day, every night was devoted to thoughts of them and some new idea or effort toward bringing them home. I had a book to do. (*Small Blessings* had made it to publication and was generously reviewed and sold pretty well.) So I returned to one based somewhat on my childhood, a novel I would not have dared to write while Muv lived and yet I felt that it was in part a tribute to her gallantry and her guts. I called the book *Jincey* and I had puttered along with it for years.

Muv knew that much about it, and she once remarked to Julia that I was writing a book called *Jincey.*

"And Celestine never even *knew* Jincey Peacock!" she added wonderingly.

I hadn't known Muv's childhood friend by that name but I had been interested in her name and borrowed it for my little-girl character. Larry had liked the start I had on the book well enough to take it with him when he changed jobs and went to Simon & Schuster. He encouraged me to finish it, and I worked along between covering the day's assignments, writing my column, going to court with Mary, writing letters to friends in Texas, where Bird and Sibley might be, and putting my head down on my desk and crying.

When I got close to the end I rented an apartment on a lovely quiet little island called Isle de Chien off the coast of Florida and went down there to wrap it up. Jack drove me down and left me with the admonition to let somebody see me and know that I was all right every day. It didn't seem likely that I would be otherwise but he knew I would probably swim and most certainly take walks into the pine woods and palmetto thickets, and he considered drowning and snakebite possibilities. Because of that promise I dropped by what was the island's social center and closest thing to a commercial establishment, an old Quonset hut that stocked a few groceries, beer, soft drinks, and cigarettes and visited with the proprietors, Dewey and Doris Covington, every afternoon after work.

Walking along the shell road with the snowy dunes and the waters of the gulf on one side and the woods with palmetto and beach cedar dark green against the white sand on the other side was pure pleasure until one afternoon I saw a young boy and girl running toward me.

"Bird and Sibley!" I cried and started running toward them, arms outstretched.

They slowed down and looked at me in bafflement. They weren't my missing grandchildren, of course, but a couple of youngsters from a sailboat beached on the bay side. I cried all the way back to the hut.

The book did get finished but it suffered a severe setback when Larry again changed jobs, going to Harper & Row. This time he couldn't take it with him. Both he and I hoped that because Simon & Schuster insisted on keeping *Jincey* they liked it and would promote it assiduously. They didn't. They gave me an editor who apparently liked the book so little she couldn't bear to read it. After she questioned me about a few southern colloquialisms she didn't understand I think she threw up her hands. The picture on the jacket didn't resemble anything or anybody in the book, and the flap said the story was about the "coming of age of a lovely girl." Jincey never got older than about seven years, and she was a stringy-haired, freckled-faced child whose own mother regarded her as hopelessly plain. I howled when she showed up on the jacket with red curls, looking like Little Orphan Annie, but it was too late to make a change, they told me.

In the long run I don't suppose it made any difference. The book went out of print almost before it hit the bookstores. Reviews were good. Sales weren't, but it did have the distinction of being banned by the library in one small Georgia town where my books always had a good reception. The reason was a couple of plain country expressions for urination and defecation, words that were respectably used at that time and place. (Years later, when a movie producer asked for an option on the book, I was so grateful to him for liking it I didn't even care whether or not he paid for it.)

When he first heard that I had never been to Europe, Jack started a campaign to get me there. He thought it was one luxury that I would appreciate and really needed like a hyacinth, for my soul. He had gone to study French in Switzerland for a time after he returned from his service in the Navy, and had stayed for a holiday, getting around on a borrowed motorscooter to France and Germany and Italy and going home to Biloxi laden with gifts for all his relatives. He wanted me to see all the things in England that I knew from books, and one summer he and his mother (and my son, Jimmy), and I embarked on a two-week tour of England, Wales, and Scotland.

The three of us were to go back together or with our friend Don Tolbert two or three more times. And one summer the same group took Muv to France. It was her first trip abroad and totally memorable for us all. She walked all over Paris in her bedroom shoes, totally irreverent, for, as she told us all, Paris was "just like Dothan, Alabama." Even the Chamber of Commerce in that small town in the wiregrass section of Alabama forty-five miles north of Muv's Alford, would not make that claim.

She came to love it all, except for the unfortunate tendency of the French to speak French, which she called "that foreign language," until we stopped for lunch one day at St. Tropez. The beach was filled with young women swimming and sunbathing nude from the waist up.

Muv stopped stockstill, her bedroom-slippered feet rooted in the sand.

"Julia! Julia! Come quick!" she cried. And then, overwhelmed, she whispered, "Lord, oh, Lord!"

We finally got lunch and got Muv away without any international incident, but it shook her faith in the French, and she insisted that the next time anybody in her family went abroad they should confine themselves to decent, respectable England.

That suited Jack's stepfather, Lee Morris, fine. He had never gone with us on one of our trips but he suddenly made up his mind he would like to venture forth. As a young man he had shipped on a freighter, which landed at Liverpool, but shy and nervous about being loose in a foreign land, he had stayed on shipboard. Now he was ready to see what Jack and Julia and Jimmy and, in her way, Muv thought so great about foreign travel.

We planned a trip for early fall in 1977, and Lee began systematically to get ready for it. Morning walks were a custom with him and Julia but with the trip abroad in prospect he stepped up distance and speed. They bought good walking shoes and were breaking them in for all the sightseeing they intended to do in England. Every morning they went out earlier and walked longer.

One morning when the moon was still shining, they got to Biloxi's beach drive just as an all-night beer party of teenagers was breaking up. They thought the young people had gone and they began their hike when suddenly a speeding car came bearing down on them. They were knocked down and run over, suffering so many broken bones they were in the hospital in intensive care and in casts for weeks.

Jack had been at the family's fishing camp on the Pearl River with his cousin Billy and he got to them right away, staying beside them in the hospital and then taking them home.

Lee, who had regained consciousness muttering, "Now I won't get

262

to go to England," did not mend. They found while treating him for his accident injuries that his lungs were in trouble. He had a spot they thought was cancer.

Jack couldn't leave his mother, whose pelvis was shattered, until she was able to walk, but he knew it was imperative to get his father to a lung specialist as quickly as possible. He called an Atlanta doctor and subsequently put Lee on a plane, which John and Ted and I met.

The airport was crowded, it was raining, and there was a delay in getting a wheelchair for our patient. Lee looked small and lonely standing at the ramp of the little plane that brought him from Biloxi, and I remember vividly the picture John, still a high school boy, made picking him up in his arms gently as he might a baby and bringing him into the terminal.

It was winter, the bitterest one Atlanta had had in years, when we were able to bring Lee from the hospital to Sweet Apple. Julia, moving about painfully with a walker, came to join him. We had no more than settled them in the downstairs bedroom and turned up the furnace than an ice storm struck and the electricity went off, taking with it heat, water, plumbing, and stove.

Snow and ice covered the roads. I was unable to get out of the woods and to the office. We camped out by the fireplace, wrapping Lee in quilts and putting him in a rocking chair close to the fire.

A soup pot became a fixture on the coals, potatoes in their jackets in the ashes. Food, such as it was, did not run out during the weeklong icy isolation, but Jack stayed on the telephone, the only working utility in the cabin, trying to find a motel for his parents. We were terrified that pneumonia might strike his stepfather and even his mother, who was valiantly trying to wait on her husband despite her own injuries.

The day he found one and the roads were again passable I went back to work and Jack packed bags and took Julia and Lee to a restaurant for a hot meal and to Day's Inn for a warm bed, a working bathroom, and television. They stayed one night and called us to come and get them.

There were terrible periods when both Jack's parents were in nursing homes, then back in their own home again, and then, inevitably, Lee, terminally ill, needed round-the-clock care. He died in 1979 with Julia and Jack at his bedside. I went down to Biloxi the next day and stayed for the funeral, which brought out scores of people who, surprisingly, knew Lee Morris, a gruff, sharp-spoken little man, as a person of carefully hidden kindness and generosity, the very person, in fact, who had spent his vacation helping take care of my mother in her last days.

Torn and aching from one more futile trip to find her children, Mary had settled into a job which amounted to janitorial work at a company that made displays for conventions and advertising exhibits. One day when she had time on her hands she undertook to use one of the power machines in the plant, maybe figuring that if she acquired skill in that field she could get a better job or perhaps not caring what happened to her.

The machine sliced into her hand, cutting it severely.

A bearded young fellow, who was considered the most skillful and creative in the plant, rushed to the rescue, taking her to the emergency room for stitches, scolding her, and eventually teaching her the ways of the dangerous tools. When she brought him out to the cabin I liked Ronald Vance immediately. Only a year or two older than Mary, he seemed vastly more mature—a former teacher at a New England college, quiet, bookish, and, like Cricket, a musician, with the difference that he had set aside his French horn and his records to earn a living. He won my heart by enjoying walking in the woods and he was unstinting in his admiration for my favorite view from a great boulder jutting out over the river.

He came with Mary to a family Thanksgiving dinner and her Uncle Ervin and his wife, Lil, liked him tremendously. Susan and Edward approved him. Shortly before Christmas when we were having Sunday-night sandwiches and coffee by the fireplace he and Mary told us they wanted to get married. Ron's parents came down from Virginia for the ceremony, a simple civil rite, which I did not attend for the reason that I was at Sweet Apple whipping up a reception.

It was a happy occasion and we took pictures to send to Bird and Sibley in care of their Indiana grandparents, feeling some obscure kind of obligation to keep them informed but also hoping that they would care and wish their mother well.

Mary was happy with Ron and they promptly fell into the family's old-house pattern, buying a terrible old duplex in a close-to-town neighborhood called Candler Park. It was a street beginning restoration, but the house they acquired hadn't been swept or had the garbage taken out in years. It sagged, it smelled, and the day the last tenant moved Ron walked into the kitchen and fell through the floor to the basement.

This one really was hopeless, we all said, shaking our heads. We spoke from vast experience in shoring up decaying, dejected abodes. But we all went with rakes and brooms and mops and Jack's truck to haul off a yardful of old batteries and tires and bottles and cans and clear a path so they could move in the better side.

It seemed that in no time at all Susan and I were arriving with brushes and paint cans to spruce up yet another room for another baby.

David, fair-haired and blue-eyed, was born, the image of Bird, Mary said. The rest of us weren't sure of the resemblance, but his mother hung pictures of his missing brother and sister and we tried to find that they were look-alikes because it seemed to cheer Mary.

And then when David was little more than a toddler and Mary was pregnant with another one—a little boy to be called John Steven—we got a call from Bird. He was passing through Atlanta on his way from Indiana to New Orleans and had an hour's layover at the airport. Would we, he suggested diffidently, want to spend it with him?

Would we?

Mary and Ron and baby David and I were at the airport an hour before Bird's plane was due, and Mary and I trembled and wept and laughed with excitement as we paced the waiting room.

The boy who left us when he was thirteen years old was now a man, nineteen, six feet three and heartbreakingly handsome. We hugged him and clung to his arms and wanted to keep touching and patting him but were seized with a shyness that made conversation awkward. What do you say after six years of alienation? What questions dare you ask?

Just when we realized frantically that our hour was almost up and he would be boarding his plane and going off again Bird said to his mother with a touching sweetness, "I'd like to spend the day and go back tomorrow but it would cost me another twenty-five dollars and I don't have that much."

"We'll pay!" Ron and I cried together.

Bird went home with his mother and stepfather and I went to work. They all came to Sweet Apple for supper and Bird spent the night. Jack was away but Bird wanted to look at the lake where he had learned to swim and spent so many hours fishing and splashing about with his cousins. We drove the truck over and I choked up to see him take his baby brother, David, on his shoulder and carry him down to the little beach he had helped to build.

Bird elected to sleep in my room instead of in the big room in the annex where all of them had slept dormitory-style in that earlier, happier time. From the rope bed under the eaves I looked across at the strong young body sprawled across the double bed.

"Bird," I said before we went to sleep, "I worried that you might be hungry."

He smiled gently, the smile I had loved in the little boy whose picture hung over my dresser all the years.

"I was never hungry," he said.

Far worse than bodily hunger is the hunger to be in touch with and at peace with people you love. The children had teased me about becoming the family's matriarch after Muv's death, and I quickly declined the role. A matriarch is not only supposed to be staunch and steadfast, a tower of strength, but very wise—the one in the family who knows what everybody else should do. I wasn't any of those things and, being usually at odds with my own life, how could I direct theirs?

They didn't ask it. Susan and Edward moved to New Jersey, following Edward's new job. I rode up as far as Asheville, North Carolina, with Susan and the children and dogs—the first lap on their trip to their new home and a stopover for me to work on a book with the famous wildlife artist Sallie Middleton. (It was subsequently published under the title *The Magical Realm of Sallie Middleton.*)

Mary's fifth baby, John Steven, was born prematurely by Caesarian section, an event that nearly cost her life and was followed by a year's vigilance with a monitor for the little boy, another candidate for SIDS. He emerged from it a lusty, rosy child with no hint of the peril he had endured, but we were all shaken by the experience and doubly anxious to be reassured about all the others.

John stayed behind his parents to finish his last two years of high school at Woodward Academy, where he especially wanted to play varsity football. He divided his time between the school dormitory, Mary's house, and mine, and we loved having him, although he was a constant reminder of his cousins who were still missing.

But Bird did call once or twice, and we had a letter or two from him. Sibley was doing well in high school but not disposed to be in touch with us. She lived with her father, again divorced, in Shreveport, Louisiana. Both children had jobs, Sibley playing with the symphony orchestra in Marshall, a small city across the state line in Texas. Bird was working after school at McDonald's and insisted on paying for the phone calls he made to us "because I'm making money now," although we urged him to call collect.

By the summer of 1981 he had managed to get a government loan and had spent a year at Louisiana State University, responding with grace and good humor when Mary and I dispatched a gift or a little money to him. It wasn't much but during the long silence letters and gifts had been returned to us, sometimes "Addressee Unknown." We still did not dare to send anything to Sibley, who had bailed out of her senior year of high school and enrolled at Centenary College, where she had first taken music and then switched to pre-med, which she subsequently gave up when she went to Ireland for a summer job with some schoolmates.

Perhaps as a form of therapy but also because I owed Harper & Row a book, I had done a novel called *Children, My Children*. In it, I wrote about some of the feelings I had experienced with the loss of Bird and Sibley and some of the things I had learned from the experiences of others. The locale was generally the Florida island we had discovered when I was finishing *Jincey,* and I spent a few weeks there, coming to love its beauty and comparative isolation—no phones, no pavement, no stores, no traffic.

To my complete astonishment *Children, My Children* was picked for the Jim Townsend Fiction Award, which has been presented semiannually since the death of the founder of the *Atlanta Magazine* and the mentor and friend of most Atlanta writers. When I learned my novel had won out over several excellent ones from my compatriots, I was inclined to believe the judges, knowing that I was old and tired, had given me a sort of now-or-never, Jack Benny–type recognition. Larry, who came down for the presentation luncheon, reassured me by showing me the names of the judges, only one of whom was local. The others, agents and editors, were from New York and Los Angeles.

Larry's presence in Atlanta for the award was a wonderful surprise but even more surprising was Bird's. He arrived in town and accepted cheerfully when I mentioned the luncheon. I hadn't wanted him to read the book. I would never have suggested exposing him to the anxieties and grief we suffered. But he sat at a table with Larry and our bookseller friend Faith Brunson, his friend since earliest childhood, and when somebody asked him he said, "I read it. It's a good book."

Before summer had ended Bird had come back to us. He moved in with Mary and Ron, who had sold their first house and bought another bigger, older, slightly less dilapidated one on the same street, also with restoration in mind. He transferred from LSU to Georgia State and took a job as a copy boy with the newspaper, making friends and progressing to a variety of jobs. When I looked up and saw him striding across the room on some errand or other, my heart lifted and I almost wept with happiness and thanksgiving.

There was still Sibley to miss and grieve for. Bird heard from her but we didn't, and he didn't share his letters from her. But one day he left a letter he had written to her in my car and he called me and asked me if I would mail it. The address on the envelope broke my heart. Not my namesake, Sibley, but a renamed stranger, Sybil. I didn't mention it to Bird but he must have remembered that I would have seen the address and he called to offer halting comfort.

"You know how girls do," he said. "They're always changing their names."

I knew it was more than a girlish whim. It was total rejection, but I said no more about it. And in a couple of years Sibley was to change another part of her name. She had gone to Ireland with some school friends to work in a castle one summer. She met a German artist named Norbert Schaum and decided to marry him instead of returning to college. The wedding was to be solemnized at her father's parents' home in Indiana at Thanksgiving. Bird was invited. The rest of us were not.

Mary and I went through a period of fresh misery. We remembered how all little girls plan their weddings, and Sibley and I had mentally staged hers in the small white clapboard 1836 Presbyterian church in Roswell, which I joined soon after moving to Sweet Apple.

"That's all right," Mary finally said. "We'll give Bird the trip. He'll be there for all of us."

We took him to buy clothes and Ron gave him a credit card to get a U-Drive-It to travel in. I polished the antique family silver, which had been given to me by Jim's mother that day when we told her we were engaged. The eldest granddaughter should have it, no matter what, I said, enveloping it in white tissue paper and satin ribbon and writing a note of love and good wishes to go with it.

It was nearly two years before we heard from Sibley again. She had a baby, a little boy named Vincent, and they were in California waiting for Norbert to sell their house in Ireland, get his papers in order, and come to join her. She called me one night, and when she said, "This is Sibley," not Sybil, I was so delighted I didn't hear anything else for a time. She had changed her name back and she loved us and missed us. She said nothing about coming home, but one afternoon about a month later I drove into the yard on Candler Street and Mary was sitting on the back steps alternately laughing and crying.

"Sibley's coming home!" she called out to us. "She wants to see us. She's bringing my grandchild!"

And then she put her head down on her knees and cried in earnest.

We all hugged and patted her, attributing some of her emotion to the fact that she was having postnatal tremors. Her own baby, a girl child called Betsy (whole name, Elizabeth Jean Mary Everitt), was a little over a month old.

"Just think," I marveled, looking at the little boys playing in the backyard, "they're uncles. Betsy's an aunt. You're a grandmother and I—good heavens, I'm a great-grandmother!"

Where had the time gone? How did we all come to this point where there were so many of us, such an amazing tangled skein of kinship, with babies being uncles and aunts, my own youngest a grandmother, me a great-grandmother? What happened to that scared child who stubbornly refused to leave the front steps of the old rooming house in Mobile, terrified that the one person in the world, the only person she had, might not return?

Ah, I thought, if only Muv could see us now!

She had once said in some moment of sere introspection, "Well, you don't have to *understand* life, you just have to *live* it."

We had been living it—ah, how we had lived it!—and it seemed to me that we were in the midst of what an old hymn called "billows of blessings."

Sibley and Norbert and the most enchanting baby boy, Vincent, arrived in March of 1986. Susan and Susy had come down from New Jersey for John's twenty-third birthday, to check on Ted, who was a student at nearby LaGrange College (Aunt Pittypat of *Gone With the Wind* is said to have gone there) and to spend a few days with Jack and me at the beach cottage he had built on the little island I loved. (I helped to build it. I had blistered knees to prove it after the flooring was finished.) We came back from the beach to find the cabin full of family, Vincent already in the battered old Kitty-Koop, which had served nearly all of our babies, a tall, fair-haired young man, and a slim, dark-haired girl seated by the fireplace surrounded by the little uncles, the baby aunt, the young grandmother, all beaming, all proud and awed, as I was that there were so many of us and we were together again.

It had been ten years since we had seen Sibley off to New Orleans, a little girl uneasy to be flying alone, uncertain as to what awaited her at her destination. But she was our same Tib, except more beautiful, more poised, with the sheen of motherhood and wifehood on her. She and Norbert decided to settle in Atlanta, where there seemed to be a ready market for his skills as an artist and a woodworker. She came to work part-time as a secretary for me, and as I approach the little office and see her dark head bent over the typewriter or leaning into the telephone, my heart lifts and I am filled with gratitude for the goodness of life.

One night Jack and I went to be with the family of a friend of ours who had died. She had been ill a few months, but it seemed to us that her death had come with a terrible suddenness. We had not been prepared to lose so close and cherished a friend. We talked with her daughter and grandchildren and stood awhile among people she had helped, listening to their accounts of her kindness and concern for their problems. We talked to a tall, handsome man who was the eldest of her several brothers and who spoke movingly of their growing-up years on a farm in Tennessee and how each child helped the one just younger to a college education.

Back home we sat awhile in the car in the backyard, sad and wondering at the mystery of life and death and perhaps feeling our own mortality.

Suddenly Jack asked the old question we had put aside twenty-five years before: Would I marry him?

I have forgotten what pretty answer I made but it must have been, Yes, thank you very much!

For the things that bothered me so long ago no longer seemed real.

The difference in our ages was reduced to nothingness by the ancient wisdom, the bone goodness, the bonny humor of this man. Neighbors of ours lost a son in a terrible accident and Jack, who was on a trip with another week to go, canceled it and came home to stand by and help them in all the quiet, unobtrusive ways he knew. "You walked with us all the way," the boy's mother wrote us.

Jack Strong had walked with me and my family all the way. He had been with us in mourning and in rejoicing. He gave my mother some of the happiest times of her life, and he was there to serve her when she was ill and close to death. He got up in the night to go to a sick baby, a vomiting boy, to get a drunk friend out of jail. My friends became his friends, his friends mine. Our families were joint kin or, as it says in the Book of Ruth, "thy people shall be my people" equally dear to us both. We knew each other's best stories and we laughed at the same things.

Julia, Jack's mother, once said in a tone of wonderment, "You all *talk* to each other!"

We never could wait to talk to each other, phoning back and forth, saving up things to relate at the end of the day, writing letters if all else failed.

Would I marry him? The wonder was that we had waited so long!

We talked about it over a period of weeks and agreed that it must be done quietly with a minimum of attention from anybody else. One Sunday most of the children were in the country, except Susan and the New Jersey contingent and Jimmy in Florida, and Jack lined them up on the rock steps in front of the cabin for a group picture. While he focused the camera he said casually, "Tine and I are getting married."

When the excitement subsided they all promised to let us do it our way. Mary took off the plain gold wedding band, which had been Muv's and which I gave Ron to put on her finger when they were married.

"Here," she said, kissing me. "Your turn. It's too tight for me anyhow."

It was too tight for me, but Jack took it to a jeweler to be stretched, admonishing him not to obliterate the words inside, which said: "Evelyn, wife of W. R. Sibley, December 13, 1924."

We called my absent children and Jack's mother and aunts and a week later the two of us and the Reverend Cyrus Mallard walked into

271

the sweet old Presbyterian church in Roswell for the ceremony, solemnly promising that we were not entering into matrimony "unadvisedly or lightly but reverently, discreetly, advisedly, soberly and in the fear of God."

The next day we left for Florida, going by Alford and putting on Muv's grave the bridal bouquet of garden flowers Jack had brought for me.

Adults, I have always noticed, are cautious and reserved about claiming to be rich. It may be a form of superstition, a sort of oriental fear that exulting in something invites the jealousy of the gods, who will smite you down. Children don't feel that way—and I am with them.

Recently among my mother's things I found a few yellowed, dog-eared columns of mine that she had saved. One of them marveled at the attitude of Susan, a child who was unafraid of rejoicing in wealth. She was with me at the grocery store when I bought not one loaf of bread but *two,* one of them raisin.

"Gosh, Mommy's rich today!" she caroled across the grocery store. Having a dime to buy an Eskimo pie instead of "just hunkies that cost a nickel" filled her with a sense of plenitude. She measured wealth by having something to give away. We not only got hand-me-downs from our affluent friends, we got hand-me-downs that we could pass on to the "less fortunate." She counted the street light "almost in our front yard, our very own street light . . . Light all night that you don't have to pay for" as a bonanza. Living close to the fire station "and every time the trucks go out we can hear them . . . That's rich, isn't it?"

Two of her blessings I found most humbling were my makeshift efforts at decorating. We couldn't afford linoleum for the kitchen floor so I painted it red. We couldn't afford real curtains for the living room so I made some out of twenty-nine-cent-a-yard muslin and dyed them yellow.

"A ruby floor and golden curtains!" Susan proclaimed to her friends.

And then at dusk, after she had a full day at the church day camp, I heard her report to Sally Jane, the downstairs tenants' daughter, "I'm real rich today—I learned a new song."

Who but a child has the sense to measure riches by the rescue roar

272

of a fire truck, a song, the radiance of light not paid for?

With such teachers as my children maybe I have learned. For I now know that I am rich, indeed. I have a husband, funny, steadfast, *there*. I have many children and many, many grandchildren—even one great. I have a job that grows more rewarding with each passing year. Even the books I thought were long out-of-print and forgotten have been reissued by a newcomer to the field, Peachtree Publishers of Atlanta. Even the one I thought was dead, the novel I most wanted to write, has gone to seek its fortune in Hollywood. (Hope in itself is riches.)

Suburbia surrounds us. Woods are giving way to mansions and landscaped yards. Change not of my choosing is all around me. But it hasn't engulfed and overwhelmed little Sweet Apple yet.

And sometimes when I drive into the yard and see the slanty roof, the gray-weathered logs of the old cabin, when I find a rose I thought was dead suddenly blooming, when I hear a whippoorwill tune up in the woods, and take off my shoes and stockings and wander through the tall grass to help Jack harvest the tomatoes he planted, I know that I am fortunate among women.

Years ago my friend Jack Spalding pegged my good fortune for me. He was a reporter on the *Journal;* I was a reporter on the *Constitution*. By sheer coincidence we both turned up at the state hospital for the insane at the same time to do stories. We were invited to a patients' dance that afternoon and we went. When we walked in, a gray-bearded old gentleman wearing an old-fashioned Boy Scout uniform with leggings and a Sergeant York–type hat asked me to dance.

Not knowing what else to do I accepted and we stomped and whirled around that blazing-hot concrete auditorium to the recorded "Tennessee Waltz"— the only tune the patients wanted to hear—for two solid hours.

When the dance finally lumbered torturously to its end, my pal Spalding came to walk me back to the hospital administration building. I lit into him.

"You saw I was stuck!" I cried. "Why didn't you rescue me?"

He grinned. "What are you complaining about, old girl?" he asked genially. "You never got such a rush from *sane* people."

He was, now that I think of it, absolutely right. It is one of the compensations—and they are, believe me, many—for being turned funny.